SOUTHERN MIGRANTS, NORTHERN EXILES

CHAD BERRY

Southern Migrants, Northern Exiles

UNIVERSITY OF ILLINOIS PRESS
URBANA AND CHICAGO

Manufactured in the United States of America
∞ This book is printed on acid-free paper.

Library of Congress Cataloging-in-Publication Data
Berry, Chad, 1963–
Southern migrants, Northern exiles / Chad Berry.
p. cm.
Includes bibliographical references (p.) and index.
ISBN 978-0-252-02429-0 (alk. paper)
ISBN 978-0-252-06841-6 (pbk. : alk. paper)
1. Migration, Internal—Southern States—History—20th century.
2. Migration, Internal—Middle West—History—20th century.
3. Poor—Southern States—History—20th century.
4. Labor mobility—Southern States—History—20th century.
I. Title.
HB1971.A3B47 2000
304.8′0975—DC21 99-6511
CIP

1 2 3 4 5 C P 6 5 4 3 2

For my grandparents, Ruby and Alvin,

and the hundreds of thousands

who came with them

By the rivers of Babylon—
there we sat down and there we wept
when we remembered Zion.
On the willows there
we hung our harps.
For there our captors
asked us for songs,
and our tormentors asked for mirth, saying,
"Sing us one of the songs of Zion!"

How could we sing the Lord's song
in a foreign land?
If I forget you, O Jerusalem,
let my right hand wither!
Let my tongue cling to the roof of my mouth,
if I do not remember you,
if I do not set Jerusalem
above my highest joy.

—Psalm 137:1–6

Thus says the Lord of hosts, the God of Israel, to all the exiles whom I have sent into exile from Jerusalem to Babylon: Build houses and live in them; plant gardens and eat what they produce. Take wives and have sons and daughters; take wives for your sons, and give your daughters in marriage, that they may bear sons and daughters; multiply there, and do not decrease. But seek the welfare of the city where I have sent you into exile, and pray to the Lord on its behalf, for in its welfare you will find your welfare.

—Jeremiah 29:4–7

Contents

Acknowledgments

EARLY IN THE SIXTH CENTURY B.C.E., after a long struggle for Jerusalem, and hence the kingdom of Judah, to maintain its identity and a degree of autonomy, Jerusalem was destroyed, and Jews were forced into exile in Babylon. As all exiles are, this one was painful and difficult. In Babylon, they lived in clustered communities, where they nurtured their own culture and struggled to preserve the memory of Zion, remembering with fondness what life was like in Zion, even though, with time, some exiles were doing quite well economically. After fifty years of captivity, a new emperor allowed exiled Jews to return to Zion. But ambivalence was strong. Some made the decision to return to Jerusalem, while others stayed on in Babylon because they had been gone so long that it was now home.

This Old Testament story has uncanny parallels to the story here. White upland southerners found themselves economic exiles in a strange land. They, too, often lived amid their kindred and nurtured their transplanted culture in the North. Many of those who stayed in the North prospered economically, so well that when the time came to return, as when retirement dawned, they faced the difficult decision of whether to return South—to Zion—or to remain in the North—in Babylon. Ambivalence about exile for twentieth-century southerners was just as strong as it was for Old Testament Jews. Although *exodus,* which entails leaving a foreign land spent in bondage for the freedom of the promised land, has often been used to describe migration stories, I have chosen *exile*—having to leave one's homeland for a strange, unknown one—as the guiding metaphor for this story.

As the grandson of southern migrants, I cannot remember my first trip to the South. Family folklore proclaims that my grandparents were able to talk my parents into letting them take me "down home"—from Indiana to Tennessee—for the first time at the age of six months. But I remember well successive trips: enduring the incredibly long and arduous drive, eating the home-cooked goodies that my grandmother would take along in a basket ("If you keep eating like this, the fried chicken will be gone by Kokomo," she would tell me), meeting and becoming reacquainted with distant cousins and kin in the South and marveling at the differences, and wondering about the beautifully adorned graves of my forebears on Decoration Day at Crossroads Methodist Church, my grandfather's family's church, and at Mount Pleasant Methodist Church, home to my grandmother's ancestors.

I never guessed that one day I would be writing a book about the experiences of my grandparents and hundreds of thousands of others like them, but the seed was planted by my grandparents. Like Old Testament exiles, they hoped that the culture of their Zion would never be completely lost or forgotten, so in many ways I became the repository of this body of knowledge. There were others along the way who sparked, nurtured, and advised me in this chronicle. The late Clarence and Lolita Stillman sparked an interest in local history. At the University of Notre Dame, three people in particular taught me different things in different ways: Barbara Allen, Lynwood Montell, and Thomas Schlereth. I can show my gratitude only by giving my own students as much generosity and attention as each of them gave me.

At Indiana University, I received several grants-in-aid from Research and the University Graduate School and from the Department of History, for which I am grateful. A graduate fellow designation from the Indiana Historical Society greatly facilitated my research. Again, however, people made the difference. Lorna Lutes Sylvester taught me a great deal about nineteenth-century migration to Indiana, and she and Susan Armeny showed me how beneficial an editor can be. James H. Madison taught me that local history matters, Henry Glassie how important each word can be, John Bodnar how important the big picture is, and David Thelen—well, he taught me too many things to list here, not the least of which was expanding my horizon. Life in Bloomington would not have been the same without Jan and Tom Weir, Martha and Alex Urbiel, Jennifer and Mark Branning, and Laura and Patrick Ettinger.

Librarians and archivists helped immensely, including those at Indiana University, Bloomington; the University of Illinois at Chicago; the Harold Washington Library Center in Chicago; West Virginia University; Samford University; the Mishawaka-Penn Public Library; Appalachian State University; Alice Lloyd College; the Columbus Public Library; Maryville College; the Country Music Hall of Fame; the Urban Appalachian Council; and especially Shannon Wilson, Gerald Roberts, and Sidney Farr of the Hutchins Library at Berea College.

Others have offered invaluable support. Jim Palmieri helped me decipher microdata census material. Gordon McKinney has been most generous, along with Ivan Tribe, Margaret Ripley Wolfe, David Whisnant, Jim Gregory, David Kimbrough, Michael Maloney, Phil Obermiller, Roger Guy, Bruce Tucker, Loyal Jones, Bill Weinberg, Laurel Shackelford, Elizabeth Haiken, Steve Aibel, Todd Gitlin, Nancy B. Cain, Tony Shuler, Matthew Jewell, Sarah Best, and Denise Giardina. Lea Ann Sterling and Anne Ragsdale deserve special thanks for introducing me to interviewees. Judy McCulloh's guidance throughout the publication process has been rewarding; I'm honored that my title can be a part of her long, impressive list. Jane Mohraz's suggestions prove that copyediting is not a dying art. I am grateful for her work on the manuscript. At Maryville College, I enjoy the best possible colleagues. I would like especially to thank Roger Myers, Susan Schneibel, Peggy Cowan, David Powell, Carl Gombert, Margie Ribble, Charlotte Beck, Lori Schmied, Karl Jost, Paul Threadgill, Frank van Aalst, and Dean Boldon.

To my family I owe a great deal. My parents, Tom and Nancy Berry, deserve thanks for sending me to such a fine school. I thank Jeff and Pam Gardner for raising such a wonderful daughter. My own daughter, Madelaine, as an infant allowed me to type the first life of this manuscript while she slept on one side of my desk. I hope my son, Nat, in one day reading this, will not forget what his great-grandparents had to endure. And I thank my wife, Lisa, so much for so graciously making the sacrifices that this effort demanded.

Most especially, I thank the people who trusted me enough to sit down with a tape recorder so that I could preserve their stories. This book is really about and for them.

SOUTHERN MIGRANTS, NORTHERN EXILES

Introduction: Of Dollmakers, Job Seekers, and Divided Hearts

> Some go when they do not wish to go, but others stay. Even when hungry, they stay because they have a greater hunger; hunger for home, for old familiar scenes, for peace, for the known and the understood, the ties of kith and kin. Those who do go look to the day when they will again walk the paths in their own land in better times.
>
> —*Mountain Life and Work,* 1961

> If I would've had employment down here, I would've never left. I didn't like the fact that I had to leave. I went because I had to.
>
> —Daymon Morgan, 1993, Bad Creek, Ky.

IF *The Grapes of Wrath* is the representative novel of the "Okie" migration westward, Harriette Arnow's *The Dollmaker,* published in 1954, is the counterpart for southern white migration to the midwestern states of Illinois, Indiana, Michigan, Ohio, and Wisconsin.[1] Gertie Nevels and her husband, Clovis, live in the valley of the Great South Fork of the Cumberland River in southeastern Kentucky during World War II. The region is hardly isolated; the effects of a world war have easily penetrated upland southern life. Her brother, Henley, has just been killed in action, and the community's doctor and most of the other men (except

Clovis) have gone away: the doctor to Oak Ridge and the men to the army or to such northern cities as Muncie, Gary, Cincinnati, and Detroit. Even the preacher "left God's work fer Oak Ridge." Suddenly, men were earning regular and substantial paychecks. Notices nailed to trees were patriotically calling on Kentuckians to help the war effort: "MEN, WOMEN, WILLOW RUN, UNCLE SAM, LIVING QUARTERS." "GIVE, RED CROSS—JOIN THE WACS—GIVE BLOOD—WORK AT WILLOW RUN."[2]

Arnow's main characters could not be more different from one another. Clovis loathes farming—the "old fashioned" life of eastern Kentucky—and yearns to answer the call of northern industrialists. Gertie, however, is very much at home in this often difficult region, gaining both her inner and physical strength from nature and the land. The novel opens with her stopping an army car en route to Oak Ridge and pleading with the officers to take her youngest son, Amos, who has diphtheria and is near death, to a doctor. When the army officers refuse, Gertie performs an emergency tracheotomy on Amos using her whittling knife and a straw quickly made out of a poplar branch, much to the shock and horror of the men. Convinced by her desperation, the men agree to take them to a doctor. On the way, and in a fidgety attempt to make small talk, an army officer asks her about the main crop of eastern Kentucky. "A little uv everthing," Gertie answers, more concerned about her son. Arnow writes:

> "But what is their main crop?" he insisted.
> "Youngens," she said, holding the child's hands that were continually wandering toward the hole in his neck. "Youngens fer th wars an them factories."[3]

Gertie belongs very much to the land that another Appalachian writer, James Still, called "earth loved more than any earth." When Gertie is given her dead brother's cattle money, the three hundred dollars, along with money she has secretly saved for years, is sufficient to buy the Silas Tipton Place, meaning the Nevelses will no longer be renters. Tipton, Gertie recounts, "went off to Muncie to work in a factory. He wanted his wife an youngens with him, so he sold his place. It's a good place—old, a log house—big an built good like they built in th old days." Later, when she takes her five children there just before the deal is final, the house seemed divine: "Now in the yellow sun . . . all seemed bathed in a golden halo and Cassie [Gertie's daughter] called that the house had golden windows." The reader sees the landscape of the Big South Fork through Gertie's eyes:

> She climbed to the edge of the cornfield above the house and stopped and looked back. Gray rains and curls of fog from the rising creek and the river made the hills across the creek seem one black iron mountain smudged

> and indistinct. Her father's farm and the hills beyond the river were blotted out so that she could see little but her own. Just below her was her house with the blue smoke rising, and set in the curving sweep of grassland, as green almost from the warm fall rains as grass in the spring. She saw the apple trees, black-trunked, gray-twigged in the rain; the pear trees, the peach, and rising like an outpost in the fog, the great poplar by the spring, its arms held up as if reaching for the sky. She wished she could see the cedar bluffs above the creek, with more cedar for fence posts than she would ever need, and the old sugar trees with their gray scarred bark, and the beech trees with their thin fine twigs that would on winter nights make a lace-like pattern against the stars.

Because of her brother's death and the money she is given, she realizes that the war takes and gives, and she is about to be set free "so that she might live and be beholden to no man, not even to Clovis. Never again would she have to wait to bake bread till Clovis brought home a sack of meal." "'I've reached the land of corn an wine,'" she recites to herself, "'and all its riches freely mine; here shines undimmed one blissful day where all my night has passed away.'" Gertie is about to enter Zion.[4]

But the deal is never to be finalized. Clovis discovers in Cincinnati that the army does not want him for several months, and, realizing that the war is giving him the opportunity to find a well paying job, he secretly goes to Detroit—where he has wanted to go for years—and easily gets a job in a Willow Run plant.

Arnow creates two more people who, like Gertie and Clovis, are light-years apart in their attitude about Gertie's following Clovis. Her mother-in-law, Kate, warns Gertie not to follow. "You won't leave us an foller him there?" Kate asks. "Deetroit's so far away—might nigh as bad as bein acrost the waters. He'll like it there. All that machinery'll just suit him—fer a while. It'll be all over one a these days; and he'll come back an git him another truck. But if'n you foller him he might never come back." It is Gertie's ignominious mother, however, who forces her to go, quoting the apostle Paul: "There he is," she says scornfully, "away off in that cold, dirty, flat, ugly factory town, a haven to mix up with all kinds of foreigners and sich, a haven to pay money to a union. . . . He could be took in th army, an you'd never see him agin. . . . 'Wives, be in subjection unto your husbands, as unto th Lord.'"[5]

Gertie packs her children on a northbound train infused with the smell of sweat and vomit. Looking around her, she sees "the red-necked, loose-jointed older men in overall pants so new they still smelled of the dye" and women, like herself, in new rayon dresses and new imitation patent-leather shoes with red mud on them, all purchased by northern wages. Gertie and her children are suddenly bound up in a real-life nightmare that would forever be etched into their minds, particularly their first glimpse of "Deetroit" from a taxi's window:

> Gertie looked . . . and through the twisting, whirling curtain of smoke and snow she saw across a flat stretch of land flame and red boiling smoke above gray shed-like buildings. Closer were smaller smokes and paler lights about black heaps of rock-like stuff strewn over a gray wasteland of rusty iron and railroad tracks. She jumped, Cassie squealed, and even Enoch ducked his head when there came an instant of loud humming, followed by a bone-shattering, stomach-quivering roar. The plane was big, and seemed no higher than the telephone poles as it circled, fighting for altitude. There were several loud pops, but the roar gradually lessened as the plane climbed higher, then was drowned in the clank and roar of the steel mill.

To their horror, the taxi driver informs them that they are home, in "Merry Hill," government wartime housing, which, Clovis repeatedly reminds her, he was damn lucky to find.[6]

Away from the Kentucky landscape, Gertie is reduced to weakness and misery. What follows are months of newness: learning new words (*credit, communism,* and *adjust*), new things (an Icy Heart refrigerator—the ironic symbol of technological achievement), a new residence (Merry Hill), new people (a black person on the train northward, the caustic Roman Catholic neighbor, Mrs. Daly), a new identity ("My country is Kentucky," she tells the school's principal), even new burial customs ("It ain't like back home, Gert," Clovis remarks as their daughter is taken to the morgue).[7] She tries tirelessly to scrimp in an effort to resave money so that her family can return and buy the Tipton place, but Clovis berates her for buying the cheapest grades of meat and food, reminding her that he is making good money and implying that he has no intention of ever returning to Kentucky. Even time is different, she discovers, as she whittles on a piece of wood:

> The night sounds of Detroit came between her and the thing in the wood, but worse than any noise, even the quivering of the house after a train had passed, were the spaces of silence when all sounds were shut away by the double windows and the cardboard walls, and she heard the ticking of the clock, louder it seemed than any clock could ever be. She had never lived with a clock since leaving her mother's house, and even there the cuckoo clock had seemed more ornament than a god measuring time; for in her mother's house, as in her own, time had been shaped by the needs of the land and the animals swinging through the seasons. She would sit, the knife forgotten in her hands, and listen to the seconds ticking by, and the clock would become the voice of the thing that had jerked Henley from the land, put Clovis in Detroit, and now pushed her through

> days where all her work, her meals and her sleep were bossed by the ticking voice.

She is constantly encountering the snowy cold and the equally frigid ethnic groups that mutter repugnantly, "Hillbilly." Once a woman as strong as a man, Gertie remembers, "It wasn't the way it had used to be back home when she had done her share, maybe more than her share of feeding and fending for the family. . . . She'd bought almost every bite of food they didn't raise. Here everything, even to the kindling wood, came from Clovis." Gertie now seems only able to watch as her family disintegrates. Her youngest daughter, Cassie, is killed by a train; her oldest son, Reuben, flees Detroit and returns to live with his grandparents; and Clovis, seeking vengeance for a fight, commits a murder with Gertie's whittling knife.[8]

Ultimately, it is Gertie's talent with wood that saves the family momentarily from ruin. Reluctantly, she saws up a venerable block of wild cherry she had been carving on for years to make dolls she would sell to earn money. But here the novel ends, although the reader hopes that Gertie finds the strength to leave Clovis in the North and return to the South to buy the Tipton place.

The Dollmaker is in many ways a great American novel that attempts to speak genuinely about an American experience. Harriette Arnow, who grew up in Pulaski County, Kentucky, in the midst of the Cumberland Valley, began work on the novel after her husband got a job at a Detroit newspaper during the war. They first moved to crowded government housing but eventually moved to a forty-acre farm near Ann Arbor, where she finished the book and spent the rest of her life.[9] Although told by someone who had first-hand experience on which to draw, *The Dollmaker* remains a fictional account. But there are real stories that have not yet been told. Travel anywhere today through the South, especially the Upland South, and knock on any door. You will be hard-pressed to find anyone whose family has not been touched by the great *white* migration, which began in earnest during World War I and continued through the 1970s. By 1960, net migration figures for the white South were negative by almost five million people.[10]

Scholarly "experts" and journalists have had a lot to say over the years about southern white out-migration—about southern Appalachians in the 1920s, about destitute southern migrants in the 1930s, about "hillbilly" defense workers in the 1940s, and about migrants in urban ghettos in the 1960s. Rarely, however, have southern white migrants—members of an oral culture—been given the opportunity to speak for themselves. My goal here has been, through oral histories, to hear what migrants have to say of their migration experiences and to encourage them to share the meanings they have constructed out of those experiences. I have thus refused to edit sharply the large blocks of oral testimony in which their experience is embedded. My wish is for people, in the words of three scholars of Appalachia, to be "the authors of their own identities."[11]

Were one to believe many of the stereotypes about migrants, the "typical" migrant would have hailed from such a county as Harlan in eastern Kentucky's coalfields; gone to a sprawling megalopolis, such as Chicago, Detroit, or Cleveland; discovered there shoes, booze, and welfare; and become a public nuisance through violence, fecundity, intoxication, laziness, and squalor.

The record clearly refutes such falsehoods. White southerners—from the lowlands as much as the highlands, from a tremendous variety of backgrounds—were recruited and welcomed by northern industrialists and agriculturists. Generally, they found jobs quite easily (especially compared with African American and Hispanic job seekers) in midwestern factories and agricultural fields of all sizes, and, as Old Testament Jews did in Babylon, they made homes for themselves in a variety of midwestern cities and towns, often settling first in inner-city ports of entry and gradually moving to peripheral areas, where they could scratch the land for a garden. These migrants clearly refuted the common stereotype that southerners—especially people from the Appalachian Mountains—were too clannish to loosen kinship ties and leave the region for a better place.[12]

But leaving home and a way of life was never easy for migrants, so they sojourned readily and frequently between jobs in the North and homes in the South, often saving money by working through the winter in the Midwest and returning south in April to "put in a crop." Not a few migrants solved the difficulty of leaving friends and family behind in the South by making sure they came along with them to the Midwest. Some came north for only several days; others remained for several years or decades and then returned; still others decided to stay permanently, even after retirement, having lived their lives longer in the North than in the South. This is a story about diversity, not universality. The essence of southern white migratory experience in the Midwest, according to migrants themselves, was based not on weakness, misery, and victimization—in many ways the essence of Gertie Nevels's experience—but on success, on fulfilling a dream of finding a job and keeping it, of struggling and overcoming the prejudices and adjustments associated with migration, of buying a home and eventually burning the mortgage, and, of course, of having a car in which to go back south for visits.

For southerners, the highways that led northward were built on kinship, a factor that often determined where a migrant went as well as where he or she lived, worked, and even retired, again showing how the clannish view of southerners is just simply wrong. The network of federal highways and interstates also played a role in the decisions. Such highways as 23, 31, and 41 and such interstates as 65 and 75 became more than just roads; they entered the minds of people on a psychological and sociological level. Both figuratively and literally, however, the highways were divided. On a figurative level, sadness was often associated with a trip on the northbound lane to exile and jubilation was frequently associated with the southbound lane. The North offered economic rewards, but the South was home to the deeper, more spiritual values of home, family, and community.

In Gertie and Clovis—two symbolic figures representing emotional poles—Harriette Arnow was able to develop the range of emotions that migrants expressed to make sense of their lives. Gertie Nevels never finds anything in the "Hillbilly Hell" of Detroit that is an improvement over her life in the Cumberland Valley, while for Clovis Nevels, the North seems like "Hillbilly Heaven." In Clovis's eyes, the North gives him a job, at least temporarily, which provides him authority and esteem, as well as the incentive to buy, among other things, a truck and a refrigerator. As Gertie sees it, the North has taken her daughter and oldest son and destroyed her dream of owning property in her beloved Kentucky hills and living off the bounty of the land in a community of friends and family. To Clovis, the industrial North has given him everything; to Gertie it has taken everything.

Clovis and Gertie represent emotional poles of heaven and hell. Most migrants, however—as revealed in oral histories—had more complex attitudes about the Midwest. As industrial capitalism spread and as the supply of labor from abroad was cut off, industrialists looked to the South for their supply. Southerners acquired an ambivalence—a divided heart—similar to the exiled Jews of Babylon. Moving to the industrial North involved trade-offs: migrants were torn between living a familiar but often cruel and even unpredictable life in the South, close to kin and the land, and an unfamiliar northern life-style that held economic potential but was far away from land and occasionally kin. The Dolly Parton song expresses the ambivalence perfectly: "In the Good Old Days (When Times Were Bad)."[13]

Ambivalent emotions, however, did not lead to economic failure. Plenty of southerners who came north regretted having to leave their homes and families in the South. Even those whose extended families came north with them still lamented leaving the spiritual and metaphysical place referred to as "home." The emotional response to dislocation, as this study describes, was varied and complex. But the economic response was more certain and predictable, because southerners who stayed in the North achieved an impressive economic status compared with that of native midwestern whites and native whites who remained in the South, even if it came at a high price. The story of the great white migration thus entails both a divided heart—emotional ambivalence about leaving—and economic success—solving the economic problems that were the main reasons for migrating. Oral histories and economic and demographic evidence combined offer a portrait of things gained and things lost.

Take, for example, the case of Pauline Mayberry, born in 1931 in Wayne County, Tennessee, about one hundred miles southwest of Nashville. Like Gertie, Mayberry was tough as hickory. "I growed up with three boys and whatever they did on the farm I did it too," she explained. "And we went to the field, chopped cotton, went to the woods and cut wood, whatever." Born into economic hardship, Mayberry said she never knew there was an economic depression. "I just growed up not having a lot and that was it." In 1949, after graduating from high school, she found a job in a nearby shoe factory and worked until she married the following year. Like Clovis, Mayberry's husband believed married women should not work at a "public job."[14]

As it was for the Nevelses, life for Mayberry and her family in Tennessee was difficult. During the cotton harvest, she and her children got on a bus and were taken to a cotton field just over the state line in Alabama. Although she was paid only three cents a pound as a picker, "back then I could pick two hundred and fifty or three hundred pounds, and that was good money—nine dollars a day," she recalled. "There wasn't any money, hardly. My husband worked at a sawmill, and when it was raining, he didn't work. So we just barely made it down there back then."[15]

Mayberry's experiences began to diverge from Gertie's and become more similar to those of hundreds of thousands of other southerners when she and her husband packed up in the 1950s—the peak decade of out-migration—and headed for Detroit. The move was never intended to be permanent; Mayberry and her family (unlike the Nevelses) sojourned back and forth between Detroit and Tennessee for years attempting to reconcile the competing demands of money and home. "Well," she said, "that's the way most people did when they came up here back then. They would come and make them a little money and then they'd go back home, or spend it, and when it was gone come back again and stay." "The first time we came," she continued, "it was '52. And we went back and forth two or three different times. About four or five years we went back and forth that many times, I guess." It was not until 1966—fourteen years after their first move—that Mayberry and her husband decided to stay in Detroit. Although her first glimpse was unpleasant, friends and family made adjustments easier. "I'll tell you what," she said, "the first time I came, I thought, I didn't know what I was coming in to. It was the dirtiest, nastiest looking city I ever saw in my life!"[16]

In addition to sojourning, there were other attempts to reconcile their ambivalence. In 1953, thinking that life would perhaps be easier if familiar faces and voices were transplanted with them, they rented a large house on Putnam and Third streets in Detroit and transformed it into a boardinghouse for fellow southerners from Tennessee and elsewhere. Even Mayberry's children were torn between the North and the South. Her son Richard, who acquired the name "Down Yonder" from Detroit schoolmates, missed the opportunity to "get out and run the woods like we did when we were kids down there." Each time his parents shuttled between the North and the South, he and his brother had to adjust to a northern urban school or a southern rural one. After Mayberry and her husband decided to stay in Detroit in 1966, Richard and his brother returned south to live with Mayberry's mother, Virgie Rich, and finish high school, but afterward Richard quickly returned because the desire for money won out. "Mom and Dad were living here," he explained, "so I came back here and went to work with Fisher Body. It was on the assembly line—you made excellent money."[17]

When interviewed in 1992, Mayberry had been in Detroit long enough to lose her first husband to cancer and to marry another southerner, originally from east Tennessee, who had retired from General Dynamics. They were living in suburban East Detroit, with quaint, postwar brick ranch houses tightly spaced but separated by neatly manicured front lawns. Her neighbor was a Pole, but other southerners lived on the street. Mayberry, however, was even then contemplating a return to the South: "I've lived here this time almost twenty-six years, and I still don't really like it. I'd rather be back down there I think. It's too congested. There's just a house one right beside of the other, and neighbors up here are not like they were down there. They're not friendly. You know them and you speak to them, and that's about it. We've been talking about going down there and looking for a place." In 1993, they moved to Wayne County, Tennessee, Mayberry's childhood home, able to carry with them northern pensions gained from years of steady employment. For them, it was the perfect way to unify a divided heart.

Notes

1. The scope of this study is limited to twentieth-century southern white migration to the states formed out of the Old Northwest. Throughout the study, I

refer to this region variously as the North or the Midwest, but the intent is the same: the states of Illinois, Indiana, Michigan, Ohio, and Wisconsin. I limit the focus to these states because they received more southern whites than any other region except the Far West. By 1950, 60 percent of all southern-born people living in the Midwest were white, compared with 41 percent for the Northeast. As Jon C. Teaford notes, the result of white southern predominance "was a new cultural and ethnic mix that further distinguished Detroit from New York and Cincinnati from Boston." See Teaford, *Cities of the Heartland,* 193. Although studies have been published on African American out-migration, the historical record of southern out-migration is incomplete without a consideration of whites. For examples of studies of African American out-migration, see Grossman, *Land of Hope;* Gottlieb, *Making Their Own Way;* Trotter, ed., *Great Migration in Historical Perspective;* and Lemann, *Promised Land.*

2. Arnow, *Dollmaker,* 90, 14, 19.

3. Ibid., 17.

4. Still, *Wolfpen Poems,* 71; Arnow, *Dollmaker,* 18, 43, 119–20, 122.

5. Ibid., 110, 124.

6. Ibid., 130, 149.

7. Ibid., 183, 375.

8. Ibid., 187, 307.

9. *Harriette Simpson Arnow,* dir. Smith.

10. See U.S. Bureau of the Census, *Historical Statistics of the United States;* and U.S. Bureau of the Census, *Historical Statistics of the United States: Continuation to 1962 and Revisions.*

11. Banks, Billings, and Tice, "Appalachian Studies, Resistance, and Postmodernism," 295. See also Allen, "Story in Oral History," 606–11. Throughout this study, I seek balance in the overall picture of upland southern white out-migration. In letting migrants tell their own stories, I do not pretend that my qualitative data is in any way scientific or even representative. I have traveled throughout the South and the Midwest interviewing migrants and former migrants, and I have also mined extensively archival oral history collections. While I am a historian, not a quantitative social scientist, I have sought to balance this oral, qualitative data with quantitative data, especially from the Public Use Microdata Samples of the U.S. Census. But the overall quest of mine has been to let migrants share—and whenever possible, analyze—their own experiences.

12. A 1989 episode of *48 Hours* entitled "Another America" is only an example of this stereotypical notion.

13. See *Mountain Life and Work* 36 (Summer 1961): 36; and "Urban Migrants," 26. The complete lyrics of Parton's song can be found in Horstman, *Sing Your Heart Out, Country Boy,* 15.

14. Mayberry interview. Excerpted material from oral history interviews I have conducted has been transcribed verbatim, except for any false starts in the narrative that detract from the overall intent of the narrator. Spelling has been standardized, but grammar has been left as spoken by the narrator.

15. Ibid.

16. Ibid.

17. Richard was present during the interview with his mother.

1 *Footloose and Dependent: The Pioneers*

> It is almost sinful how I love these old acres here . . . how I lay store by each inch of the land, each blade of grass or grain it grows, how I believe there is no spot in the universe so perfect, so dear, and so sweet as the West Virginia mountains.
>
> —Mountain farm woman, ca. 1928

> Yes, one time I was very anxious to leave. I believe that was during the first war. There were a lot of other folks that left then and made a lot of money. My husband didn't want to go, so we stayed. We're still here, and we like it here.
>
> —Meda Arnett, 1971, Magoffin County, Ky.

FOR MOST RURAL FOLKS throughout the South, Jack Temple Kirby writes, the beginning decades of the twentieth century were a time "of danger, of loss, of falling backward while the rest of the industrialized world sped by." Anyone familiar with the history of especially the Upland South will immediately ask not so much why southerners left their region in droves in the twentieth century but why it took them so long to pack their bags, especially once the South, after the 1870s, became, in Gavin Wright's words, "a low-wage region in a high-wage country." Why, in other words, did these people from a poor region not flock to a land of relative riches sooner? The answer to the first question—why people left the South—is obvious: at best, people wanted to earn some money; at worst, people were starving, and migration would solve the problem, or so they thought.[1]

The answer to why it took white southerners so long to leave is more complex. In this chapter, I move up the beginning date of southern white out-migration from the date more commonly accepted—World War II—to at least as early as World War I, diverging from earlier studies that examine mainly Appalachian migrants. Paul Salstrom writes, for example, that "the mass migration of Appalachian whites began only when World War II created such extensive outside labor opportunities that nuclear families could migrate as parts of extended family units, as parts of what mountain sociologists," referring to James S. Brown and others, "call 'family groups.'" If mass out-migration did not really begin until the 1940s, the material for the following chapters—the cyclical pattern of migration northward and return migration to the South based on the national economy—would not exist. In moving up the beginning date, I am also expanding the story of migration to include southern whites—flatlanders as well as highlanders—since more recent studies have explored black migration.[2] Let it be clear, too, that in asking the question why it took so long to leave, I do not mean to fault southern white people. Much of this study proves that once southerners finally did leave, they enjoyed a measure of success generally unknown to those who stayed in the South. My aim here is to examine briefly why southerners began to leave the South when they did and then explore in more detail the experiences of several pioneering twentieth-century white out-migrants.

In Search of a Pull

The economic picture of the entire postbellum South has long been known to be grim. After the Civil War, farmers across the South fought another (losing) battle for self-sufficiency. The last three decades of the nineteenth century saw farmers of small acreages lose their longtime faith in the production of foodstuffs for their own tables and instead raise cotton or tobacco for the market. Cotton seemed a more plausible way to wipe out increasing debt, but as the high price of cotton was wiped out in the 1890s, so were the dreams of many farmers. Each autumn, cotton could demand money, but as the price fell, farmers realized they were without money to buy food for the winter, further increasing indebtedness. Railroads, local merchants, and commercial fertilizer only enhanced this transition from self-sufficiency to cotton-dependency. As the price buoyed up after 1900, the boll weevil infected lands eastward, though ironically, the historian Gavin Wright has discovered, the infestation served to keep prices high in areas not immediately decimated by infestation. Farmers therefore persisted in their marriage to cotton.[3]

Other scholars have examined attempts to sustain economic independence. In Clay County, Kentucky, for example, farmers witnessed a precipitous decline in their standard of living after 1860, while farmers in the Upper Cumberland of Tennessee were able to delay that decline for several decades. According to the historian Jeanette Keith, those in the Upper Cumberland were always in the middle of the commercial agricultural spectrum—seeking a middle ground between trying to participate in the market economy "without becoming dependent on it" even as progressive types were arguing for more specialization. By World War I, there was not so much a new economy as an "economy with new elements patched and fitted into old." Traditional life persisted, due particularly to some prosperous years between 1900 and 1910, but by the 1920s, many farmers had been marginalized. They had paid a high price for their traditionalism.[4]

Historians once assumed that life in the Appalachian South was rather static and isolated until coal and lumber interests began to penetrate the region in the late nineteenth century. But because of the works of at least half a dozen recent scholars, historians are beginning to see how false such an understanding is; as much or even more than the rest of the South, the Appalachian region's economic life had been harsh. Isolation, too—whether of the economic or geographic variety—is a relative term that does not apply ubiquitously or homogeneously to the region. Scholars lately have all stressed how southern Appalachia had long been controlled by outside forces, particularly absentee ownership; how a local elite dominated over lower classes; and how widespread tenantry was. Absentee landowners and speculators were in the region from the outset, and they began developing their lands after the Civil War with, in the words of one historian, "specious land claims, chicanery, ejectment, and deceit." This is not the usual picture of an Edenic Appalachia being desecrated by lumber and coal barons at the turn of the century. Since many pockets of upland southerners were already financially dependent before industrialization began to seep into the region, the picture historians have drawn emphasizes, at least implicitly, that upland southerners and their flatland cousins, long accustomed to dark economic clouds, were nervously fearful of any darker clouds. Once those clouds appeared, as they did in different times and places, southerners received their push to leave; they were merely waiting for the pull.[5]

After the Civil War, more pulls came. Southerners who eventually left the region for the Midwest frequently had already had some kind of off-the-farm experience prior to their departure. Most southerners were accustomed to ingenious ways of supplementing their rural income, whether it was hunting ginseng, poaching furs, or sawmilling; for some, temporary migration was simply added to the list of ways to make do.[6]

Several pulls originated in the South itself. Gavin Wright notes that "it was much easier for a poor southern farm laborer to follow functioning market channels within the South than to set off on his own to an unfamiliar region." One pull came from previously sleepy southern towns, such as Atlanta, Memphis, Nashville, Chattanooga, Lexington, Roanoke, and Birmingham, which had all experienced dramatic gains in population since the 1870s because they were able to absorb people from the rural backcountry. In Knoxville, for example, in-migration by both nearby whites and blacks more than doubled the population of the city between 1860 and 1880 alone. Newcomers were attracted by not only growth facilitated by railroads but also the rippling effect of wholesaling and manufacturing operations. As the authors Michael J. McDonald and William Bruce Wheeler point out, however, in-migrants "who moved from the agriculturally overpopulated hinterland in search of employment soon learned that industrialization and urban life threatened to cut them off from the traditional culture and institutions they valued so highly. They strongly resisted the threats."[7]

Historians have told how some mountaineers were attracted to coal towns that mushroomed throughout the newly discovered coalfields of the Cumberland Plateau, another pull. As Crandall A. Shifflett argues, these newcomers were not faceless victims directed by change; they came out of choice, having appreciated the conveniences—as well as the leisure opportunities—of coal town life and the prosperity of wage labor. The change was not an abrupt break with the past because migrants drew on their past to condition their present. It was only after the coal bust—after the mid-1920s and the end of the shortage of labor that led coal operators to be far less concerned with the quality of life in their towns—that conditions grew increasingly dismal and hopeless. Moreover, Paul Salstrom argues that while development of southern coalfields had delayed a subsistence crisis on the Cumberland Plateau and in much of West Virginia, income from mining, supplemented by subsistence agriculture when and where feasible, proved to be only a short-term fix, because large families—needed to keep the farm running—could not later be absorbed in the region's mines. Out-migration eventually had to occur, though only after a move to a coal mine or a coal camp.[8]

The textile boom was another attraction for approximately three-quarters of a million people who moved to mill towns, such as Bernice

Isenhour, who, born in 1912 in Patrick County, Virginia, in the Blue Ridge, moved to Fieldale in the 1920s with her family after her older brother got a job in the mill and arranged for company housing. The pull to migrate to a new cotton mill town was strengthened by labor recruiters, who fanned out from the Piedmont in search of workers. With the declining state of agriculture, it is not difficult to see why some were more than willing to give up old ways for new ones. As the authors of *Like a Family* point out, industrial capitalism's rise was inversely related to subsistence agriculture's demise: "the same conditions that crippled farmers feathered the nests of many merchants and breathed life into the small towns where they made their homes." Migration to mill towns did not happen overnight but occurred in waves over several decades. The first to be pulled off the land were female-headed tenant families—probably the most vulnerable economically—followed near the turn of the century by more families headed by men. In the twentieth century, another textile boom forced recruiters into the southern Appalachians.[9]

Other sporadic economic changes were those that could exploit the South's cheap, unskilled labor. While the region remained overwhelmingly agricultural, occasionally economic diversity led to communities of opportunity, but these enterprises, for the most part, "paid low wages and . . . added relatively little value to the raw materials with which they worked," according to one scholar. Railroads, for example, were beginning to open up more of the Upland South, sparking a number of nonagricultural industries in and near the mountains that attracted workers. Furniture making drew hundreds to High Point and other communities just east of the Blue Ridge in North Carolina after 1888; companies began mining kaolin and mica in the state as well. Tennessee also had several plants specializing in metals: the Aluminum Company of America opened a vast smelter near Maryville in east Tennessee, and in 1901 a copper mine at Ducktown, near the border of Tennessee, Georgia, and North Carolina, began operations. R. G. Hudson, who grew up fifteen miles away in nearby Blue Ridge, Georgia, said Ducktown and later Copper Hill were the only places for "public" work when he was young. And of course, iron and steel transformed such places as Chattanooga and Birmingham. But history was a burden for industrialization in the South: its late start, its lack of a technological support base, and its isolation proved difficult to overcome.[10]

When the supply of cheap immigrant labor was cut off during World War I, every southerner's option changed. Northern wartime industry pulled southerners northward to supply the great factories. Zeke Jett, born in 1893 in Breathitt County, Kentucky, recalled that after the war "people went to going out of here for public works, and plants started up over the country. And they could make a better living, and so a greater part of them moved out." "Now," he added, "when you hear tell of some elderly person like me be deceased, well, they'll give the names. They'll have boys and girls in California, Michigan, New York, and all over the country. Whereas, I'd say, thirty years before that time, everybody was right in that same creek, neighborhood. Never had gone out. But things changed after World War I in this country where there were more works, and they could make a better living." "They couldn't make a living," he concluded, "and they moved out." Other people also remember the war as a benchmark for change, just as World War II would be for a later generation. Melvin Profitt, born in 1904 in Wolfe County, Kentucky, said, "I've talked with a lot of old men, that is, a few years back, just to try to find out something that I didn't know. And they tell me that times in this county and the surrounding areas was about the same from 1875 until World War I." "Now, World War I was what made the big change," he explained. Fred Gabbard, who grew up in Owsley County, Kentucky, agreed. "A large number of the boys traveled. They went to Europe and saw other countries," he said. "It caused a lot of them, after they came home, to go back to school or to maybe even settle in other cities or places."[11]

The changes the war was bringing would be significant in years to come. People all over the South were pulled not only to new worlds abroad but also to new and different worlds at home. Jeanette Keith details the changes, especially the increasing presence of government, associated with "Sergeant York's Home Front" in the Upper Cumberland. Contrary to legend, she notes, most men "did not rush to the colors." Elsewhere, some mountaineers began working for $1.50 per day helping build eastern Kentucky railroads in the early teens, just in time for the war. Others began logging for the sawmills that sprouted across the Upland South. Riley Crabtree began helping his father log in 1915 at age twelve in Grundy County, Tennessee. "I drove oxen," he explained. "My dad used to have four yoke of oxen and drag logs off the sides of the mountain." Because eastern Tennessee's coalfields had already peaked, Riley later moved with his family to work in the eastern Kentucky mines, where the boom would not peak until 1927. After years of tenant farming, cutting timber, making rails, and "digging coal" along mountainsides for fifty cents a ton in the winters, Melvin Profitt's father went to work in the oil fields of nearby Lee County in 1917 (he would come home twice a month); Melvin went to the oil fields when he was fifteen, in 1919. The high-risk yet tempting life-style was the new boom and bust economy.

After getting laid off in the oil fields, Melvin went to work in the coal mines. In the 1920s, when he was laid off, he, like countless other miners, was forced to find other work. "I didn't love to leave," he said, reflecting the tensions of a divided heart, "but I was almost forced to." "I knowed a number of people that didn't leave that was married before I was that just wouldn't leave their wife and family for any reason," he explained. "So, I would a rather see them eat a little higher on the hog and been away from them, and had more clothing, than to have stayed here and worked, and sweated and maybe couldn't pay my bills like a lot of other people." Ed Combs, from Quicksand, in Breathitt County, Kentucky, remembers as a child watching loaded log trains traveling up South Fork Creek and how the Mowbrary & Robinson Lumber Company built a company town at Quicksand, complete with a commissary. The town's boom years were in 1917 and 1918, but once the virgin timber was gone, the mill ceased operations. "When the mill closed," Combs said, "they had to find employment. They scattered all over Indiana, Michigan, Ohio, Wisconsin."[12]

As the strength of pushes increased and as more pulls emerged, people were suddenly faced with a number of decisions: stay on the homeplace or move to a new coal camp or mill town; try to continue the traditional life or venture into the more modern; migrate temporarily, perhaps to Atlanta, Nashville, or any of a number of growing southern towns or even to Cincinnati, Detroit, or Akron, and then return home; be hungry, poor, but happy in the South or be comfortable but perhaps unfulfilled in the North; stay near family and kin or light out on one's own; be content or curious. A new northern pull brought not only the possibility of dislocation but also a divided heart to the generations of twentieth-century southerners who tried to reconcile that tension. "If only I could get a good job here at home" was the wish of hundreds of thousands, a wish that remained impossible because of the very unevenness of capitalist economic development. After World War I, more and more southerners believed that the opportunity they were seeking did not exist in the South.

The responses to this divided heart were as varied as southern whites themselves. Some were early exiles, acting on their expectations of northern life, and never looked back, but most, based on oral testimony, seem to have struggled with the decision to migrate, even when indecision prolonged their misery. The contradictions and the ambivalence that capitalism provoked were not easily overcome, and much of the story of southern white migration deals with this struggle.

The Great White Migration Begins

For thousands of southerners, the solution to problems in the South was exile, a solution that on the whole was very successful economically if painful emotionally. During World War I and throughout the early and mid-1920s, more and more southerners were attracted to the Midwest. The steel mills of Cleveland, Chicago, and the Calumet region in northern Indiana; the auto factories of Flint, Detroit, South Bend, and Indianapolis; the rubber factories of Akron; and the diversity (and proximity) of Ohio's Miami Valley industry attracted hundreds of thousands (including African Americans and Mexicans as well as southern whites).[13] There was such a housing shortage in Akron, Ohio, for example, during the 1920s that boardinghouses offered "hot beds," in which three different men would sleep in the same bed for each of the three eight-hour shifts. Beds there were also put out on porches to deal with the large number of migrants.

Furthermore, the revolutions in transportation made such life changes associated with migration a real possibility. Highway building began opening even the mountains in the mid-1920s; in years to come, these routes would largely direct the stream of migrants. As Robert S. Lynd and Helen Merrell Lynd wrote in 1937, "This migratory tendency which modern industry invites and the Ford car enormously facilitates may be expected to have far-reaching influence throughout the rest of the workers' lives." By 1924, the nation was already alarmed by "gasoline gypsies" and "auto tramps" who allegedly found it cheaper to move about the country by car than pay rent. American readers would soon be bombarded by such stories, which claimed that "their net capital is invested in a Ford that may have cost as little as twenty-five dollars. The children ought doubtless to be in school, but they are getting the education of the gasoline gypsy."[14] It was only a portent of the animosity to come.

By the late 1930s, businesses were springing up to help transport eager migrants northward and return homesick ones to the South. In 1927, the first bus line opened in southern Appalachia, but the following year, J. Polk Brooks, a migrant originally from Paducah, Kentucky, who had done a stint in a Detroit Chevrolet plant, began the Brooks Bus Line. "The longer I lived in Detroit," Brooks noted, "the more people I met from Paducah, Mayfield, and other West Kentucky towns. When people heard my wife and I were driving to Paducah they'd ask for a ride." Competition was stiff; there were at least twenty other drivers offering similar services during the late 1920s, but Brooks eventually traded in his worn-out 1924 car for a seven-passenger used car he bought from a Paducah taxi company. He made one trip a week (twenty-six hours one way) and charged passengers $12.50. In 1936, when the Interstate Commerce Commission required drivers to apply for permits, the regulation killed his competition. By the 1940s and 1950s, when out-migration was at its peak, business for Brooks was booming, and he had purchased a fleet of buses that traveled daily between western Kentucky and Detroit.[15]

Because census data for the 1920s was not as sophisticated as it would become, it is difficult to get an accurate assessment of just how many white southerners left the region. One estimate maintains that slightly more than two million whites moved out of the South in the first two decades of the twentieth century. Given the extraordinarily high birthrate in the southern mountains, it is significant that in the 1920s, eleven eastern Kentucky agricultural counties lost almost a quarter of their population. Most of the coal counties showed smaller losses or even net gains, which means that people leaving agricultural areas were not necessarily going to the mines. A study of 311 young men (sixteen and older) in Knott County, Kentucky, which had a few mines but was primarily agricultural, revealed 124 at home, 104 away from home but within the county, 56 elsewhere within the southern Appalachian region (and of those, 27 had gone into the mines), and 27 outside the region.[16]

The destinations of southerners, however, were not limited to the urban industrial venue that most often comes to mind. According to a story from Magoffin County, Kentucky, in 1907 a young man in his twenties had committed an offense for which he was banished from the county. After counting his funds (two dollars), he asked a ticket agent to sell him and his companion two fares to anyplace their money would take them. Before long, they arrived in Alger, Ohio, in Hardin County. There, they saw "great level fields dotted here and there with groups of people stooping over, doing some kind of work." They were picking onions, and the pair quickly got jobs as pickers. By the end of the season, they had made what to them was a sizable amount of money. Having spent the winter "on the marsh" (the area was the former Scioto Marsh), they told the operators of the farm that they could return to Kentucky and get as many workers as they wanted. "Being ever on the alert for cheap labor," the operators gave them several hundred dollars to arrange for transporting friends and relatives from Magoffin County to Ohio. They continued this for several years, until the migration could sustain itself. A journalist writing about "the onion workers" in the late teens traveled to Kentucky and found that the overwhelming majority of the four hundred families in a section of Magoffin County where the young man lived had been to Ohio. At the time of the article, the migration entailed about one hundred families annually. Of the total number of people who had gone to Ohio, not more than a third owned their land (the owners that left usually rented their land to kin who raised enough corn to "bread the whole clan" through the winter), and not more than half a dozen had been able to purchase land with money earned in the fields. Wages were so low that migrants barely had enough money to get back to Kentucky, although some thrifty migrants had saved enough to purchase homes on the marsh to live there permanently.[17]

Those tenants who went north to Ohio from Magoffin, Monroe, Floyd, Breathitt, Knox, and Perry counties in Kentucky often became sharecroppers in the North. To keep them working, operators gave them three to five acres and a sawmill shack in which to live. The operators prepared the soil, provided fertilizer and seed, and sowed the crop; tenants were required to pay a four-to-five-dollar fee per acre at harvest time and turn over half of the crop. They spent the rest of their time working as laborers in the larger fields for two dollars a day for ten hours' work. Children were used extensively and were paid a proportion of adults' wages. Because start-up costs were high after the marsh was drained, the operators had to use every inch of ground and the cheapest labor possible. Shacks built of green lumber developed cracks and were unbearably cold in the winter. Kentuckians who wintered once in Ohio and then left that state never to return were replaced by other southerners all too happy to move into the abandoned shack. When migrants began to stay after the harvest was over, they quickly caught the ire of natives, who complained bitterly about their reputed feuds, knifings, murders, backwardness, and ignorance.[18]

White southerners looking for agricultural work also went to other midwestern states. Their ports of entry were the Ohio River bridges, where migrant families could cross for only a few pennies. The 1920s also saw the beginning of what would become a massive agricultural migration based on "quick chilling" of fruit; former tenants and croppers traveled first to Arkansas to pick strawberries and other fruit and then followed the season up the Mississippi Valley all the way to Michigan. Indiana in the 1920s was developing a contingent of tomato pickers, many of whom were from central Kentucky. In the late 1930s, over five thousand out-of-state migrants worked in the fields; over a thousand workers were needed in Johnson County alone, which is today the home of many people born in Kentucky. Each season ads were placed in Kentucky newspapers announcing that on a particular day and time a truck would be at a designated place in town to transport Kentuckians to the tomato fields. John Brown, for example, from Pulaski County, Kentucky, went to Indianapolis both before and after his marriage to his wife, Helen. In March 1920, Helen moved there to be with him after he had gotten a job at the Campbell Canning Company. They stayed two years and then moved back to Kentucky before they settled permanently in Norwood, Ohio, outside of Cincinnati. "I didn't want to come to the city," Helen explained. "It would be a change in the life style, you know. When my husband decided to come up here I didn't want to come but I did anyway. And I was so homesick, I tell you—I thought I was going to die. I thought I was real physically sick, but I was just homesick." For their part, Hoosiers refused to work in the fields but were willing to work the two or three months in the canneries; like their Ohio neighbors, they were also very willing to squawk about those migrants who remained in the state after the season.[19]

The more popular migration to the Midwest, perhaps, was to an industrial area. For some, the transformation to midwestern urban, industrial life was tempered by intraregional moves to southern urban areas. For others, the break between a rural past and an urban future came more suddenly. Joe Wilson's father left Oakland, Kentucky, in 1919 for Anderson, Indiana's booming auto parts factories. Joe explained from his Anderson home:

> My dad came up here first, see. Him and about four or five others. He had an old '17 Model T touring car. And they heard that Indiana—Anderson, Indiana—was hiring people (which we had a bunch of little factories here and they were). And he came up here and then got a job and then when he got enough money ahead that he could have us to come up on the train, we came on the train up here, see. My sister, me, and my brother, and a baby brother, in arms, see. We rode the train up here—my mother did by herself, and she'd never been in anything like that.

The flood of Kentuckians that swept through the Miami Valley of southwestern Ohio dates from 1916, when a company recruiter from Champion Paper and Fiber Company traveled throughout the eastern Kentucky countryside nailing posters to trees advertising jobs in the Hamilton, Ohio, plant. He would then arrange train transportation to take them north. A Champion official interviewed later said it was common to lose between 30 and 40 percent of mountaineer recruits each time the train stopped; they would climb out the windows of the train, presumably drawn back to their homeplace. Once in Hamilton, those still aboard were taken to a rooming house. The official also noted the prevalence of shuttle migration; men would routinely leave the mountains after the autumn harvest to work in Hamilton and then return to Kentucky in time to plant a crop in the spring.[20]

Hazel Smith was born in 1905 in Madison County, Kentucky, near the foothills of the Cumberland Plateau, where her father was a successful merchant and farmer. When she married in September 1924, she and her husband rented some land that belonged to his grandfather, but she could see trouble in their financial future. Her solution the following September illustrates the pushes and pulls that led women as well as men to become migrants:

> I could see that we was getting in debt. We had to go in debt. We had a crop on his grandfather's farm. I seen we was going in debt and wasn't going to be able to have enough money to live on the next year without going in debt again. We wasn't getting nowheres. And so then I suggested (my older brother had done moved out here [to Norwood, Ohio]) coming here and getting a job and working a while, then going back there and paying these bills off then. Then we'd have extra money to live on. But I came—I was here two and a half weeks. I worked up here on Highland Avenue at that can company—U.S. Can. I was working there, and that's where I got the job at. As soon as I wrote back that I had a job there, he got rid of all of our furniture, turned this crop over in his uncle's name for him to pay off the bills we owed. And he come to Cincinnati. And he come on Wednesday and then on Monday he done had a job at Cincinnati Rubber Company. And he worked there as long as he worked—was able to work. Never left there. He worked there, maybe it was thirty-three years. But anyhow he worked from then on until he was a disability and couldn't work.

Although Smith took the initiative to move, she hated the city at first. "When I first come here," she said, "I thought I'd smother to death," referring to both the dirty air and the cramped conditions. "We moved down to Cincinnati, and we had some little attic rooms down there. High, and smoke and noise, and everything else, and then they was still selling coal. We had a little old gas stove, and then we had coal to heat with, see. That just about killed me for a while." She quickly came to appreciate running water and indoor toilets, however, no matter how dumpy her surroundings. Her husband made nineteen dollars a week when he arrived in 1925, and it took her managing skills to "stretch" out the money. They moved frequently in the next few years but finally settled in Norwood, along with what must have been a growing number of southerners. After her youngest child was in school, she returned to work, first at the United States Playing Card Company and then at a globe factory, a department store, and finally a dress shop.[21]

Muncie, Indiana, like other booming industrial towns throughout Wisconsin, Illinois, Indiana, Michigan, and Ohio, began attracting southerners in the early 1920s and probably even sooner, with the demands of

World War I mobilization. As one of the city's "influential manufacturers" told the Lynds:

> In 1922 we were so rushed with orders we couldn't possibly fill them or get enough men here in town to carry on, so we had to import some men from Kentucky and West Virginia. Our men from our local district here, born and bred on the farms near here, knowing the use of machinery of some sort from their boyhood, reliable, steady, we call "corn-feds." These men we brought in from the mountains we called "green peas." We brought two train loads of them down. Some of them learned quickly, and some of them didn't. Most of them have drifted back by now. We figured it cost $75–$200 to train each one of them, and there was such a demand for labor about town that they didn't stay with us. They drifted about from shop to shop, and of course when the slump came we fired them and kept our old men.

Other Muncie employers actively recruited southerners in the 1920s. Margaret Ripley Wolfe, who studied the migration of Fentress County, Tennessee, residents to Muncie, reports that a map on the front of the Forbus General Store in the county read "Muncie, 325.1 miles; Dayton, 300 miles; Indianapolis, 275." In 1990, she interviewed ninety-one-year-old Thomas C. Peavyhouse, who remembered as a young teenage boy floating logs down the Cumberland River to Nashville alongside his father. After working in Kentucky for two years, he told his brother Ray, "I'm going somewhere where I can get paid for what I do. I'm going to Muncie, Indiana. They're hiring men up there." An uncle of his had already worked there. In 1928, Tom and his brothers Ray and Clemens set out for Muncie in a Chevrolet roadster. They drove three days and two nights before reaching Muncie. Although the three found jobs, before long Clemens and Ray, homesick over their wives and the land they left behind, left Muncie for Fentress County. "On the fourth of July," recalled Tom, "I said to myself, this ain't going to work, this old nasty place. I quit a better job [back home]." But the next day, he was hired by Indiana Steel and Wire for thirty-seven-and-a-half cents an hour and would stay there for fourteen years. In July 1929, his girlfriend from Tennessee, Myrtle Choate, came to Muncie to live with her sister and her family; two months later, she and Tom were married.[22]

Robert Whitten was born in Wayne County, Tennessee, about a hundred miles southwest of Nashville near the Tennessee River (and beyond the boundaries of "Appalachia"). In the 1920s, he ventured north to deliver ice. "I worked in Michigan," he said, "two months or three [and then] I went on over to Illinois—walked over there. I just delivered ice; I got four dollars and eighty cents a day for hauling ice. I had two big horses and an ice wagon. I'd set up in there like a big one!" But Whitten found Illinois and Michigan too different from Tennessee—his heart was less divided than most perhaps—and he returned home with some capital saved, eventually opening a general store. "I went to work after I come back, by George, for a dollar and a quarter a day. That was pretty hard to lose that much, but I wouldn't a been displeased up there for ten dollars a day." Once he returned home, life was very difficult. "We didn't have the money, by God," he said, "to spare to go nowhere much." "We took the kids' gift money," he continued, "and had the mules shod. We didn't have no other money to do it with. We couldn't get a hold of no money even."[23]

Orbie Berry was also from Wayne County, but he stayed far longer in the North than Whitten did, though he, too, eventually returned to the South. I interviewed Berry (born in 1904) in 1985 for another project, but when I turned on the tape recorder, he quickly began telling me about his migration experience, which may typify the experience of other migrants.[24] Tired of working on the farm for his father, he decided at the age of twenty to go to Flint, Michigan. "Went to work for Chevrolet Motor Company," he explained. "That was in 1925. Well, they wasn't nothing down here where you make any money. You see, I hated to start out like a lot of them do, you know, and I just decided I'd get out and see part of the world. And I got a job up there you see, and it was pretty hard work, those Chevrolet people, but I never did burn out—they was lots of them did." Berry remembered with exacting detail the logistics of getting up to Flint: "I went to Florence. I got on the L&N up to Nashville and got a ticket then to Detroit. On a train. And I got to Detroit. I caught an interurban electric train seventy-five mile up to Flint. It was a better connection out—that was the reason I went that way. So that's the way I went out. Got up there about 9:30 in the night and went to a hotel . . . and I went to my friend's out on Dakota Avenue—that's where he lived. I had to transfer twice to get out there, and I walked out there and carried my suitcase."

Berry's success at finding a job quickly was partially because of the economic climate and his friend's help but also because of his own initiative and willingness to accept any available position. His story manifests little of the "dumb hillbilly" stereotype that would eventually become so popular:

> And he [his friend] wanted me to work at the Buick people. Said they paid better and done better, and I said, "Now they told me downtown, well down there where I got on the streetcar, they needed a bunch of people at the Chevrolet [plant]"—it was on the west side of Flint, Buick people on the north, see their plant was—and this boy lived up there. "Well," I

> says, "I tell you what to do—there's not might a harm there to go to work." And he says, "I'll just get in the car and we'll take you over to [Chevrolet] and see what they do."
>
> We got over there and about a hundred fellows was standing around the employment office, and the employment agent come out and wanted three men on some old punch presses. And you'd stick your hand up. And I got my hand up and looked and there was another or two, two or three had them up. And they called me and the two other fellows and so [we] went in there. And he said, "Where are you from?" And I just filled my own application out—don't go through a lot of red tape like they do now, you know. So he'd seen where I was from—from Tennessee. "Well," he said, "I'm from Missouri." You know, he wasn't too old a fellow—he was about a thirty-five-year-old fellow I guess—a young fellow. I said, "Well, I don't know anything about these punch presses"—they was a hollering out to this crowd out here like a slaughterhouse, and I said, "Well I'll take the job and see how I like it." Well, he wrote me up and told me to go to work at four o'clock. Well then it was about 12:30. And this boy, I went on back out and told him what I'd done—they'd hired me—had to be to work at four o'clock. The employment agent told me—he said, "Berry," he says (I said I got to hunt a boarding place), and he called on the phone there a minute and told me right where I'd get a room, but no board—just a room. I said, "Well a room's all right."
>
> So I went on and went to work and got off at 2:30—worked ten hours, and so that's the way I done. I worked that a way for a long time—that night shift. And so that was about the end of that now.

Although he knew he was something of a pioneer by moving north, he learned about the possibilities of northern industry from those who had gone before, suggesting an already strong migration stream from Tennessee to Flint. "Twenty-five—that was the year I went up there," Berry remembered. "I knowed this fellow Shepherd. And I knowed a few boys—some Youngbloods that went on up there two or three years before that was from Collinwood here, and a Rich fellow—he had some friends here, but he was from Arkansas. But I knew him, I'd met him here, you know. I didn't know many [people]—there wasn't many people up there from down here in them days. Well there wasn't none hardly—just what I said."

Berry continued to fill in the details of his adventure, touching on themes that for generations would predominate in the migrant experience, including suffering from homesickness, escaping to the South during the winter, buying a new car as quickly as possible, and bringing back eager friends and relatives, which further fueled northern industries. All of these motifs show his attempt to reconcile his ambivalences about migration:

I had nothing to be lonely for—there was too much excitement—everything was a boom you know to what it was here you see. Flint's a pretty good-sized town then you see. Yeah—it wasn't lonely. I didn't say I loved it, but I didn't burn out and come home. A lot of them'd get homesick, you see. I've seen them work there three weeks and get a payday or two and they'd be back. They'd say, "I'm going back to my dad." I said, "I've got a good dad," but I said I stayed there till I was twenty year old—there's more brothers younger than me that can take my place [laughs].

I stayed on then till the winter there, and there was a boy that went with me during that time (I left off a little of that). He didn't get a job on the inside. They put him out on unloading boxcars as parts went out. And it got cold out there in the winter time. And he says, "You know, I'm freezing to death out there." [And I said] "get you some more heavier clothes—there's men out there doing that, ain't they?" And he says, "Yeah." And I says, "Well you can do what the other fellows can do, can't you [laughs]"? It was bad I know out there. And I said, "Well maybe you can get a transfer—maybe on the inside somewhere." But you know, he wanted to come home too to tell you the truth. So I told the foreman, then I said, "Well it's pretty rough up here"—it was getting pretty rough then in December you know. Big snows. So I said, "Well, I'll just go with you then." And I come back and stayed till the next spring there (March) and I went back.

Of course [I] went right on in through to the employment office, and he knew me. And I says, "I'm back up here, now." He said, "Do you want to go back down there where you was at?" I said, "Well I don't mind that." I'd done built up—I wasn't on them bad jobs—they had some pretty good ones, I mean. Electric welding a little and that was very easy—spot welding. So I went on in and that was in '26. In '26 I bought a new model Chevrolet car. You can't work no longer than I did and buy a new car now, you see. It'd cost you ten or twelve thousand dollars. That car cost $695.

At that time there was different people coming up. They'd always want to ride back and get a job. I said, "They're hiring a whole lot." I'd say, "I can't guarantee you a job." And some of them I'd say, "Well, I can guarantee you a job if you want to come." I got acquainted with this employment agent and I'd meet him up at town and he knew me. Anyhow, that winter it got rough again, pretty cold, and I told the foreman, "I wouldn't mind [to] go down home and see the folks." Well there was two or three that wanted to come home with me. They was ready to get back. And I come back then and stayed I know a couple of months. Went back up there [after] the winter. And I come home one time and I'd bring three or four fellows. I had a little touring car, you know, and I didn't use it in the winter. I'd bring about four every time I'd come back [laughs]. And then on up in '27, I believe I took four or five—just loaded that thing up going back. Twenty or twenty-five dollars—it'd cost you about twenty-five or thirty if you went on a bus—they'd just say, "I'll give you what it would cost me to get there." I'd make just about as much money coming down here and going back as I did there a month or two, you know.

Even though historians know that preindustrial workers often resisted the regimentation of factory work and took time off, Berry's trips "down home" are revealing because they indicate the ambivalence associated with migration. Berry enjoyed working in the North and the money it brought, but this enjoyment was conditioned by a desire to stay in contact with the South:[25]

> As long as you kept in good ties with the company, they'd give you time off. . . . Well, I'd say, "Well I need to go home, before it gets to be bad weather, you know." I had that little old car, you know, and I still had it. . . . But anyway I worked on to December the 28th. Twelve hours a day. Then they got to working Sunday. I said, "Well, I'll just work it." The boy that was with me—the helper—he was from Canada. And he was a young fellow like myself—wasn't married. And he said, "I'd like to make all the money I can make." . . . And so we worked there through December, now, till I got ready to come home on that vacation. That was in '29. And I worked all the way from ten to twelve hours a day then. I was on days them time. They changed me from nights to days.
>
> And I'd tell the foreman, "I need to go home before it gets rough." I'd bought a new closed car—a '29—one of them new Chevrolets, but I didn't buy it then until October, getting it ready to come home—had it broke in you know. And so he said, "We just can't replace you, and if we can't get someone to keep all this down we can't run this line." I said, "I know it—I know how it is, but you know good and well that there can be somebody operate and keep this thing a going." But now it was a booming. Well, one day old Baker, the head general foreman, come down by and he'd stop and brag on us a little, and I said, "I've heard you brag on me as long as I'm going to hear it." He said, "Why Berry?" I said, "Well, I've just been aiming to go home here for a month before it got bad weather and it's done now getting to be bad, time I go down and stay two weeks." I said, "Give me a tool clearance." I said, "I've been a going down to the superintendent and he'd just say 'We just can't do without you now—just wait a little longer.'" He started to walk away and I said, "Wait a minute here—you know what I asked you. Give me a tool clearance." That meant to go to the office and get your pay—check out. So he wrote it—he wrote it out. And after the whistle blowed there at four o'clock . . . I just stopped. Just never did start to change—that whistle blowed at four o'clock and [I] just shut her down. And this boy he knowed what I meant—I told him what I was aiming to do.
>
> I went down there and the superintendent seen it was a tool clearance to check everything out. He just tore it in two before he said a word. He said, "You're wanting to go home, I guess." I said, "That's where I'm a fixing to go. Why are you tearing that up for?" He said, "Go. You'll be back ain't you?" I said, "Yeah. I'm going to stay two weeks."

Both the Chevrolet people and Berry himself believed that he really would be back to his job after a few weeks of visiting and tending business "down home." But what they did not yet realize was this sojourn would be Berry's last as a southern migrant. As the economic conditions of boom were replaced by bust, thousands of migrants such as Berry would be pushed out of factories; with no place else to go, they went back home to tough out the Great Depression.

Notes

1. Kirby, *Rural Worlds Lost,* 52; Wright, *Old South, New South,* 76. For a discussion of earlier migrations, especially in the nineteenth century, see Hsiung, *Two Worlds in the Tennessee Mountains,* 103–27; and Salstrom, *Appalachia's Path to Dependency,* 1–59. Jeanette Keith also notes that out-migration to western lands left a number of farmers in the Upper Cumberland of Tennessee who were satisfied with status quo methods. Keith, *Country People in the New South,* 13–14.

2. Salstrom, *Appalachia's Path to Dependency,* 40; Brown, "Family behind the Migrant, 153–57; Schwarzweller, Brown, and Mangalam, *Mountain Families in Transition.* On black migration, see Grossman, *Land of Hope;* Gottlieb, *Making Their Own Way;* Trotter, ed., *Great Migration in Historical Perspective;* and Lemann, *Promised Land.*

3. Wright, *Old South, New South,* 107–23.

4. Billings and Blee, "Agriculture and Poverty in the Kentucky Mountains," 233–69; Keith, *Country People in the New South,* 89, 85. Keith's book is an excellent examination of a region on the eve of migration.

5. I am not going to detail the push out of the South because other historians have already done so. Much new Appalachian scholarship is represented in Pudup, Billings, and Waller, eds., *Appalachia in the Making;* McKinney, "Economy and Community in Western North Carolina, 1860–1865," 163–84; Hsiung, *Two Worlds in the Tennessee Mountains,* esp. 8–19; Dunaway, "Speculators and Capitalists," 67; Dunaway, *First American Frontier,* 249; Rasmussen, *Absentee Landowning and Exploitation in West Virginia,* 6; and Inscoe, *Mountain Masters, Slavery, and the Sectional Crisis in Western North Carolina.* On differences of development throughout the region, see, for example, Waller, *Feud;* Dunn, *Cades Cove;* Eller, *Miners, Millhands, and Mountaineers;* Pudup, "Town and Country in the Transformation of Appalachian Kentucky," 270–96; and Hofstra and Mitchell, "Town and Country in Backcountry Virginia," 619–46.

6. Even by 1860 in Appalachia, nearly two-fifths of households were earning income from nonagricultural sources. Dunaway, *First American Frontier,* 249.

7. Wright, *Old South, New South,* 78; McDonald and Wheeler, *Knoxville,* 11.

8. Shifflett, *Coal Towns;* Salstrom, "Newer Appalachia as One of America's Last Frontiers," 92.

9. Isenhour interview; Hall et al., *Like a Family,* 24. For a thorough picture of the transformation because of the mills, see Hall et al., *Like a Family,* 3–43, esp. 10, 6, 33; and Wright, *Old South, New South,* 124–55.

10. Wright, *Old South, New South,* 162–73; Keith, *Country People in the New South,* 76–89; Hsiung, *Two Worlds in the Tennessee Mountains,* 128–61; Eller,

Miners, Millhands, and Mountaineers, 93–110, 121–22; Quinn, "Industry and Environment in the Appalachian Copper Basin," 576; Hudson interview.

11. Jett interview, 11; Profitt interview, June 23, 1975, 7; Profitt interview, Aug. 11, 1975, 10–11; Profitt interview, May 30, 1975, 3–5; Gabbard interview, 7.

12. Keith, *Country People in the New South,* 143–69 (quote on 145); Crabtree interview; Profitt interview, June 1, 1975, 13–14; Combs interview, 3.

13. For Mexican immigration, see Vargas, *Proletarians of the North.*

14. Lynd and Lynd, *Middletown,* 61n17; Sanderson, "Gasoline Gypsies," 265. See also Keith, *Country People in the New South,* 103–17.

15. In 1954, Brooks received a letter from Denver that included a check for fifteen dollars. It read: "You won't remember me, but back before the war I was flat broke and you hauled me from Paducah to Detroit on your bus on credit. You did me a big favor and I never forgot it. I now am on my feet and so I am sending the money I owe you for my fare." Joe Creason, "Paducah to Detroit," *Louisville Courier-Journal,* Aug. 15, 1954. I thank William Lynwood Montell for bringing this article to my attention.

16. P. Daniel, *Standing at the Crossroads,* 79; Williams et al., *Family Living in Knott County, Kentucky.* See also Galpin and Manny, *Interstate Migrations among the Native White Population.*

17. Gibbons, "Onion Workers," 413–15.

18. Ibid., 406; McWilliams, *Ill Fares the Land,* 130–33.

19. McWilliams, *Ill Fares the Land,* 142–46, 148–56, 283; Brown interview. As part of an agreement to use this interview, I agreed to change the name of the interviewee.

20. Wilson interview, Feb. 19, 1982, 1; Holly Wissing, "Kentucky Migrants Area Labor 'Backbone,'" *Cincinnati Enquirer,* Jan. 27, 1974. By the 1950s, 36 percent of Hamilton's manufacturing workers and 38 percent of Middletown's workers were native-born Kentuckians. A study of Inland Container Corporation's 220 Kentucky natives in Middletown found that over 50 percent were from Wolfe County. See Wissing, "Kentucky Migrants Area Labor 'Backbone.'" Since other studies have reported labor recruiters traveling to Texas to lure Mexicans and to Mississippi for African Americans, it is likely that many employers from Detroit and elsewhere made the trip to Tennessee and Kentucky and West Virginia to induce white southerners northward. See Vargas, *Proletarians of the North,* 13, 20–21; and Marks, *Farewell—We're Good and Gone,* 23. For evidence of southern white labor recruiting, see Clarence Senior to James S. Brown, Aug. 5, 1959, Urban Migrant Project, folder 7, box 278, Records of the Council of the Southern Mountains, Southern Appalachian Archives, Hutchins Library, Berea College, Berea, Ky.

21. Smith interview. As part of an agreement to use this interview, I agreed to change the name of the interviewee.

22. Lynd and Lynd, *Middletown,* 58n13; Peavyhouse quoted in Wolfe, "Appalachians in Muncie," 176. See also C. L. Jones, "Migration, Religion, and Occupational Mobility of Southern Appalachians in Muncie, Indiana," 167.

23. Whitten interview.

24. What follows is largely a chronological transcript from an interview with Orbie Berry. It is significant because this testimony was unsolicited, affirming how important moving northward still was in Orbie Berry's life many years after he had moved back to the South. Orbie and Irene Berry interview.

25. Raymond Paul Hutchens found that "blowing out" to the South and returning sometime later with a friend or relative at a migrant's former job was generally accepted by employers as long as it did not occur too frequently. See Hutchens, "Kentuckians in Hamilton," 54.

2 *Up North and Down Home: Southern Migrants and the Great Depression*

> Times is hard, and we aim to put in a crop if we can get back. You can always make something to eat on the farm.
>
> —Millhand, ca. 1930

> Dear Uncle.
>
> How is work up there? There are several coming up there. Do you think I can get a job if I was up there? If you do, write and tell me if I can. I had better close, hoping to hire [hear] soon.
>
> Your nephew.
>
> —Letter from Arkansas to Flint, Michigan, ca. 1935

BY 1930, SOUTHERN WHITES had begun to establish footholds in many midwestern communities where employers were demanding labor, a demand that simply could not be met with local labor. Migrants who were looking for jobs went to many different places, including the Midwest's largest cities, such as Chicago, Detroit, Indianapolis, Toledo, Akron, Dayton, Cleveland, Cincinnati, and Columbus, but also smaller towns, such as Muncie, Anderson, Marion, Fort Wayne, South Bend, the Calumet's cities, and Terre Haute in Indiana; Findlay, Lima, Sandusky, Springfield, Barberton, Canton, Hamilton, and Middletown in Ohio; and Flint, Kalamazoo, Battle Creek, and Pontiac in Michigan. A

1936 survey of Henry County, Indiana, for example, reported a number of Kentuckians working in New Castle's Chrysler plant. Eager southerners intent on what they thought would be a good wage also went northward to work in the rich, flat agricultural lands of the Midwest in such diverse places as Johnson and Henry counties in Indiana, the fruit belt in southwestern Michigan, and Hardin County and other areas of northwestern Ohio.[1]

The exile northward was never a one-way movement, but the migration patterns that were initiated in the 1920s and the struggle over whether to remain on the land in the South or pursue wages in the North were suspended by the hard times of the Great Depression because, for the first time in a decade or more, the South was no longer alone in its economic problems. In some instances, the depression frightened many who had come north into retrenching, either by planting a bigger garden, cutting back still further on household budgets, or taking in a fellow southerner as a boarder to increase income. But it also forced many to return to the South, whether they wanted to or not, reversing the northward trend of the 1920s. In many cases, the Great Depression resolved the ambivalence associated with migration because suddenly there was little if any reason to move to the North. Some were sufficiently shocked by the bust that they returned to the South and never again left, but plenty of those back-to-the-landers, along with fellow southerners who had not yet seen "the North," simply tarried, staying in the South until miserable economic conditions pushed them out or rejuvenated midwestern cities pulled them out, whichever came first.

By 1935, the blip on the migration scale was gone, and thousands again faced the difficult choice of whether to leave the South for the North. The great white migration was flowing again, though still not as voluminously as in the 1920s. It would take a massive economic mobilization for another world war to get surplus southerners to go northward again en masse. Ultimately, it seems that the Great Depression would actually intensify the desire to move northward once jobs became available during the 1940s (indeed, the 1950s would see the greatest volume of out-migration), although ambivalence and a yearning for the South continued in the hearts of most southern migrants.

Viable Colonies

In 1929, Vivien M. Palmer, from the University of Chicago, was studying the composition and complexity of Chicago's neighborhoods. While poking around the North Side, she ran across a small community of Tennesseans, who, she said, were the neighborhood's newest arrivals. Discouraged by bad conditions at home and enticed by the "tales of high wages and better living conditions here," people from the western flatlands and eastern mountains of Tennessee had come to the city. The principal "colony" was near Wolfram and Damen. There, "families have crowded together in order to meet the high rents and the crises of unemployment and in this section," according to Palmer, "single dwellings often house two or three families." Palmer's short description of the "colony" reveals how functional it was, even at the beginning of the depression. Kith and kin were bound in a collective world that tried to ease divided hearts by helping new migrants find housing and jobs but also keeping the unemployed fed and housed. Her description also explains how the city's "natives"—in this case, Germans and Poles—were beginning to raise eyebrows in kitchens and lodges about the "queer" people who were flocking to their neighborhood. The pattern was set that would be replicated in migrant destinations across the Midwest.[2]

Census data indicate just how many white southerners had moved to sixteen midwestern cities by 1930. Detroit had over 66,000 white southerners inside its city limits, Chicago close to 50,000, and Indianapolis almost 30,000; even Flint, Michigan, had over 8,000 southern exiles. Hamilton, Ohio, had approximately 11,000 white Kentuckians in 1930, nearly one-quarter of its native-born population. Southern whites constituted one-fifth of Akron's native white population; Akron was more "southern white" (defined by the proportion of white southerners) than was Cincinnati, where southern whites made up 16 percent of the native white population. Indeed, in years to come, Akron would scornfully be said to be the new capital of the state of West Virginia.[3]

The census tabulations also hint at the migrants' destinations. The data, for example, disprove distance determinism. Flint had more whites from Arkansas than from any other southern state. Tennessee had the second largest number of out-migrants, the majority going to Detroit and Chicago, although large numbers of Kentuckians, of course, went to Evansville, Indiana, and Cincinnati and West Virginians to Akron and Columbus. White Tennesseans, however, outnumbered Kentuckians in several cities, including Akron and Flint, and were roughly the same in Toledo, which demonstrates the prevailing migration streams from Tennessee to Akron and Flint; Orbie Berry was clearly among his own in Flint. In addition, many more whites from Georgia came to the Midwest than did those from the Carolinas, who presumably ventured up the Atlantic seaboard. The number of West Virginians living in the Midwest was also significant, because of the depressed nature of coal mining and subsistence farming there, especially in the southwestern areas.[4]

Migration streams are also possible to identify. For instance, if Evansville is discounted as the most "southern" city listed, Akron seemed to be the white southerner's destination of choice, since it had the highest percentage of southern whites, at almost 75 percent. Even in the case of Georgia, which had the smallest percentage of white migrants of the ten southern states listed, almost half of those going to Akron were white; more than half of the Alabamans and two-thirds of the Mississippians who went to Akron were white. If one assumes that the migration dynamic—where kinship support combined with employment opportunity—was properly functioning in Akron, then prejudice there must have kept African American migrants out in the 1920s; only 135 of almost 19,000 southern migrants to Akron were black. Flint, Michigan, also had a high percentage (60 percent of in-migrants were white); along with Detroit, it was a very popular destination for whites from Arkansas. Indianapolis, Toledo, Dayton, and Cincinnati, according to the averages, received about equal numbers of white and black southerners. Conversely, Youngstown, Gary, and Cleveland were the least popular destinations among white southerners; less than a third of each city's southern in-migrants were white by 1930. State-by-state migration streams are also evident. By 1930, kinship and racism were influencing the destinations of white southerners, but the worsening effects of the Great Depression would push many southerners, whites in particular, back to their homeplaces.[5]

You Can Go Home Again

Orbie Berry's experiences in Flint, Michigan, in the 1920s were typical for the pioneering migrants who left their homes for the North. Many easily found jobs in the booming economy, whether as workers in steel or automobile production, construction, petroleum, or any of a host of jobs that required strong backs but little prerequisite skill. But Berry's experiences with an increasingly uncertain economy were also typical. Not accustomed to seeing a "panic" in the urban, industrial North, Berry was deeply affected by what he saw, and he, like thousands of other southerners in the North on the eve of the Great Depression, began to think that perhaps the support of kin back in the South and even an infertile patch of land might outweigh the risks involved in trying to hold on to one's job in the North. In short, economic instability helped make

Orbie less ambivalent about working and living in the North; he opted to return to the South to escape the industrial system.

Having decided to leave his new car in the South and take a bus north, Berry described what, unbeknownst to him, would be his last trip back to Flint as an employee:

> And I got a bus (the busses was going back then—it was cheaper to ride the bus). . . . We got to Cincinnati to change and that bus station was just full of people. And I wondered well what in the world? Anyway I went up to the bus agent and asked when we'd get a bus out to Detroit. And he says, "About thirty minutes." Well I just turned around and this fellow says, "Where're you going?" I said, well, I was going to Detroit. And he said, "Everything's been a laid off. They've just shut everything down." I thought he was pulling my leg. But I seen all of them people there—people coming back you know. They was mostly from Detroit. Well, I went on to Detroit and then didn't stay there but a few minutes . . . and we got over to Flint and it was eleven o'clock in the night. And the old lady at my boardinghouse (I'd a been a boarding with her for years), there was a light on. I said ole Miss King's up—the landlady, so we went in and [she] said "Lord have mercy, Orbie, they've shut everything down. Shutting it down." I said, "Well we heard that in Cincinnati that they was doing that." I went on and went to bed but I got up when I always did you know and [was] down there at 6:30. We went to work at 6:30.[6]

Berry was soon faced with the frightening specter of a huge industrial plant virtually deserted and dangerously quiet. Nevertheless, he entered the plant:

> And the watchman at the gate up there where I went in he said, "Berry—they've been a collusion here since you left." And I said, "Well that's what I've heard in Cincinnati that they was shut down." I just went on down through the plant. Everything was standing—there was no machines a-moving. Well I worked my way through, and I got to the superintendent. And I said, "Lord have mercy, what in the world has happened here? Everything was busy when I left." He said, "Berry—don't get mad at me. This come down from headquarters." So he says, "You get your hind end and get back home. We ain't going to lay everybody off. We just shut down here for these two or three days to get cleaned up. Go back and don't come back tomorrow—come back the next day."
>
> Well that's what I done. And I went back down there, and I didn't even operate the big machine after a while cause they had parts down there. So anyway we went to work a little that evening, and they paid us now. And the next day they went in, why, I worked five hours. The line was just shut down. And the next day we worked nine hours on the day shift when you didn't work overtime. And they took on that a way about three days or three and a half as long as I worked.

The shutdown affected Berry deeply, forcing him to think about the realities of industrial wage labor and to weigh the advantages and disadvantages of life in the North versus the South. Once again, it was time to go "down home" for a visit:

> And they went on there then before Christmas, and I said, "Well, I've got some business down there that I need to see about, kindly, I ought to." And he [his foreman] said, "Business?" I said, "Well yeah, I loaned a fellow some money down there and he went crazy and he's in the asylum and I've got to sell a farm—I got a mortgage in." He'd run a store—is what I loaned him this money for, see. He said, "Well, if you're doing that we're dragging around here anyhow. You ain't going to stay too long?" I said, "Well no, a week or two." And I come home and that's about the way it went off.
>
> So I just finally decided I wouldn't make enough up there and quit. But now he told me, he said, "Don't check out—you're going to come back." I said, "Well, I may never be back." But I didn't want to leave so much pay up there and be out, so I checked plumb out then. That was when they shut down. I said, "They's other people that need the job worse than I do." I said I knew, boy, I seen them crying on the street during the time them days I wouldn't be a working. They was laying them off you know—pitiful.

In 1929, Berry returned to Wayne County, lured back by family and friends and the way of life of agriculture, to eke out a living. After all, at twenty-five years of age he had saved his money and would not be starting out like the other young men he knew. He had bought and paid for a small farm. "That's the reason," he recalled, "I knowed what I could do when I come back—I had learnt [farming] when I was a kid. So I come back and oh, a couple years or three years I married. So when we married I rented that farm, and I let a fellow rent it—he thought it was all right. He made three or four bales of cotton on it. Got a pair of mules, you know, [and] a fellow could live on such as that. Work out at a sawmill."

But like many future migrants, Berry was still divided about where to reside. Even after he married Lillie Langford, he was attracted to the wages of the North and tried to persuade his new wife to pack up and move there with him. His explanation to her that Flint was not like Detroit or, for that matter, Youngstown suggests the varieties of the migration experience. Plenty of southerners went to Detroit, of course, but Berry preferred Flint because, in his words, it was more like nearby Florence, Alabama:

> I said, "Well, Flint's a good town—it's more like Florence (she was used to Florence), it ain't like Detroit." I said "Detroit's a crowded-out place,"

> you know, it was rough down there, all them plants. They wasn't but a Buick and a Chevrolet and a little Fisher [plant] up there in Flint and a lot of other little old things. . . . But she didn't much want to go, and I said, "Well, I'll tell you—we can make money up there, I can." "But," I said, "I can do all right here as far as that goes." See I had that farm, had to take it over—had that—and I had a good car and this and that and money I'd saved up, see. And so we moved [to the farm]. That was in '33—the first of '33. And the things was hard then. They was walking the roads hunting jobs.

He began clearing his acreage with local help for fifty cents a day and began raising corn and cattle. He would never permanently leave Wayne County again, although in 1936 he took his wife to visit Flint, perhaps one last time to see if he belonged in the North or the South. To his dismay, there were new watchmen, new foremen, and new machines—all of which made his job in the 1920s far different. He went back home, determined to stay put permanently. Berry became, by Wayne County standards, a successful farmer, buying more land throughout his life, until, at his death, he owned hundreds of acres.[7]

Berry was certainly not the only southerner to go back home during the depression. Although the census limits precise figures about migration, migrants from the South who ventured northward during the 1920s came back to the land in the depression. Otha Lindsay, for instance, grew up in Cosby, Tennessee, at the base of the Great Smoky Mountains. In 1922, he went to Cleveland, Ohio, and got a job at American Steel and Wire, but after fifteen years, he, too, decided to return to the South. "Cleveland's a wonderful place," he said. "Only reason we came back was that things got slow up there and I had a farm here to fall back on." When Sally Etter's mother was pregnant with her in Whiting, Indiana, she was frequently "sick to her stomach," Sally explained. "And, of course, that was a good excuse that, you know, she would be better if they came back to the clean air" of western Kentucky. So her father quit his job at Standard Oil and headed south on U.S. 41.[8] Orbie Berry, Otha Lindsay, and Sally Etter's parents made the choice themselves to return to the South, but for many others, the choice was made for them when they lost their jobs.

The problem with the growing dependence on industrial capitalism was that just as migrants were beginning to adjust to the new life-style, they were frequently forced to abandon it for the farm. The decision to return to the farm forced them to try to revert not only to a deteriorating home, rusted tools, overgrown land, and broken fences (with little or no capital) but also to the life-style of the past, with different social relations and practices. Fortunately, perhaps, divided hearts came in handy when southerners were forced to move back to the South. Indeed, some southerners may have welcomed economic downturns because the decision to move back was easier to make. Orbie Berry certainly did not seem to mind returning, at least temporarily.

Michigan's fluctuation in population during the depression reflects the back-to-the-land movement that reversed the northward trend from the 1920s. Researchers during the depression found that Michigan's population began declining in 1930 and continued to decline through 1935, at which time in-migrants seemed to begin returning; seven out of ten migrants who had moved to farms between 1930 and 1934 had left the farms again by 1935. Demographers at the time seemed surprised to learn that men and women flocked to the state when jobs were easily found but that during lean times, when not only finding a job but also keeping one was difficult, migrants stayed away. Between 1930 and 1935, a net out-migration reduced Michigan's population by more than seventy thousand people, but between 1935 and 1940, the state gained at least that many. Losses "to neighboring and to southern states in the first half of the decade," the sociologist Amos H. Hawley found, "were more than replaced in the last half." Denver Mattingly, for instance, was making eighty cents an hour at the Hudson Motor Company in Detroit. Although he was never laid off, he was getting only twenty-two hours a week working nine-hour shifts, insufficient to support his family. Because "there are 71,000 in Detroit out of work," he decided to move back to his father's place on Muncie's Creek in eastern Kentucky. The reasons for his departure from Kentucky in the 1920s, however, were still there to face him when he moved back: the farm could not feed the extended family. Mattingly moved in the first place because his younger brother's labor made his unnecessary.[9]

The problems Mattingly faced were also confronted by thousands of other southern men and women. Any history of migration risks understating demographic factors that greatly influenced migration; recall that the southern birthrate—particularly in the highlands—was the nation's highest. In the southern Appalachians, the excess of births over deaths was greater than two per year for each hundred people. Had the region's population been undisturbed by migration before the Great Depression, it would have increased by more than 2 percent each year. Yet no increase actually took place until 1930 because the increase was skimmed off by out-migration. Put another way, a population index of 100 meant that there were just enough children to replace those removed by death for one generation (twenty-eight years). An index of 150 meant that the population would increase by half at the end of a generation. In Kentucky, for instance, the index in 1930 was below 100 in only 5 of the state's 120 counties, and they were all urban areas (suggesting that these areas would decline in population without in-migration). In contrast, seven eastern counties had indexes above 225, and Leslie County's was 260, the nation's highest. In other words, Leslie County had 2.6 times the number of children needed for population maintenance, and not surprisingly, because the county could not support such a burden, it experienced a net loss of one person out of every four during the 1920s. Such an index meant that the county's population would have doubled every twenty-four years. In eight other eastern Kentucky counties, the population would double in less than thirty years, and in eighteen others, in less than forty years. Had some wall been erected around the state of Kentucky, keeping migrants from leaving, the population would have doubled in seventy-seven years. Just as the New World was a safety valve for Scots-Irish, the Midwest would become such for the many Scots-Irish of the southern highlands.[10] Severe problems were in store for the region (and other rural areas, such as the cotton South, which also had high rates of natural increase) when the population increases continued and the out-migration reversed.

Another problem was that people were returning not to the richer lands (these were obviously tightly held and land values were high) but to the poorer land. Those who migrated in the 1920s were escaping worn-out land; in the early 1930s, they returned to the same infertile farms. Moreover, returnees were increasing the number of farms and often decreasing the acres per farm, particularly in the hilly regions, where tillable land was already in short supply. Between 1930 and 1935, the number of farms increased in the United States by almost 10 percent. Not surprisingly, increases were also registered around industrial towns and cities: Jefferson County, Alabama, which surrounded Birmingham, saw a 100 percent increase in the number of farms. Miners and mill workers were forced to farm the land they inhabited. All of these factors—the mounting population, returnees from the city to the country, the increase in the number of farms and the decrease in acreage, especially on worn-out soil—combined for the first time in U.S. history to produce a massive *rural* relief problem.[11]

In spite of a land that could not support them, returnees funneled back to the hills, perhaps believing it better to go hungry among kin than to beg in the North among strangers. Depression researchers' statistics tell the story. The 1930 population of Jackson County, Kentucky, not far from Lexington, was only slightly more than 10,000, but 300 to 500 families were believed to have moved back by 1932 from northern industrial areas, largely from southwestern Ohio's Miami Valley. In June 1934, there were more than 1,300 families on relief, between a fourth and a third of whom were returnees. Knott County had a similar experience. Seven hundred families returned to farms between 1930 and 1933, a figure that includes those returning from the North and ex-miners who were victims of shutdown and bankruptcy. Of the 4,400 people who lived on farms, a quarter farmed less than three acres. In 1934, 1,780 families were on relief. "The southern Appalachian plateau is poor beyond description," Nels Anderson wrote:

> These are not areas into which other industries have migrated to use the labor supply left stranded by the lumber industry. The great proportion of the people try farming; and when they do not succeed, the more energetic and restive families and individuals move away, following the roads that lead to the industrial town and then on to the industrial city. Had industrial employment not declined after 1929, the annual exile might have gone on. But the economic system turned into reverse, and that brought into prominence the problem of depressed areas where people grow up so they can move away.[12]

In 1930, Mary Breckinridge, who worked for the Frontier Nursing Service in eastern Kentucky, was weary of telling hungry men who came begging for work that she had none. Hugh Morgan, for example, had gone to Hamilton, Ohio, during the teens to work for the Champion Paper and Fiber Company and made $3.98 per day. Ten years later, his wages were a dollar less per day. Frustrated, he went to a nearby Ford plant and made $6.00 per day, and after a year he was making $7.20 each shift. But suddenly the work week was reduced to three days, and soon thereafter he was laid off. He had little choice but to return to his family's house in eastern Kentucky, but again, as in Denver Mattingly's case, Morgan's father had more than enough labor and mouths to feed with four sons still at home. "It will be seen that the mountain country is having troubles of its own," Breckinridge wrote in 1930. "Is it fair that it should be asked to shoulder the cities' unemployment as well? The industries which entice labor away from the mountains, and keep it employed through years of claimant prosperity, should help tide these workers over the lean days." "But they have drawn the labor out and used it," she concluded, "and now they cast it back upon the mountain country which did not share the prosperity of the city, and which is now asked to add the cities' unemployment problem to its own struggle for existence against the forces of nature."[13]

In 1931 and 1932, Malcolm Ross traveled to the coalfields to tell the country about the machine age that had come to the hills. What he found was a strong back-to-the-land movement among hungry and desperate miners. Even if a union emerged and mining stabilized, he wrote, "there still remains a surplus of people who cannot be used underground. Already the pressure of hunger has sent them by tens of thousands back to the soil. In the yards of their shacks the miners have planted seeds supplied by the Red Cross and their States. The operators approve, and sometimes set aside blocks of land and lend horses to do the plowing." Ross was advocating companies' leasing land to out-of-work miners. The alternative was to continue the process of taking away land from people who still managed to own it. "The process still goes on. In a courthouse square in West Virginia farms were being auctioned for taxes one day last winter. A farm was sold under the hammer for $6," he observed.[14]

In 1935, the Federal Emergency Relief Administration (FERA) published a study of six of the rural relief problem areas in the United States based on extensive fieldwork in June 1934. It included the Appalachian-Ozark area, which stretched westward from the Blue Ridge in Virginia through West Virginia and most of Kentucky and Tennessee (encompassing even the western parts of the states, not usually designated as a part of "Appalachia"), and into the Ozark region of Missouri and Arkansas. Families there owed very little money for either real estate or equipment and were farming on very small farms, indicating subsistence farming. In 1934, three-quarters were trying to survive on farms of less than fifty acres. The median size farm for the "problem area" was twenty-seven acres.[15]

The authors of the FERA study saw the curtailment of nonfarm work as a large factor in rural relief in the Appalachian-Ozark area. Wages from lumbering or mining or mills nearby constituted a considerable amount of their income, since in 1929 the income from the farm after expenses were paid was frequently under a hundred dollars. The average southern Appalachian farmer worked fifty-three days off his farm for wages in 1929, a figure that does not include the wages of older boys who often went with their fathers and contributed to the family coffers. "Since the industrial depression shut off employment opportunities for many who would normally have migrated from this area to northern cities and also curtailed employment in the mines and factories of the area," the study noted, "the increasing population has had to depend upon agriculture for its subsistence."[16]

In the eastern cotton belt, adjacent to the Appalachian-Ozark area on the north and including most of Mississippi, Alabama, Georgia, South Carolina, and interior sections of North Carolina, conditions were only slightly better. R. G. Hudson, a Georgia native, tried to explain the reason for the problem. "See, the South took a real beating in the '20s and '30s when the price of cotton dropped to five cents a bale. I'm talking about the whole South. And it was just a general migration from the South when the cotton fell so bad. I think it was in the early '30s that it dropped down to just nothing," he said. "There was no reason for industry to come down there and fight this big expense of moving anything when they could come up to Ohio or Illinois or Indiana and start it so much easier," referring to expensive transportation. Approximately a third of those heads of households in the eastern cotton belt who were receiving relief were employed in June 1934, more of whom were white than black. Less than a quarter of white farmers owned the land they tended, although the overwhelming majority were in debt; the rest were renters. But even in the cotton South, farm size had also shrunk in just four years, suggesting a reverse migration not unlike that farther north.[17]

People all across the South were simply waiting until better times would pull them out of the region; optimistic miners were waiting for another coal boom that was just on the horizon. Carter Goodrich warned against assuming southerners were there to stay:

> I believe that it would be most unwise to try to hold the population in the areas which people have characteristically found during the depression. . . . Whatever direction migration in the future should take as a long-run matter, it seems to me clear that it cannot be the direction that migration has taken during the depression. . . . Attempts to make the migrants take deep root in these communities are not likely to succeed. In a number of these states . . . these particular counties began to lose population even between 1933 and 1934, with what little pick-up there was then. You are not likely to succeed in planting them there, and it is more important to say that it would be tragic if you succeeded.[18]

Toughing It Out in the North

Not all migrants who came to the North before the depression went home, of course, and even during the depression people who were desperate in the South trickled into midwestern towns and cities. Several studies completed in the 1930s provide virtually the only extant traces of what life was like for southerners in the North. Perhaps not surprisingly, most of these authors failed to consult migrants themselves. They did, however, speak readily to community elites from business and industry, and their comments reveal more about the growing stereotypes and scorn that were beginning to take root in northern cities after only a decade of significant migration than about what life was actually like in the North for southern migrants.

In 1934, just when reverse migration was leveling off, the Civil Works

Administration conducted a survey of the housing situation in Flint, Michigan, which provides information about the time of migration, age and sex distribution, occupation, place of birth, housing, and residential segregation among southern migrants, white and black. Flint had a total population of 144,000 people, of whom almost 8 percent were southern white. The data show, for example, that more African Americans than whites left just after World War I but that more whites than African Americans left after 1924. Key differences between the migration of whites and blacks are age and sex distribution; white southerners had a significantly higher ratio of young adults than did either African Americans or the population at large. Young white males between nineteen and thirty-five years of age often came to Flint to find a job, perhaps with the intention of saving money and returning south to buy land, marry, and begin a family (many may also have come out of youthful wanderlust). The smaller yet significant number of young white women migrants, often invited by an older sister to help out with nieces and nephews, probably came out of sense of adventure and a desire for the independence that "public work" could provide. Not surprisingly, there was a higher percentage of males among southern whites than among either African Americans or the general population.[19]

Data show that while the overwhelming majority of white southerners living in Flint were unskilled, there were a few semiskilled workers. Of the skilled workers who were southern white, the majority were in particular factory positions, though a sizable number were foremen. Over half of the semiskilled southern whites worked as machine operators, and practically all of the unskilled worked in auto factories. But even by the 1930s, Southern white males had more foremen relative to their proportion of the population than native whites did. Southern whites were moving up the job ladder.[20]

Southern whites were recruited not only as foremen but also, perhaps paradoxically, as union leaders. According to migrants themselves, they were in midwestern cities for a reason: to get jobs and earn money. They maintain that southerners—men and women—were "hard workers," a comment heard over and over in oral testimony. Although in this early period, they may also have been made foremen because the company felt they were "safe" employees—that is, they were assumed to be both antiunion and anticommunist—to companies' chagrin, they often became fiery and fervent unionists. Some southerners' gregarious and jocular personalities may have made them popular among the rank and file.

Migration streams to Flint were established after just a decade of migration. One factory executive explained the familiar story of one person unleashing the floodgates of migration. "After the World War," he is reported to have said, "our personnel director discovered that it was no longer possible to get cheap labor in the North even for the unskilled jobs. He was a southern gentleman who knew conditions in the South. He knew how plentiful labor was down there. So he asked his friends in different towns in Missouri and Arkansas to advertise for workers and send them up to our factory." Most important to management, however, was that "these people could do the unskilled jobs all right and were glad to get whatever wages were given to them," an eagerness that migrants often mistook for sincere appreciation of southerners as good, decent workers. Since, to management's delight, workers sometimes came regardless of factory needs, wages were pushed down because of periodic labor gluts. Before long, certain communities were largely transplanted to Flint. According to the housing survey, Kennett, Hayti, and Cape Girardeau in Missouri and Paragould, Arkansas, supplied workers for Flint.[21] Recall that the man who hired Orbie Berry in Flint's Chevrolet plant was a thirty-five-year-old Missourian.

The relatively low status of both southern white and black migrants in Flint is evident in housing, although southern whites were more mobile and often lived in poorer housing than did either black migrants or the general population. While almost half of Flint's total population were homeowners, only 27 percent of southern whites and 24 percent of African Americans owned homes in 1934. The housing survey found that southern whites had far less residential stability than African Americans had, which is reflected in both return migration and the temporary nature of white migration. Among southern whites in Flint, four-fifths had lived there five years or less, compared with three-quarters for African Americans and three-fifths for the general population. Surprisingly, a much higher percentage of southern whites than either the native or black population lived in houses without running water. White migrants, like blacks, may not have cared about a luxury they may not have had in the South but, unlike blacks, may have been willing to do without to save more money before they returned home. One other surprising result of the survey disproves the widely held notion that southern white homes were filled with boarders. Although the survey was conducted at the end of a period of southern white out-migration from Flint, the percentage of white southern families who kept boarders was far less than that of the general population and the black population (which was disinclined to return south and thus probably more likely to have boarders).[22]

The survey also revealed southern whites to be far less segregated than was supposed, although the findings need clarification. Because the survey includes migrants who came to Flint before 1914 and also a cross-class sample based only on nativity, one would not expect such an early migrant to be living in the same neighborhood as, say, a migrant just up from Kentucky. As southerners' standards of living increased, of course, they, like many other groups, moved out of their port-of-entry neighborhoods. Southern whites were scattered throughout forty-one city districts and forty-six out of the forty-nine metropolitan districts. The 1,269 migrants from Kentucky, for instance, lived in eighty-one of the ninety districts. Conversely, most African Americans were concentrated in five districts. As one might suspect, the southern white migration experience was much more varied than the African American experience.[23]

It was Detroit, Michigan, however, that was the mecca for those hopeful of a job in the fantastic new automobile factories, and it only took a small number of migrants across the South to make Detroit (pronounced *DEE-troyt* in the southern vernacular) as well known to the home folks as Roosevelt and Ford were. Automakers that had provoked the exile a decade or so earlier watched the natural forces of migration take over in the 1920s and supply the companies with fresh shipments of unskilled workers (and, they thought, "safe" workers regarding radicalism) who were eager for the work and the wages, whatever they may be. The hardship of the next four years pushed as many as thirty thousand white exiles back, of course, but by 1935, economic prosperity seemed imminent, and Detroit's automobile industry was having its best year since 1929.

Humming factories began working two, sometimes three, shifts six and seven days a week. The factories were once again hiring, but according to Louis Adamic, who wrote an article in the *Nation,* the relief rolls were not falling proportionally. Some auto plants had increased their employment as much as 100 percent, but the number of those on relief fell by only 20 percent. The reason, he argued, was a fear of unionism. Often passing over experienced Detroit automobile workers for those less experienced and, it was assumed, less militant, labor agents once again fanned out from Detroit, concentrating on southern white recruits. As Adamic explained:

> These hill-billies are for the most part impoverished whites, "white trash" or a little better, from the rural regions. The majority of them are young fellows. They have had no close contact with modern industry or with labor unionism—this, of course, is their best qualification. Their number in Detroit is variously estimated as between fifteen and thirty thousand, with more of them coming weekly, not only in company-chartered buses but singly and in small groups on their own hook, for no one has a better chance of employment in Detroit these days than a South-

> erner of unsophisticated mien. They are employed at simple, standardized tasks in production departments . . . at 45 or 50 cents an hour, except in Ford's, where the wages are slightly higher. These workers are happy to receive this pay and are much "safer"—for the next few months, anyhow, while big production is on—than local labor, poisoned by ideas of unionism and perhaps even more dangerous notions.

One of the results associated with this preference for "green" southerners, according to Adamic, was that Detroit natives practiced southern dialects and drawls, applied for jobs, and were hired "as soon as" they spoke. Sadly, "another good way for a man to get a job in Detroit, I am told," Adamic wrote, "is to look and act stupid."[24]

Because they often functioned as union blockers, southerners attracted more than their share of scorn from Detroit natives and those, such as Adamic, who were hopeful of union efforts. "The hill-billies," he wrote, "with their extremely low standard of living and lack of acquaintance with modern plumbing, are looked down by all but the most intelligent local workers, both native and foreign-born; they are despised also, indeed, mainly—because they take employment away from the old-time automobile workers." Adamic was also pessimistic about the time it would take migrants to become passionate for unions: "Any kind of solidarity between these newcomers and old-time Detroiters is out of the question in the immediate future." Adamic was apparently unaware that a good number of these "hill-billies" from the coalfields knew as much about the effort to establish a union as a number of "old-time automobile workers" did. When workers throughout the industry in December 1936 began their sit-down strikes, southern migrants were sitting down with the old-timers. Unlike many natives, southerners had apparently little to lose.[25]

Just about the time this importation was occurring, Elmer Akers was conducting a study on southern whites in Detroit. Though most media were silent about the hordes of migrants pouring into Detroit and other areas of the Midwest, Akers's study offers a revealing snapshot of the white migration that was beginning to regain its former stamina.[26]

Akers found that hamburger stands employed southern young men almost exclusively. "Yes, it's true," explained one manager. "We do employ southern fellows. It's because they are patient and obliging with customers." The manager continued, "They don't get mad and show irritation if a customer complains about the food or the service. They are always cheerful and like to talk. I guess it's all part of the southern hospitality you hear about. And if a man or girl comes in and don't want much, because maybe he has only 15 cents, they don't think nothing about that, but just treat that customer the same as if he had plenty of money." Workers were begun at fifteen dollars a week and given board. No training was required, and although the average wages were lower than elsewhere, this work was assumed to be more steady than factory work. Young white southerners, Akers reported, also seemed better able to "endure the heat," statements uncannily resembling reasons used to legitimate African American slave labor in the South. Similar chain migration ensured that restaurants had a steady supply of eager young men just up from the South. Akers also found southern men predominated in dairy bars and gasoline stations.[27]

Turnover in these occupations was high because virtually every southerner dreamed of getting a job at an automobile plant; smaller restaurants and gas stations and other small businesses, which hired migrants by the hundreds, were simply feeders to the auto industry, which hired them by the thousands. Akers interviewed auto management when it was willing to divulge information, though many managers were reluctant to give precise figures about employed migrants, lest the fires of the "hire only Detroiters" sentiment from earlier in the depression erupt again. For instance, an industrial relations spokesperson in a car factory estimated only 15 percent of its thirty thousand employees were southern-born, although others, including southern workers, privately estimated between 30 and 50 percent were migrants. One personnel manager in an auto plant of five thousand, however, estimated that half were southern white migrants. By 1936, when increasing labor militancy seemed to indicate the inevitability of a closed shop, some companies apparently had grown tired of the preindustrial habits of southerners. Akers reported that many began reducing the number of migrants they hired, citing the undependable nature of migrants and their frequent visits to the South. One company official told Akers that he "got tired of seeing southerners. You can tell a southerner as soon as he opens his mouth, you know, if not by his appearance. I would tell them, 'I don't want you fellows from the South. You don't stick to your job. The first thing we know you are gone some place else, or back south.'" "We're not trying to discriminate against southerners," he concluded, "but we do want people who work steadily." A manager of a carbonated beverage company concurred: "You can't depend on them. They're here one day, and gone the next. They don't think about our side of it."[28]

More significantly, however, northern industrialists were discovering southern migrants were often enthusiastic about unionism; passionate churchgoing in the South was sometimes transformed into fervent unionism in the North. Such transformations often took time, much to the chagrin of labor organizers and even labor historians. The historian Peter Friedlander, for example, who studied the development of the United Automobile Workers (UAW) in Detroit, points out that southern whites, along with blacks and Poles, were slow to join unions and were underrepresented in union activity before 1937. A more revealing glimpse of union activity among southern white migrants, however, is not possible in Friedlander's study because most of his data on southerners stem from talking to *non*southerners, a problem common in the history of southern white migration. Had Friedlander interviewed southern workers, he might have discovered that some believed they did not need to join a union because they were not intending to stay either in the particular position or in the North. Buried in his notes is an extremely important point for a discussion of southern whites: "It seems that of those southern-born workers who supported the CIO [Congress of Industrial Organizations], a large number of them came from this group of occupationally mobile, acculturated urban workers," the very ones who had relinquished their ties to the South. Eventually southern activity in the nascent UAW increased. Once they were converted to labor's cause, Friedlander argues, they rarely backslid.[29]

Friedlander is closer to the mark, however, when he criticizes southern whites for their conservatism and racism. Not only were they slow to join the movement, southerners were not attracted, Friedlander maintains, to the Communist party in the way that African Americans were. Friedlander indicts southern migrants with a virulent racism that became anticommunist as much as racist, and he insists that southern support for the labor candidate Homer Martin was partly because of his racism. Friedlander notes that wherever there was support for Martin in National Labor Relations Board elections in 1940, there was likely to be a large number of southern whites, including those from such areas as Pontiac, Flint, Lansing, and Norwood, Ohio, where 60 percent of the workers were believed to have been southern highlanders. Martin's greatest strength was in Flint's Chevrolet plant, particularly in the final assembly line, where southern white workers, such as Orbie Berry, predominated. Although Friedlander points to the amazing mélange of workers that came together eventually in the UAW, he is unsympathetic to the enormous changes that southern whites experienced—some more than others—in their move from a southern rural culture into a northern urban one.[30]

If some white southerners, at least initially, were cool to radicalism, they were not always passive workers. One company official from an auto plant lamented that most southerners were in the CIO and "were the most troublesome group." A spokesman for one of Detroit's largest parts factories (and whose CIO representative was a white southerner) described the cunning of southerners. "Do you know how they work it?" he asked. "A southerner who has worked here in Detroit several years, having a good work record, etc., will come into another plant than the one in which he works and on the strength of his qualifications get a job, then turn the badge he was given over to his freshly arrived southern friend." "We may employ him for months," he admitted, "without discovering that we haven't employed the man we thought we had. They are not reliable. And we prefer to employ citizens of Detroit, or at least of Michigan—fellows who don't change their name every fifteen minutes and try to trick you at every turn." Asked about the sudden burst of southerners in union membership in less than one year, he replied, "Just as soon as they saw it gave them some kind of power and—or so they thought—a chance at more money, they all joined. Whatever one of them gets into they will all be getting into pretty soon."[31]

Management's sudden change of feeling for migrants forced those hungry for a job to do more than lie, change one's name (which became virtually impossible after Social Security registration), and get a work badge from a friend or relative. Akers reports a host of tactics southerners used to gain entry into factories, including recommendations from employees, friends, relatives, and "established" people in the city. Drivers, or "bootleg bus services," hauling groups of migrants northward often provided these letters and collected a fee of as much as thirty-five dollars once a passenger was hired. Others went to private employment agencies that were willing to bribe personnel managers. Another ingenious and somewhat surprising tactic, given southerners' reputation for political apathy in the North, was having a representative of the Southern Voters League pressure managers to hire certain southerners just up from the South. The "grapevine telegraph" operating in Detroit and throughout the South also brought willing migrants to hiring windows as soon as positions were vacant. Some job-hungry migrants sought out companies known for filling entire departments with white migrants, particularly once some companies, in part out of jingoist local pressure, began openly discriminating against southern white employees, preferring instead to hire only native-born (read native *local*-born) employees.[32]

Southern whites who came north brought a certain amount of independence with them, and because of it, they were often scorned by those unsympathetic to their plights and stereotyped even by those who were more understanding. In employment especially, they suffered the condescension of other whites angered that southerners rather than their Polish cousins or WASPish brothers were getting jobs. One could argue that southern whites were scorned as much as, if not more than, foreign immigrants or African Americans were because they were presumed to be "American" and their shortcomings and differences with "mainstream" American culture made them unacceptable. Southern whites, however, may well have taken pride in this same "Americanism," and thus their hatred for African Americans in the South was supplemented in the North with nativist scorn for many foreign immigrants, particularly, it seems, the Polish. As a young southerner in Detroit explained in the 1930s, "The people up here think we don't like it because the Negroes are given equal rights with white people. But I don't think that's so, so much. What we don't like is that you northerners seem to think the foreigners have more right to work and to a place here than the southerners do."[33]

Elmer Akers's study of Detroit marks an early example of the work of others, particularly professionals, who spoke *about* and *for* southern white migrants. Early in his study, Akers candidly writes that "if they have any ambition—and rarely will you detect it—you will finally conclude it is to get enough money to go back home and buy a farm of twenty or thirty acres or possibly more," apparently an ambition northerners did not respect. Akers continues his discussion by distinguishing between the "rigidly truthful, scornful of charity, clannish, [and] proud" mountaineers and the "lazy, shiftless, untrustworthy, slovenly, and devoid of self-respect" lowlanders, a distinction not often made in the literature. Akers was also an early writer to raise the specter of maladjustment among migrants, an ascribed characteristic that would haunt southerners throughout the century:

> Our impression is that the sense of inferiority has stronger sway over their conduct than has any genuine pride. . . . Reared in a folk culture with the patriarchal type of family in which the children are severely ruled by the father, and trained to a stoic concealment of emotion, their minds and personalities are at least frequently stamped and handicapped for life with inferiority-superiority feelings. This characteristic of mind and personality, combined with a pitifully meagre education and almost total unfamiliarity with the ways and demands of a high-speed industrial society makes their difficulties of accommodation to Detroit almost insuperably great.

Akers's comments make one wonder how southerners even made it to Detroit.[34]

If automakers criticized southern migrants after their industry was unionized, others in Detroit were critical from the start. Grocers and druggists accused them of being cheap buyers. "They always buy the cheaper cuts of meat, the cheaper grades of cloth, and so on," a Detroit grocer told Akers, adding, "And five families of southerners won't buy as much in a drug store as two northern families." Southern whites were as vulnerable to charges of frugality in the North as they were to accusations of reckless spending in coal camp commissaries. A personnel manager of a plant where southern whites made up a quarter of the work force criticized them for their obsession for buying low-priced jewelry, especially watches. Others also charged them with making a trip to the grocery before each meal, not realizing that many did not have refrigerators or were accustomed to shopping at a store around the corner. Northern landlords were also reportedly disinclined to rent to southerners because they were bad housekeepers and often skipped out on rents, charges that indicate middle-class standards of homemaking were not important to some migrants, who never regarded Detroit as home and were intent on saving money and returning south. Landlords who did rent to them usually charged at least fifteen dollars more a month, not only because they considered them risky tenants but also because they assumed the apartment would be occupied by two families. By the 1930s, midwestern property owners dreaded southerners almost as much as they did African Americans. One resident explained:

> These southerners don't take any care of the premises. In fact, they just don't give a damn about it. If you once let southerners into your house you can hardly rent it to any other class of people, because the southerners let it get so dirty and run-down. The . . . insurance company owns a lot of property here in Detroit, and they don't want southerners. On some streets they just won't rent their properties to them. I'm not prejudiced. I'm telling you the facts you'll find anywhere around here. I haven't told you a thing you haven't heard already, I expect. But I live in a neighborhood where there are a lot of southerners, and I know a good deal about them.

Not surprisingly in the face of such hostility, southern white women who ran boardinghouses were, Akers noted, particularly popular because they provided welcome refuge and became mothers away from home to young exiles.[35]

From Southern Soil to Northern

Whites who left the South were very visible to natives in rural areas as well. Throughout Indiana, there were 125 canneries in 1925, and their seasonal nature often demanded workers from afar to process the bounty, much of which was in tomatoes. In 1925, the state's canneries employed more than fourteen thousand people, divided equally between men and women, although sixty-six plants employed people under age sixteen. Johnson County, for example, had twenty thousand residents in the 1930s, but its agricultural productivity made demands for labor that local residents either could not or would not satisfy. Seven canneries in the county employed close to four thousand workers, half of whom were women. Even tiny Trafalgar had a cannery that employed almost two hundred people. Tomato growers and canners needed an additional seven thousand workers during the August through October season alone. Consequently, the migration from central Kentucky only increased during the 1930s.[36]

A 1936 county planning board report gave a great deal of attention to the plights of the annual "pickers and canners" from the South. It noted that living conditions of Kentuckians were miserable; migrants lived in barns, tourist cottages, tents, an abandoned hotel and slaughterhouse, and even a stack of straw. A Whiteland merchant complained that the average ration of a Kentuckian was a loaf of bread and a can of beans a day, since those intent on returning were doing all they could to save anywhere from $50 to $150 in wages. The report also bemoaned the local cannery that annually advertised for jobs in the Louisville papers, bringing the eager "in trucks and dilapidated automobiles of all kinds." While mainly sympathetic, the report was designed to propose ways to stop the annual migration, because seasonal labor needs, the board maintained, could be filled with nearby Indianapolis residents.[37]

If hordes of Kentuckians coming to the county and funneling local money out were not bad enough, migrants that stayed on in the county after the season was over were an even greater problem in the eyes of the authors of the report. The problem, of course, was that although migrants were warmly welcomed during the harvest season—indeed, they were often *delivered* by trucks to the county—they could not always afford transportation back to their Kentucky communities because their wages were so low. A 1935 study of families that were on relief found that nearly one-third were born in Kentucky. In Greenwood, Pleasant Township, the site of a Stokely Brothers cannery that employed fifteen hundred people, almost half of the township's relief population was born in Kentucky. Relief families with both heads of the family born in Kentucky, the study found, were clustered around towns that had canneries: Greenwood, Whiteland, Franklin, Trafalgar, and Edinburg. Only Bargersville, which had a cannery that employed over two hundred people, did not have a Kentucky family on relief. The authors of the study maintained that Kentucky families had come to the county during the late summer harvest and canning season and had stayed afterward, "eking out an existence until they established residence and then going on relief." The authors asserted that although Johnson County was originally settled by Kentuckians, "the earlier immigrants . . . were of a much higher type than the recent ones." Since 1920, migrants, or "squatters," had come principally from the south-central Kentucky counties of Adair, Casey, Pulaski, and Taylor.[38]

The authors of the planning board study even did genealogical checking of Kentucky-born relief cases. They found that eighty clients had the same surname from Kentucky that they fictitiously called "Adair"; another fifty clients had a close relative of the "Adairs." More shocking to the researchers was that half the "Adairs" had married "Adairs," and "evidently this has been going on long enough until the whole stock is inbred." The study continued:

> The average age of the girls at marriage is 14, some of them having been married at the age of 13. The record of the whole family is filled with desertions, divorces, premarital children, and illegitimate children. Criminal records are not unknown, but there does not seem to be very much crime as yet. Although the "Adair" family is not as bad as the famous "Jukes" family, the level of intelligence is quite low and the fertility is quite high, a child a year is the average. The move from Kentucky does not interrupt the processes of nature. The "Adairs" bring part of their children with them and the rest are born here.

Information obtained from Kentucky stated that the "Adairs" were as much of a problem in their home county as they were in Johnson County. Most of them lived on a very unproductive highland. According to the study, it was known as "Adair Ridge. Here they produce children and send them into the surrounding counties. In Adair County practically the entire family is on relief."[39]

Migrants from Kentucky, Tennessee, and West Virginia had also continued to answer calls for labor in the onion fields of Ohio's Scioto and Hog Creek marshes. In the teens and twenties, prices, profits, and demands for weeders soared; in 1917, onions had sold for twelve cents a pound, and in 1929, growers were believed to have gained a million dollars a year from the 21,000 acres planted in onions. More and more southerners were coming to work the June-to-October season. Children in particular were highly valued because their tiny hands were said to be more nimble among the young, grasslike stalks of onion seedlings. For adults, the weeding method was to "hunker" down on all fours and travel down the rows.[40]

By 1934, problems were emerging for the hordes of southerners working on the marshes. Onion prices had been falling for several years; in

1932, onions were selling for twenty-one cents a bushel. Weeders' wages decreased dramatically, from thirty cents to as low as ten cents an hour, because growers complained they were losing money, although they denied access to their accounting ledgers. Acreage also decreased; in 1934, only 3,500 acres were planted in onions. Weeders suddenly were faced with lower wages and fewer jobs. They also had grievances against low prices for onions that were sharecropped. Incomes in the marsh had always been supplemented by onion sharecropping. The grower "fitted out" the cropper's soil and planted the seed and then charged the cropper anywhere from $3.50 to $12.50 per acre. Croppers were concerned that their onion crop at season's end would mean indebtedness to the grower. Finally, some weeders were concerned about the number of children in the fields. When an average weeder's work week began to be as short and inconsistent as a coal miner's, as many as eight hundred weeders struck, demanding thirty-five cents an hour and leaving the young onion crop to be choked by weeds.[41]

Media coverage of the strike that began on June 20, 1934, was nil at first. The press was concerned with Adolf Hitler, summer lightning storms, the death of John Dillinger, a taxi strike in Cleveland, and other strikes in San Francisco and Minneapolis. A week after the strike, however, reporters were being sent to the marsh, particularly after two strikers were shot and killed, and observers began hailing the strike as one of the first attempts at an agricultural union. "Us are the strikers," said a young man "in patched overalls" with "the simplicity of the Cumberland Mountains," the reporter Ralph Kelly wrote. The young man explained: "It don't do us no good to work when we have to go on the relief anyway. If there ain't no more cash than what we've been getting, we figure we might just as well not work." In the last month, he had worked three days a week for $1.25 per ten-hour day, and over the winter, he was fed by relief money and tried to survive in an abandoned cabin with no lights or water.[42]

Leading the charge for the Agricultural Workers Union (an American Federation of Labor affiliate) was Okey O'Dell, a migrant weeder from West Virginia who came to the fields in 1928 to be with his parents, who had long been weeders. "Those growers have been going down to Kentucky and West Virginia for years to get cheap labor. They bring our people up here and work them a few days a week in the summer, put them in shacks not fit for a hog, and pay them 10 cents an hour," he told a reporter. "In the winter time they let the county feed them." As a West Virginian, O'Dell was not ignorant of the business of unions. "I come from West Virginia," he said, "down in the hills. I've been around coal strikers. I've never been in a strike myself, but I know how it is done." He continued:

> Five years ago the growers paid 25 cents an hour. That's no good for killing kind of work, but we didn't kick. This year it's been hell. The boys stood around and said we ought to do something. I went and got those union men, and we talked it up. The idea took hold quick. June 16 we told the growers there would be a strike. They didn't pay no attention. Some walked out the 20th.
>
> They're willing to pay 15 cents now but they will have to come up a lot higher. Thirty-five cents is little enough an hour. The growers say they don't make money but that's a lie.

As the hot summer dragged on, most strikers persevered, in the face of evictions and hunger. Violence continued. Onion warehouses were set afire, the house of McGuffey's mayor was bombed, and a jailed O'Dell was dragged from the courthouse by an angry mob and beaten. By late summer, Secretary of Labor Frances Perkins ordered the labor conciliator Robert C. Fox from Indianapolis to Hardin County to attempt a settlement. In the end, most strikers had to settle for fifteen cents an hour, if they even had jobs at all, because growers were changing their onion fields into potato fields, requiring far less human labor. With no agricultural employment, southerners were forced away from the marsh. Some probably went back to the South temporarily, but a sizable number no doubt went to nearby industrial areas, such as Dayton and Columbus. Nevertheless, the strike was a significant event in the lives of many southerners and proved that white migrants were anything but ignorant of unionization.[43]

By the middle of the decade, southern white migrants, like those obstreperous weeders from the Scioto Marsh, were gradually being "discovered" by the rest of the country. No longer could hundreds of thousands of southerners pack up and move, as they were about to do as the country braced itself for another world war, without being noticed.

Notes

1. The Virginias, Carolinas, Georgia, Kentucky, Tennessee, Alabama, Mississippi, and Arkansas combined lost more than 3.8 million people to interstate migration in the 1920s. U.S. Bureau of the Census, *Fifteenth Census of the United States: 1930,* vol. 2, *Population,* table 30, 185; Schort, *Preliminary Survey of County Planning Problems in Henry County, Indiana,* 3.

2. Palmer, *Social Backgrounds of Chicago's Local Communities,* 34. For information on the same colony two decades later, see Killian, *White Southerners,* 104–5.

3. Evansville, Indiana, had the largest percentage of southern whites among the cities I checked. In 1850, for instance, 26 percent of Vanderburgh County (where Evansville is located) residents were born in Kentucky. See Rose, "Hoosier Origins," 201–32; and Galpin and Manny, *Interstate Migrations among the Native White Population.* Evansville is somewhat of an anomaly. Located farther south than either Louisville or Cincinnati, it has, many would argue, more of a "southern" flavor than the two upstream cities. The changes associated with crossing an Ohio River bridge and arriving in Evansville may have been less distinct than crossing a bridge into Cincinnati. The percentages of southerners among the native-born white population were Cleveland, 3.0; Columbus, 6.7; Dayton, 10.0; Springfield, 4.9; Toledo, 4.4; Youngstown, 2.0; East Chicago, 5.7; Gary, 6.0; Indianapolis, 9.6; Chicago, 2.2; Detroit, 6.4; Flint, 6.3; and Milwaukee, 0.6. On average, southern white migrants constituted 5.4 percent of the native-born white population in these cities. I have not included quantitative data in table form here, choosing instead to summarize in broad strokes the quantitative specifics. Readers interested in such data, however, are encouraged to request them from me in care of the press.

4. Compilations from U.S. Bureau of the Census, *Fifteenth Census of the United States,* vol. 2, *Population,* table 37, 208, 210–11, and table 38, 217–18; ibid., vol. 3, *Reports by States,* part 1, table 58, 62, table 15, 715; ibid., vol. 3, *Reports by States,* part 2, table 15, 494.

5. Ibid. It is possible that Arkansans who traveled up the Mississippi and Wabash valleys picking fruit and vegetables and ending the season in southwestern Michigan's orchards accounted for the concentration in Flint. Needing work, they could have easily migrated to Flint and Detroit.

6. Orbie and Irene Berry interview. All the Berry quotes in this section are from this interview.

7. Some scholars who have studied southern white migration have found a relationship between a person's social class and the period when the person migrated out of the region; that is, those who moved early were often from a fairly high social class, a trend perhaps explained by more education, higher aspiration, and greater familial resources. This was certainly true of Orbie Berry. See Schwarzweller, Brown, and Mangalam, *Mountain Families in Transition,* 216.

8. "Cocke County Boasts Scenery and Moonshine," mimeographed clipping [from *Harlan Daily Enterprise*], Urban Migrant Project, folder 3, box 278, Records of the Council of the Southern Mountains, Southern Appalachian Archives, Hutchins Library, Berea College, Berea, Ky.; James and Sally Etter interview, 7. After Sally married, she and her husband moved back to Whiting until retirement, at which time they returned to Ohio County, Kentucky. See also "Flight from the City," 32–33.

9. Lively and Taeuber, *Rural Migration in the United States,* 33; Webb and Westefeld, "Industrial Aspects of Labor Mobility," 796; Hawley, *Population of Michigan, 1840 to 1960,* 10; Beynon, "Southern White Laborer Migrates to Michigan," 337; Breckinridge, "Corn-Bread Line," 423 (Mattingly quote).

10. Oyler, *Natural Increase and Migration of Kentucky Population,* 235–37.

11. Woofter, "Rural Relief and the Back-to-the-Farm Movement," 382–85.

12. Thompson, "Industrialization in the Miami Valley"; Anderson, *Men on the Move,* 224.

13. Breckinridge, "Corn-Bread Line," 423.

14. Ross, *Machine Age in the Hills,* 235–37.

15. Beck and Forster, *Six Rural Problem Areas,* 77–78. The other five "problem areas" were the eastern cotton belt, the western cotton belt, the lake states cut-over area, the spring wheat area, and the winter wheat area.

16. Ibid., 78–79. See also Shifflett, *Coal Towns,* 199–212.

17. Beck and Forster, *Six Rural Problem Areas,* 83–84; Hudson interview.

18. Quoted in Woofter, "Rural Relief and the Back-to-the-Farm Movement," 385.

19. An intensive search for the original data turned up nothing. The results of the survey are reported in Beynon, "Southern White Laborer Migrates to Michigan," 336–43. A similar study was conducted in 1935 for Cincinnati and is reported in Leybourne, "Urban Adjustments of Migrants from the Southern Appalachian Plateaus," 238–46.

20. Beynon, "Southern White Laborer Migrates to Michigan," 338–39.

21. Quoted in ibid., 339. For evidence of southerners' mistaking employer motives, see Alvin and Ruby Berry interview. Streams were also strong to Detroit; Paducah, in western Kentucky; and Jonesborough, in eastern Tennessee, proving that people from throughout the South were migrating northward.

22. Beynon, "Southern White Laborer Migrates to Michigan," 339–40.

23. Ibid., 340–43.

24. Adamic, "Hill-Billies Come to Detroit," 177–78. The auto factories, Adamic maintained, denied the importation of southern labor, and newspapers and city boosters went along with the denial; thus, little attention was given to southern whites in the city.

25. Ibid. Joseph Wilson, a migrant from western Kentucky, was hired at GM's Anderson, Indiana, Guide Lamp plant in September, 1935. A year later, the workers were striking, and Wilson quickly threw his support to the union: "They come and asked you how you felt about the union. I don't know nothing about the union, so I asked one guy, 'What do you mean, union?' I said, 'I don't know what the hell you're talking about, see.' So he told me, 'We're going to group together, and we're going to try to form a union here so that we will have some say over what's happening to us.' We didn't have no say so over it at all. Because they'd tell you you've got to run so many parts an hour and tomorrow you'd come in, they'd add fifty or sixty more parts on it. You thought you was going as hard as you could go here, see. And if you didn't make it, you went out the door, see. You had no security of a job at all." Wilson interview, Feb. 19, 1982, 16.

26. A 1936 school census conducted in Detroit and Highland Park tallied 2,547 southern white families, nearly a third (848) of whom were from Kentucky and half as many (447) from Tennessee. Missouri totaled 352, West Virginia 284, Arkansas 193, Georgia 121, Alabama 98, Virginia 68, North Carolina 41, South Carolina 30, Mississippi 27, and Louisiana 18. Akers included Missouri in his definition of "southern." Akers, "Southern Whites in Detroit," 20.

27. Quoted in ibid., 21–22.

28. Ibid., 23, 41–42. Southerners, Akers discovered, often sent money back south for a parent to keep until their return. In one post office branch in a "southern white neighborhood," Akers found that in one morning, eight out of the thirty-four money orders were addressed to southern states: three each to Kentucky and Alabama, and two to Tennessee. Ibid., 48.

29. Friedlander, *Emergence of a UAW Local, 1936–1939,* 121–31, 45, 55, 66, 100–

101, 146n69 (quote), 17. Generalizations about southern white migrants' labor unionism are difficult to make; a revealing labor history of southern whites is yet to be written.

30. That southern whites did not join the Communist party as frequently as blacks did also implies that white southerners were experiencing sufficient mobility in what was, after all, often a racist labor force. Ibid., 101, 121–31.

31. Akers, "Southern Whites in Detroit," 26–27, 27, 28.

32. Ibid., 32–36, 45–46.

33. Quoted in ibid., 74–75. White southern migrants in the 1920s no doubt swelled the ranks of the Ku Klux Klan in the Midwest.

34. Ibid., 7, 5, 7–8. Akers's distinction between mountaineers and lowlanders is unique in that most commentators assumed *all* southern white migrants were from the Appalachians. Another exception is Killian, *White Southerners.* It is also unique because it holds mountaineers in higher esteem than other southern whites. For more on stereotypes, see chapter 7 herein.

35. Akers, "Southern Whites in Detroit," 15–18, 67.

36. Matthews, *Children in Fruit and Vegetable Canneries,* 3, esp. 55–84.

37. O'Harrow, *Preliminary Survey of County Planning Problems in Johnson County, Indiana,* 5. The report lamented that "payrolls are loaded with transient Kentuckians, while many employable citizens of Indiana are on relief rolls because of lack of employment." Ibid.

38. Ibid., 5–6.

39. Ibid., 6–7.

40. "Labor Conditions in the Onion Fields of Ohio," 325–27.

41. Ibid., 328–30.

42. "2 Striking Onion Field Workers Shot," *New York Times,* June 29, 1934; Ralph Kelly, "Luxuriant Weeds Aid Onion Strikers," *Cleveland Plain Dealer,* July 3, 1934 (quotes). See also "Onion Fields Won't Import Labor, 600 Strikers Assured," *Cleveland Plain Dealer,* June 27, 1934.

43. Quoted in Ralph Kelly, "Onion Strikers Hold Big Parade," *Cleveland Plain Dealer,* July 4, 1937. See also Ralph Kelly, "Strange Is Strike in Onion County," ibid., July 5, 1934; "Warehouses in Onion Strike Region Burn," ibid., July 7, 1934; "23 Are Arrested in New Skirmishes of Onion Strikers," ibid., July 10, 1934; "Evicted Strikers Lie Out in Rain," ibid., Aug. 7, 1934; "Strikers Face Eviction," ibid., July 29, 1934; "O'Dells Defy Aroused Mob at M'Guffey," ibid., Aug. 26, 1934; "Onion Strike Head Seeks U.S. Action," ibid., Aug. 27, 1934. Elizabeth Faue, in her study of Minneapolis, also found that migrants from the hinterland—particularly women—were often vociferous supporters of labor struggles. See Faue, *Community of Suffering and Struggle.*

Ruby and Alvin Berry with Thomas, their son, Akron, Ohio, 1940s.

Orbie and Lillie Berry, 1930s. After their marriage, Orbie tried to persuade Lillie to return to Flint, to no avail. They spent the rest of their lives in Wayne County, Tennessee. (Photo courtesy of James D. Berry)

Patricia and R. G. Hudson, shortly after their marriage, 1948. (Photo courtesy of Patricia Hudson)

Jesse and Emma Martin and family, Butler County, Kentucky, 1950s, before their move to Indianapolis. (Photo courtesy of Emma Martin)

Reuben and Mary Tune, 1950s. (Photo courtesy of Reuben and Mary Tune)

Aerial view of the Ball-Band plant, Mishawaka, Indiana, 1930s.
Ball-Band was a magnet for southern migrants.
(Photo courtesy of Mishawaka-Penn Public Library)

Migrant child from Arkansas, Berrien County, Michigan, July 1940
(Photo by John Vachon; courtesy of Library of Congress)

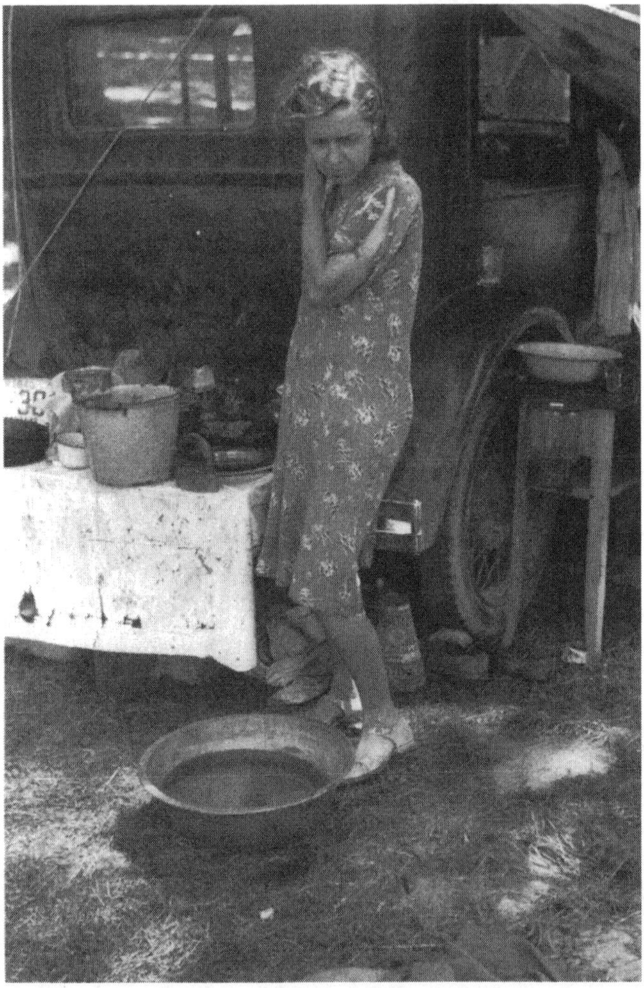

Migrant woman from Arkansas in roadside camp, Berrien County, Michigan, July 1940. (Photo by John Vachon; courtesy of Library of Congress)

Arkansas farmer now a fruit picker in Berrien County, Michigan, July 1940 (Photos by John Vachon; courtesy of Library of Congress).

South State Street, Chicago, Illinois, July 1941. Taverns that advertised cheap beer and liquor were popular haunts of southern migrants. (Photo by John Vachon; courtesy of Library of Congress)

Children playing in an Uptown alley. (Courtesy of Archives and Special Collections, Berea College)

Window display at the Chicago office of the Council of the Southern Mountains. (Courtesy of Archives and Special Collections, Berea College)

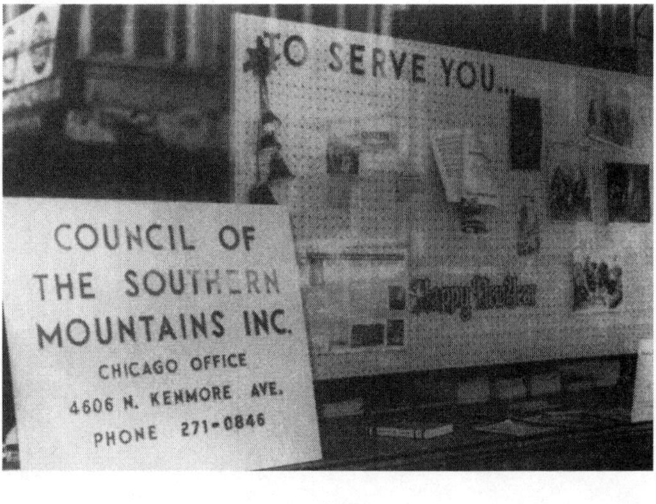

3 *The Discovery of Poverty and Migration*

> A combination of the improvement of present laws, with certain extra-legal action, presents the only method of combating the deteriorating influences of immigration of sub-normal human beings.
>
> —Dennis O'Harrow, *Preliminary Survey of County Planning Problems in Johnson County, Indiana,* 1936

IN 1936, A REPORT WRITTEN about Johnson County for the Indiana State Planning Board recommended steps to limit the number of Kentuckians and other white southerners recruited to the county to harvest tomatoes and work in the canneries. The language of the report was stern: "It might be well to note that some states have enacted legislation which has been designed to prevent such situations, by sterilization of defectives and unfit." The report also concluded that canneries were most responsible for the influx of migrants and urged employers to rely on local labor, assuming that area residents were willing to do the hot, miserable work for the low wages. The following year, a front-page plea in the *Detroit Free Press* asked for twenty dollars to send Jim and Joe, two brothers whose family had come north from Tennessee in 1935, to summer camp. The article was much more sympathetic—even melodramatic—than the Johnson County report. "The boys," it stated, "brought up in the hills, among the trees, have never known any playground except the alley. Their parents are finding it hard to adjust themselves to city ways, harder yet to find steady work." It continued, "The family table often lacks food. The family living room becomes a furnace in warm weather. If some . . . readers, perhaps those who were born in the hills, who played there as children and who love the out-of-doors, will help, the camp director will crowd in two more cots, set two more places in the dining room, find two more swimming suits, and Jim and Joe will have their chance at 10 days of happiness."[1]

In Johnson County and Detroit and in myriad other places, Americans seemed suddenly to discover in the 1930s that the land was teeming with migrants who were distressed and often destitute. Southern white migrants in the Midwest, of course, were not the only group discovered; much attention was given to the hundreds of thousands of people from Oklahoma and Arkansas who were flocking westward, and the migration of African Americans and even Mexicans northward continued during this period. New Deal researchers and crusading journalists discovered that people of many different backgrounds and even classes throughout the country were adrift. Migration seemed the *only* prospect for countless Americans if they wanted to stay fed and alive.[2]

Because of this discovery, a number of programs, mostly federal ones, were designed to address joblessness, homelessness, and hunger, especially since many states were passing legislation designed to keep migrants out. One program in particular, the Federal Transient Bureau, was organized to address locally the thousands of uprooted migrants. But other New Deal programs, such as the Tennessee Valley Authority (TVA), the Civilian Conservation Corps (CCC), the Works Progress Administration (WPA), the Resettlement Administration, and even the Agricultural Adjustment Administration (AAA), although at least implicitly designed to serve the needs of both a migratory and a potentially migratory population, often had the unintended consequence of inducing southern white migration because the programs loosened ties to land. As the federal government penetrated virtually every nook and cranny in the South, southerners would never quite be the same. Even Congress "discovered" the large migrant population, and in 1939 it organized a House committee, popularly known as the Tolan committee, to investigate the migration of destitute people. The hordes of people hunting work in the Midwest could no longer be ignored.

Unsettling Settlement Laws

Poor relief in the United States had legal precedents and social customs dating back to Elizabethan England, which dictated that the right to relief was based on the individual's permanent residence. If a poor person needed relief but was staying in a place different from his or her permanent residence, the community could return a "dependent nonresident" to the place of origin. By the twentieth century, according to Helen S. Hawkins, "passing on" was the accepted American method of dealing with migrants in need of relief. If a migrant was fortunate, he (and many who were charged were men) might be fed a meal and allowed to sleep in the jail the night before his return, but as the Great Depression worsened, even this token concern vanished. Communities such as those in Johnson County, Indiana, which were popular destinations of migrants, increased enforcement of their poor laws. Newcomers who could not produce enough money to cover their food and expenses were arrested for vagrancy and jailed; they were then escorted out of town. Some communities began dumping migrants across state lines, as if they were stray kittens, and some states, such as California, even hired border patrols to prevent the entry of destitute migrants.[3]

Settlement laws were responsible for the callous and uncompassionate treatment of destitute migrants. Before the depression, most states had settlement laws of one year; interstate migrants who had yet to satisfy the one-year residency requirement in a new state were legally without a state, a home, a vote, and a political voice. The settlement laws were particularly troubling for southern white migrants who were already notorious for their shuttle migration, especially during the summer shutdowns in the automobile industry; one could easily lose settlement in the original state for an absence of anywhere from six months to three years. In Michigan in the 1930s, one had to earn two hundred dollars in a twelve-month base period to be eligible for unemployment compensation; fewer than half of migrant applicants could meet the requirement. Not surprisingly, many were forced to return to the South. But as the depression lingered and as the number of unwanted interstate migrants increased, many states began strengthening settlement laws expressly to prevent newcomers from obtaining settlement and, therefore, public relief. In 1931, Wisconsin, Illinois, Indiana, Michigan, and Ohio all had one-year residency requirements before a person could apply for public relief. Nine years later, Illinois and Indiana had changed their laws to three years; in Illinois a relief applicant had to live at least three years in the municipality, and in Indiana an applicant had to reside at least one of the three years in the same township. One bureaucrat from Chicago admitted that the law was designed to "affect those persons coming in from other states" and that "if the problem in the South was met in the South, it certainly would relieve the problem in the Northern States." Charles B. Marshall of the Indiana Department of Public Welfare said sarcastically,

"It is interesting to note the great excess of natives of Kentucky and Tennessee who live in Indiana over Hoosiers living in Kentucky and Tennessee." Mayor Edward J. Kelly of Chicago warned flatly, "We are not hanging up any wide open WELCOME signs for any and all individuals to come here . . . because they have been unable to earn a decent livelihood in other cities." Each state's settlement law indicated the extent to which migrants were welcome and common. California, for instance, went from a one-year law to a three-year law and then a five-year law. However, no settlement laws, as such, existed in Tennessee, Kentucky, Georgia, or Arkansas, where relief was always negligible in the first place. Alabama and Mississippi had six-month laws.[4]

As each state scrambled to extend its settlement law because an adjacent state had increased its own, the poor were caught in the middle of an inhumane game of returning the unwanted to their states of origin, where they were unable to earn a living. In November and December of 1938, for example, township trustees in Indiana deported 264 people, of whom 113 were sent to Kentucky, 41 to Tennessee, 9 to Georgia, 3 to West Virginia, and 2 to Alabama; 58 percent of the deportees were from Kentucky and Tennessee, and 64 percent were from southern states. Only 52 were returned to Illinois, Michigan, and Ohio combined. Eleven people from Dudley Township in Henry County (noted for its concentration of Kentucky migrants) were returned to Kentucky, for example, which cost the township fifteen dollars for "furniture & family by truck." Another Kentuckian was returned from Shelby County by ambulance, costing the county fifty dollars.[5]

Considerable constitutional controversy emerged over settlement laws, as states continued to strengthen laws designed to keep poor migrants out of their state. In 1939, the Supreme Court in *Hague v. CIO* prohibited municipalities from selectively deporting individuals, although two years later, in *Chirillo v. Lehman,* it permitted states to return to their state of residence those relief applicants who had not satisfied a state's settlement law. The most important case concerned Fred F. Edwards, who was convicted on February 17, 1940, for bringing his wife's brother-in-law, Frank Duncan, from Spur, Texas, to Yuba City, California. According to California law, "every person, firm or corporation, or officer or agent thereof that brings or assists in bringing into the State any indigent person who is not a resident of the State, knowing him to be an indigent person, is guilty of a misdemeanor." Illinois, Michigan, Indiana, and Ohio, as well as twenty-four other states, had similar laws. The constitutional question centered on interstate commerce: whether an able-bodied but unemployed person could migrate from one state to another or whether the state could prohibit entry because of "moral pestilence." In short, did humans have the same freedom of movement as articles of commerce? In *Edwards v. California,* the Court ruled that states could not restrict interstate migration by punishing those who helped people move across state lines.[6]

Although the mythology of "America" was based on the notion of a land of economic opportunity, where citizens could advance from rags to riches and where a nation of immigrants had seemingly legitimated the myth through migration—whether moving *from* a different continent or *to* a far-off corner of the United States—in the 1930s those who had decided to improve their lot by moving were rejected. One reason, of course, was that American society assumed migrants who were poor had moved to a new place, such as the Midwest, not to find a job but to receive the relief benefits, particularly since poor relief in the South was at best sporadic and at worst nonexistent. In Indiana, township trustees, who were responsible for relief, were required to observe three principles when returning nonresidents: the return should be "to the social and economic benefit of the client"; local officials at the destination must approve the return before a nonresident was handed over to them; and plans "for his care upon . . . arrival must be made." But Charles L. Dawson, secretary of the Indiana Township Trustees Association, explained that most of the state's returnees were from Kentucky and that returning a destitute nonresident to that state was not in the best interest of the person since there was no federal aid to dependent children or to the blind; relief in Kentucky, he pointed out, was rare. Furthermore, he noted that Kentucky officials seldom granted permission (or even answered letters) because they realized that the Kentuckian was much better off in Indiana.[7] As historians have argued, states and local communities were so overburdened by an anachronistic relief system that instead of answering the calls of the poor with social *welfare,* they responded with social *control.* Another common reason for migrants' facing hostility was that no community, in the throes of the worst economic crisis the country had faced, would welcome a needy stranger whose purpose in migrating was to compete for what few jobs existed.

A Transient Program for the Transients

For a time, the Federal Transient Service (FTS) changed this. Proof that the government had begun to notice (because of the tireless efforts of reformers and even private charities that no longer opposed a public relief program) that migrants were wandering the country in search of food, shelter, and work came early in the New Deal. In May 1933, passage of the Federal Emergency Relief Act established historic legislation that provided federal relief for the "indigent newcomer" by reimbursing states fully for relief given to nonresidents. Eventually, every state except Vermont organized a transient bureau, and states were reimbursed over $88 million for aiding more than a million nonresident citizens.[8]

The case of a Hopkins County, Kentucky, man in the 1930s was probably typical of the southern transient relief cases. He came to Detroit in 1922 after working in the coal mines of western Kentucky, and for several years he worked the mines in the busy winter months and then worked in Detroit's factories in the spring and summer when mining slumped. By the late thirties, however, his wife was dead, he was receiving aid in the Detroit transient bureau, and his three children were living wherever they could with Kentucky kin. Elmer Akers found plenty of other southerners seeking help from the Detroit transient bureau; about one-fourth of the eight hundred daily cases were from southern states, a figure he found surprising because he maintained "nearly all the southern whites in Detroit have relatives and friends there, and doubling up . . . is so common a practice we had come to suppose that most of them would do this rather than go to such places as the Transients Bureau."[9]

The FTS was not only a relief agency but also an information clearinghouse. For two years, the FTS set up transient bureaus in cities across the country to provide relief to those migrants falling between the cracks because of settlement laws. Aware of the stigma involved with social welfare, FTS reformers conducted monthly surveys of registrants in thirteen transient bureaus between May 1934 and June 1935, hoping to tackle hearsay head on. Data revealed that people were moving not to find the best relief payoff but to find work and that the reason they were distressed when they did not find a job at their destination was that a settlement law prevented them from getting public relief. Another view held that young men, who were believed to be the majority of "transients," were on the road because of simple wanderlust. A Florida psychologist, for example, wrote that "transiency is the result of a deep inner need to escape from a human condition into an unknown condition, to remove the old and discover the new, to break restraining bonds and find freedom, to renounce the too obvious 'real' for the more glitteringly 'unreal.'" In spite of his explanation, in April 1935, the overwhelming majority of "unattached transients" had migrated to seek a job or had been promised one if they moved; only 8 percent had moved because they were seeking adventure. The major difference between the American population and transient bureau clients was that the migrants were simply testing American mythology that held migration was the answer for one's economic distress.[10]

Researchers at the time also learned that entire families had packed up and moved in a desperate attempt to better themselves. FTS studies in 1934 and 1935 found that approximately three-quarters of those migrant relief cases surveyed said they moved to find a job. Over half had moved to a specific location because friends or family members were there or had once been there. Like unattached migrants, these families were often young, native-born, and educated. They also were small (most contained two or three members), and the number affected by separation, divorce, or death of a spouse was smaller than in the general population. The findings indicated that there was very little movement from bureau to bureau. Migrant families moved to a city and stayed there; few families stayed on transient relief for long. Anywhere from 20.0 to 40.0 percent of each month's case load left the program within that month, contrasted to a 5.6 percent rate for resident relief during the same period. The migrant family population, unlike the resident family on relief, was not chronically receiving relief; rather, researchers discovered, it was constantly replacing itself.[11]

In spite of studies that disproved many conceptions about the migration of the poor, the FTS, in Helen Hawkins's words, became "as transient as the group it served." In 1935, when federal relief was reorganized under the WPA and the Social Security program, the transient service was abolished. Those who were able were given WPA jobs, while those who could not work were returned to their place of legal settlement or were assigned to the care of the state or municipality in which they resided. Harry L. Hopkins said that "the final victory for the transients is only won when, working side by side the local man, he is known simply as a working man worthy of his hire." Although Michigan's transient service was kept alive, most migrants were forced to turn again to private agencies, such as the Salvation Army and Travelers' Aid, for relief.[12] The temporary benefits of the FTS were now gone, and the problems that led to this historic legislation—settlement laws, poverty, and unemployment—only increased.

Alphabet Soup Feeds the Hungry and Moves Them Along

Prior to the New Deal, the South and its people lay largely beyond the concern, influence, and scope of the federal government. One of the astonishing things about the policies of Franklin D. Roosevelt's administration was that many of the programs designed for the country at large actually penetrated the hills and hollows of the South. In my own fieldwork in the South, it was impossible to find an aged person who did not know through experience about some New Deal program. Roosevelt, in describing the sweeping scope and vision of the Tennessee Valley Authority in 1934, reminded the nation that the mountaineer family "certainly has been forgotten, not by the Administration, but by the American people." The New Deal programs had an extraordinary influence on migrants and migration. Some of these programs had effects—good and bad—that were apparent soon after their initiation; others took generations.[13]

One of the most common and best-known programs of the "Second New Deal" was the WPA, which, among other things, replaced the programs of the Federal Transient Service. The goal was indirect relief, or "public" work, which purportedly would restore human dignity lost because of the Great Depression and, some reformers believed, the direct relief of the first New Deal. The WPA was the nation's most comprehensive attempt to give every able American man (as well as a few women) a job that would provide minimum sustenance. Between 1935 and 1943, more than $11 billion was spent constructing roads, bridges, parks, airports, and buildings. Soon after the massive public works program was in place, desperate southerners began trekking to county seats to sign up, and before long, men were building roads that in years to come—beginning with the industrial mobilization for World War II—would enable them to migrate northward in search of a job. Earl Cox, from Fannin County, Georgia, remembered that people in his northern Georgia county were not doing much of anything before WPA work arrived. "It was the best thing that ever happened to us," he said flatly. "There was a lot of people that was hungry and couldn't pay their taxes or anything else until they started that." Frazier B. Adams, born in eastern Kentucky in 1907, said that although some people called it "we piddled around," the WPA "was really beneficial to the people. They built roads, bridges over small streams, constructed school buildings, and cleared forest and things like that. It really gave them work and was a good thing." Alice Allen, who lived in eastern Kentucky, said WPA workers "went around on these creeks and things where these little paths where people had walked were, and they dug them out with a pick and a shovel until they made a pretty good road where a car, I guess, could go over the road."[14] Ironically, a program designed to feed, clothe, and house the poor actually helped southerners leave a destitute region by providing an easy route out; all that was needed was a broken-down Model T (with plenty of oil), a brother or uncle or friend with a car, or a bus line running northward.

Although predating the WPA, the Civilian Conservation Corps also had a profound effect on southerners on the verge of becoming migrants. The CCC gathered up young men and moved them to almost fifteen hundred distant camps around the country, giving them a glimpse of life elsewhere and encouraging them to loosen their ties to the homeplace. Like the armed forces (which would receive many men from the Corps), the CCC had strict requirements: one had to be out of school and work, between seventeen and twenty-four years of age, between sixty and seventy-eight inches in height, over 107 pounds, have at least three "masticating teeth above and below," and, in some cases, have prior experience with the WPA. Young men (no women were allowed) as "soil soldiers" built fire towers, trails, and roads; planted trees; fought fires; conducted biological studies; and even constructed flood control projects.[15]

Dewey Thompson, born in 1913 and raised in Hardin County, Tennessee, grew up working on his father's eighty-acre farm and in sawmills. For him, like most southern yeomen, life was "hard work." When the depression came, he was eager to start working on the CCC, so he went across the state line to Florence, Alabama, to sign up. But regulations held that either the applicant or his parents had to work on the WPA before he could join the CCC. "Well," he told them, "sign me up on the WPA then!" He worked two weeks building roads ("Back then there wasn't no roads") in Lauderdale County, Alabama. Two weeks later, he went to the CCC camp in Bessemer, Alabama, near Birmingham. Although the program was limited to nine-month stints, Thompson managed to stay three years, cutting fire breaks and doing general forestry work, all for thirty dollars a month. He kept five and sent the remaining money home to his father, in hopes that his parents would be able to make the payments to keep the farm. They could not. After leaving the CCC, Thompson went back home to work in the woods. In 1938, he and his sweetheart, Marie, ran away to a preacher's home and were married. "My dad was one of those old fashioned dads," Marie Thompson said, "so we had to elope. Back then you did what your parents told you to do." They rented a little log cabin for two dollars a month just north of the state line. That two dollars, Marie said, "was hard to get back then just like three or four hundred dollars is now." Although Dewey had twenty-five dollars when they married, he was soon laid off, and to get by, he made a few cross ties until he was called back to the sawmill; Marie hired herself out to work in the nearby cotton fields. "Life wasn't easy," Dewey explained, "but I don't know ——."

Marie interrupted, "We was happy as we could be. We was a lot happier than people are now with everything. We probably didn't know no better, but we was happy." By December 1943, when Dewey was drafted, they had managed to buy a fifty-acre farm in Hardin County, Tennessee.[16]

Allen Barkley, born in 1922, lived near Big Cypress Creek on a two-hundred-acre farm in middle Tennessee. His family grew "everything just about that we eat. Raised everything with horses," he said. "We'd plow on them hillsides and them roots knocking your toe nails off; a little cussing and fussing went along with all that. As we growed on up, the times was hard, you know, and we had a little bad luck there. So I took off to CC camps. I spent six months on there up at Sewanee and Monteagle, Tennessee; down at Waynesboro, Georgia." By now used to traveling to find work, Barkley went to Logansport, Indiana, to work on the Pennsylvania Railroad:

> Coldest confounded place ever I seen. It was warm here, man, as it could be. I wore a pair of slippers and dress clothes. I got up there and hired in, and I didn't have no money to buy no more clothes with, so I went on out there to work in that snow and ice. Of course them shoes would get wet and I'd get in there to one of them stoves, and I burnt the bottoms out of them. But I made it that way until I got a pay day, and got me some shoes and clothes. And I got my call to the army. And I thought boy, I'll sure be glad to get out of this place.

Unfortunately, he was sent to even more frigid Fort Sheridan, Illinois, "right up on that lake up there."[17]

Other New Deal programs also either pushed people away from their homes or pulled them out. The minimum wage legislation of the National Recovery Administration, for example, prompted bottom-line accountants in the tobacco industry to mechanize, and in turn, hundreds of workers lost their jobs. "What has become apparent," the historian Pete Daniel writes, "is the key role the Agricultural Adjustment Administration . . . played in turning the South from sharecropping to agribusiness." The AAA's crop-reduction programs reduced the demand for farm labor and, because prices were stabilized, also provided landlords the capital to mechanize. A one-row cotton chopper could block out an acre in forty-two minutes, whereas it took more than twelve hours by hand. According to H. L. Mitchell, secretary of the Southern Tenant Farmers' Union in 1940, for every tractor put in use on a cotton plantation, two to four sharecropper families were displaced; with no place to go, many ended up in regional cities, such as Memphis, or farther north, such as Chicago. Thad Snow, from Missouri, said that in the 1920s, there was a "tremendous migration" from his state's cotton counties to industrial centers and that throughout the 1930s, the sharecropping system had continued to wither. "The high yield areas are cultivated by day laborers," he said. "The plantation is an industry rather than a farm. They have only occasional work and it is often not much over 60 days in a year, and they will certainly migrate if they get a chance to go. A great many white people have already migrated from our country."[18]

Dewey and Marie Thompson remembered those difficult days when they were forced to cut down some of their cotton. When cotton prices sunk to "a nickel a pound," Marie said, "they were cutting the cotton down and stuff." "We cut down some after we got married," she continued. "We'd planted it, and then you couldn't get nothing for it—it was too much cotton being made, so they had some of it cut down. Well, we just had to do what we had to do. You hated to do it, but you knowed that you'd get a little bit more for what you did have, you know." Reuben Little, born in 1888 in Perry County, Alabama, northwest of Montgomery, "was raised in the timber. There was 4 years when I left the farm and cut timber, sawmill contracting, cutting timber for 4 years, and then I went back on the farm." In 1930, he became a sharecropper. "I made six bales of cotton, and I couldn't get an offer on it, not even a penny a pound," he said. "I borrowed money from the bank through the landlord, and I had to turn it over to them, and I turned it over to them and went back to sawmilling in 1931," he continued. "And then I went back on the farm in 1932 or 1933, the first year that they plowed up cotton." Matt Butler grew up in Lawrence and Wayne counties in Tennessee growing cotton on rented farms after his father lost their 120-acre "level farm" after World War I. In 1936, he went to Arkansas to grow cotton "because you could make two bales of cotton over there [for every one in Tennessee], and you didn't have to put any fertilizer on it." In the Mississippi River bottoms, he explained, "all you had to do is go out there and plant that cotton and cultivate it and pick it when it matured." The tractors that large landowners purchased because of AAA policies could not get around the many cypress stumps near the river, but Butler and his mules could, so he rented the small perimeter lands that were full of stumps. When the Arkansas landlord bought a harvester, he wanted to reduce Butler's share from 50 percent to 40 percent, since Butler would not have to gather his crop. Butler was angry, and he was tired of his young daughter's having to "wade the mud" to get to school, so he left. He farmed in Wayne County for two years, but because the people in Arkansas wanted him back, he returned, until the boll weevil in 1945 prevented him from farming in Arkansas at all.[19]

Those who lived within the wide-ranging watershed of the Tennessee River were also affected by the government visionaries who worked for the

Tennessee Valley Authority. For some unskilled workers, TVA construction jobs offered temporary employment, but after the job was completed, skilled and well-educated employees from outside the region moved in to take the well-paid positions; those who had helped build were out of a job and often had to move. The people who lived within a fifty-mile radius of the Muscle Shoals, Alabama, TVA plant, for example, dreamed of getting a job there or working on the Wilson Dam under construction. Dewey Thompson, living across the state line in Wayne County, Tennessee, found that potential employees needed inside connections that he did not have. "I tried to get in to the TVA, but they was hard," he said. "You had to have the inside pull to get on the TVA." Others around Lauderdale County, Alabama, found that the TVA bought what land was not in the hands of landlords, particularly the rich bottomlands near the river; tenants and croppers who farmed that land lost out. One young man from the county summed up how difficult life was for him: employers refused to hire those who had worked on the WPA, while some twenty men owned the rest of the land that the TVA did not and were all farming it with tractors.[20]

If the TVA could not provide a job, many southerners discovered that it could take away their house and flood their land. Frequently the TVA, like many other New Deal agencies, merely loosened people from their land (as it simultaneously strengthened ties to the national government) and made the decision to migrate no longer a choice but a necessity. In the summer of 1933, the TVA began buying up expansive tracts of land for an immense dam just below the confluence of the Clinch and Powell rivers in eastern Tennessee.

Those who were removed for the Norris Dam remembered not only how they were pushed out but also how ambivalent the exiled were about an old way of life and a new. Claude Longmire was seventeen when the TVA bought his father's farm. "I've always felt," he said, "that for TVA to break them up was probably the best thing that ever happened to those people. Because most everybody that left there bettered themselves." Hubert Stooksbury agreed: "That was the best thing, of course, that ever happened to them, to move, but at the time they thought it was very cruel." Others, however, were not as positive about the experience over forty years later. Myers Hill was forced from his family's land in Union County at the age of twenty-six. "I think it was a problem to them. Some of the older people I don't think ever was really adjusted to the new localities," he explained, articulating the trade-off between two ways of life. "They tried to make the best of it, of course, but even though they had better living conditions, they were still, I don't think, quite as well satisfied." He concluded, "A lot of them would rather have stayed on, even though their living conditions wasn't as good as they were where they moved." If the older people were struck hardest in being forced off their land, the dislocation actually served to send many younger people northward. "My daughter was here yesterday," Vera Stiner explained, "and I talked to her about the old conditions, you know, and she wanted to know why people left the area—young men, most of them, when they grew up—to Indiana, Ohio, Michigan, to work, because we didn't have any industry in the area at that time. And very little in Knoxville at that time. So they went to the industrial North."[21]

If southerners found it difficult to believe that their house might in the near future be covered with ninety feet of water, they found the government's actions around the new town of Oak Ridge, Tennessee, even more mysterious. Charles Brummett, who grew up nearby, remembered having to move off his family's land in 1941 when the government acquired it. "The farm that I was raised on," he said, "it was inside the area that the government bought. I forget how many thousands of acres they bought there. But everybody, they came and they surveyed around for—I don't know—how many weeks. Nobody knew what they were doing." He continued:

> And then so they worked out there for a long time just, you know, doing that. And then in '42, they called us all in the area where I lived to one of the high schools. And one of the guys was telling us that the government was buying—I don't know how many acres it was. Boy! It was a lot. Up in the thousand, you know. And they said it's for the war effort. That's all we knew. And [he] said, You will be given a certain amount for your place, you know. They will appraise it, you know. And then when they settled with you, we had no choice, you know.
>
> In the meantime, you'd be looking for a place, you know, to move. So they told us what they would give us and boy! It was nothing, really. But my parents moved out of that area in '43. I think about January '43 to Clinton, you know. But nobody around there knew what it was. They just said it's for the war effort. And then when they started working inside the plant and everything, everybody had to [be] cleared through the FBI and everything to work inside.
>
> It really hurt a lot of people. Some, you know, that never lived nowhere [else] in their life before. And there were, you know, some of them [that] were getting up in years. Some of them, I think, it caused them to [lose] their health, you know, to go bad and to die later. To me it was kind of exciting, you know. I was going into service anyhow. And I wasn't thinking anything about it, you know—having to move out.[22]

Even smaller New Deal projects affected communities. After years of lobbying by local boosters and politicians, in 1934 Congress allocated fifty thousand dollars to survey the "Natchez Trace," a trail that ran from Nashville, Tennessee, to Natchez, Mississippi, with a goal of constructing a national parkway. Late in 1935, construction began in Mississippi. By 1939, construction had progressed to the point that government officials began buying up land for the right-of-way in southern Wayne County, about a hundred miles southwest of Nashville. By spring of the following year, area residents had read notices that between two hundred and three hundred local men would be employed, mainly to clear the roadway. "Natchez Trace Office Opened at Collinwood" read the banner headline in the *Wayne County News* on May 3: "First Work on Trace Will Be 9-Mile Stretch from Cypress Inn, North."[23]

When several hundred men were given jobs working "on the Trace," the federal government penetrated yet another part of the South. Many men from the area got their first taste of what it was like to earn real money. An unskilled laborer was paid thirty-five cents an hour; those who brought a pair of mules (and this was a mule culture) to the job site and were willing to use them to drag out felled trees were paid the fantastic wage of a dollar an hour—ten dollars a day—which was a 1,000 percent increase over sawmill wages, until then the most common form of "public work." Men interviewed who at the time were young said they earned more money in one day than they had seen in their entire lives up to that point.[24] Sterlin Reeves, who grew up in Wayne County, had worked as a farm laborer for fifty cents a day. At age eighteen, he went to a local sawmill, got a job, and was paid ten cents an hour for a ten-hour day. "You made a dollar a day. You worked a million days, you made a million dollars," he joked. He was thirty years old "when the Trace came through":

> And that morning when they opened that job I guess there was at least three hundred people there looking for work. I didn't go to work right then, but in a week or two I did go to work—grading out those holes where they put the culverts, and lot of them was waist down deep in water. You had to get down in there and move that mud and stuff and grade it out. And that was a little bit rougher than I liked; I quit and went to the rock quarry, and I worked that for, like, several weeks. And then I got on with the right-of-way crew and stayed with it for the first ten miles. Thirty-five cents. It beat nothing; it was a job and people was really glad to get it. It give a lot of people work that didn't have work before.[25]

Clearly, the three hundred men looking for work were trying to ease the worst parts of a life they were trying to hold on to; for many, however, work on the Trace was the beginning of the end of their familiar life-style in Wayne County.

There were exceptions, such as Ellie Williams. He was approaching forty years of age when men were getting jobs on the Trace. The year before, he had moved his family near Cypress Inn and was sharecropping on the land of Luther McFall, a half-brother to his first cousin. Since it was too early to begin plowing, McFall was paying Williams seventy-five cents a day "and dinner" to clear his fence rows. Williams recalled:

> I was glad to get seventy-five cents. I could take that seventy-five cents and go down to Ben Darby's [a nearby general store] and buy the best overalls they had for seventy-five cents a pair. (And that's something about the same thing today—you make twenty-five dollars a day on a job and it costs you twenty-five dollars to get you a pair of overalls. Just more money handled, that's all.) But anyhow when I was cleaning out around the field, Luther come up there where I was at. And he said, "Why don't you get you a job on the Natchez Trace?" And I said, "Well, I thought about it, but," I said, "I moved over here to make a sharecrop, and I knew you'd want your land cultivated." He said, "If it was me, I'd get me a job on that Natchez Trace." Well, I went and hired in. Cutting the right-of-way off. Along there about Scott's Chapel when I hired in. Between there and the highway, going to the state line. I went and hired in, thirty cents an hour. Ten hours, three dollars. Boy, I was making money.

The money Williams was making would become a sizable down payment on the house he would live in for the rest of his life.[26]

Like other construction projects, the work on the Trace lasted only a few months for the unskilled men. Once the roadway was cleared, the engineers brought in their own workers to grade, gravel, and apply a layer of calcium chloride to the surface. Those who had grown accustomed to good wages were forced after their lay-off to decide between a difficult but familiar life in the South or an alternative one, most likely in the North. Many were called into the armed forces, since by January 1942 the government had cut all the funding for the Trace. Still others left Wayne County for the North, like Sterlin Reeves, who went to Detroit after his stint on the Trace ended. But a few, such as Ellie Williams, stayed on, thankful for the money they made while they were able to make it. Williams, whose heart was divided less than most, highlighted the years of Trace construction as a benchmark for change in his community: "A lot of people got to leaving here along about then going north. And some of them saved money and came back and bought homes. And some of them are still up there. I just never did have the notion to go and never did think about going. I never was what you call money crazy. I had a family—they was growing up when the neighbors was going north. I had a house full of kids—five girls."[27]

In myriad ways, then, New Deal projects affected southerners—most potential migrants—throughout the region. After New Deal programs, migration was often a clear alternative. Southerners built roads, which would carry them out of the region; reported to distant places, where they earned money and where their ties were loosened; watched their land flooded with water; and even earned money on a government project that once it was finished, sent them searching for another job. In spite of the best efforts of New Dealers, many of the problems confronting both southerners and migrants still remained, and eventually Congress stepped in to investigate.

Congress Discovers the Destitute Migrant

The migrants kept coming northward. Between 1935 and 1940, newcomers from the southern Appalachians alone were adding up in significant numbers. For example, Appalachian migrants between 1935 and 1940 constituted almost one-fifth of all out-of-state migrants to Cincinnati and Columbus. On July 29, 1940, a congressional committee headed by Representative John H. Tolan of California opened hearings in New York City to investigate the "interstate migration of destitute citizens." In all, the committee would spend twenty-eight days (ending the hearings on September 17, 1942) listening to 371 witnesses in seven regions and would generate over fifteen thousand pages of testimony. An implicit goal of the committee was to examine ways of curtailing interstate migration, but when U.S. entry into the war seemed imminent, the committee changed its name to the Committee on National Defense Migration and officially began examining ways to ensure plenty of labor for defense needs.[28]

In the early weeks of testimony, witnesses frequently invoked Frederick Jackson Turner to remind the committee that life in the United States was based on the ability to pack up and move and the notion that one was likely to better oneself in the process, never mind those who failed. But by the twentieth century, this mythic history had been replaced by the realities of depression and disappearing potential. Said one witness, "Modern migrants seek to improve their position as did pioneer migrants, but the chances of improvement are impressively less."[29]

The Tolan committee also heard testimony that argued against medieval notions of human frailty as the cause of poverty as well as the belief that people migrated because they were given care along the way, a charge often raised earlier against the Federal Transient Service. What is obvious today evidently was not so apparent in the 1930s, as testimony by Bertha McCall, of Travelers' Aid, indicates: "Well, . . . the family as a whole, when it picks up and goes, does so because it does not have enough to live on well where it is and thinks that the next field is much greener than the one where it is, and it keeps going in that way. . . . I would say from my experience in all of these years, in Travelers' Aid, that you would find a large percentage of people who move, moving because there is something pushing them, a pressure pushing them out—a magnet drawing them rather than just a human frailty." When asked if care and attention while migrating did not increase the number of migrants, McCall replied, "Well, that's one of the great criticisms that was made of the Federal Transient Program. I happen to be one of the people that does not believe that is the real reason why they go. There were other good conditions why they go. I mean you would move from your community if you were not able to do well in that community and you found another community in which you could do very much better." John H. Tolan asked her, "In the early days of this country people migrated and as they got to the States of destination they found jobs. Now, do you not think the tendency in America today is to want them to come in if they have got some money and they do not want them to come in if they have not got any money? That is our problem, is it not?" "Yes," McCall answered. In a later hearing, Pare Lorentz, the *McCall's* photographer who had spent five years with migrants, was more blunt: "I think what you are facing is chickens coming home to roost. You have not a new problem of migrants, but you have an accelerated tendency that we have been fiddling around with for 10 years."[30]

The committee traveled around the country and held hearings in various cities. Local politicians, welfare bureaucrats, private relief officials, academics, local employers, and union officials were summoned, but even more significant were the migrants themselves that committee investigators searched out and put on witness stands. These witnesses, unlike the thousands for whom they spoke, had their names and often their experiences memorialized in the official testimony.

Spurgeon Hayden, for example, who testified before the committee in Chicago on August 20, 1940, was typical of the thousands who had left the South late in the depression for a northern industrial city. At the time of his appearance before the committee, he was forty-three years old and had seven children, the oldest eighteen and the youngest thirteen months. Born in Mississippi, Hayden had been a sharecropper and had had various other jobs off the farm. "I worked in the saw mill, corn press, and so forth," he said. "I dug ditches, worked in the saw mill, and I farmed some," earning a dollar a day in the mill, sixty cents a day for plowing (sunup to sundown), and fifty cents a hundred picking cotton. As a sharecropper, he had about fifteen acres in cotton and five or six in corn, and he had a garden, some chickens and hogs, and a milk cow. But when asked about his success he answered, "I didn't do so well," adding that "sometimes we would and sometimes we wouldn't" have enough food to eat. If he was lucky, he would make twenty-five to thirty-five dollars after his crop was harvested. "Cash money was scarce. When they pay a man 60 cents a day from sunup to sundown, that ain't much money," he observed. On December 7, 1939, he came to Chicago on a train. "I was about 2 years or longer saving that up to get here," he said, and, after selling his chickens, hogs, and cow, he had thirty dollars when he arrived. But his lot in the Midwest had been little better. He had painted "a little. I have calcimined. I tear down paper, clean buildings, and all like that" for $1.50 per day. In 1940, he had not had a regular job; from January to March he was unemployed and was forced to seek help from United Charities, which gave him ten dollars a week for the three months (the public relief agency refused his request because he was not yet a resident of Chicago). Asked why he chose to leave Mississippi, he replied, "I just got tired of that job we had. We didn't have enough to live. We couldn't send the children to school." He had, he said, "heard a whole lot of talk about Chicago. I didn't have no friends here, but my folks had been here, and gone back, and I talked to them." He told the committee, "I would rather stay here. I ain't done bad here. Of course, it is a little tight now, because I ain't got no job. It is kind of tight. Times is kind of tight anyhow. It's a whole lot better than in Mississippi."[31]

Reuben Little, who had to turn over his cotton to the bank in the early 1930s, later moved to Autauga County, Alabama, where he contracted malaria (when he was farming the bottoms of the Alabama River) and got into skirmishes with the landlord. In 1940, the family—three boys and three girls—was living on relief in Lowndes County because Little had a history of "nervous problems." Because Little was unable to farm, the landlord hired two of the boys for ten dollars per month, plus room and board. When Little went into a hospital, the landlord changed the unwritten contract with the boys. "He told them that he would stop their board but would give them three pounds of plate meat [salt pork] and a peck of meal apiece instead of boarding them," he told the committee at its Montgomery hearings. "They took it up and didn't know no better than to do that." Eventually, the landlord evicted them, and Little was desperate about his next move. "I can't take no manual labor myself and I am not able to do it," he said, "and the doctor has told me not to do it and I tried to find a light job like night watching or something like that, but I can't find it." Sorrowfully, he told the committee, "I never owned any land in my life. I have owned two or three head of stock, that is all."[32]

Committee investigators also uncovered many who were agricultural migrants, not simply those seeking industrial jobs. The committee learned of the long route that berry pickers trekked as they followed the season northward. George Friday, a farmer from Coloma, in Berrien County, Michigan, testified that "we gave quite a lot of work to workers that work in the South part of the year and come through and work north." Estimating the composition of at least five thousand migrants in his county alone, he said, "There are probably more families that come in from Arkansas than any other State in the Union. There are a lot of them that start in the South that have not had any home for years. There are probably two-thirds of them, or better than half of them, at least." Although he said preference was given to single workers, many families came, and children aged ten or over were expected to contribute their labor for piece wages. Those who had never before worked in the county had the hardest time finding employment, since farmers there relied on largely the same group of people year after year. Frank Collins, for example, was born in Swain County in extreme western North Carolina in 1896 but was living in Belle Glade, Florida, near Lake Okeechobee, in a Farm Security Administration migratory labor camp when he was called before the committee. Until 1940, he testified,

> I have always had to leave Florida in the summer due to having no place to live in the summer season, and I would go to Kentucky and Michigan and up through Indiana coming back and working in Kentucky around Paducah in the strawberry section going up, and around Benton Harbor [Michigan] I would work some. And I would work in the strawberries and the cherries going up, and I would come back through Indiana and work in the tomatoes, and then it would be about vegetable time in Florida, and between those two times maybe we would have a few weeks off.[33]

Troy Coldiron, who was fifty-nine when he appeared before the committee in Chicago, had been living in McGuffey, Ohio, on the Scioto Marsh, for eight years. Born in Kentucky, he came to the marsh, he said, "because I couldn't get anything to do, and I just came here to this place, came down and wanted to live in it." His family, which included six children, lived in "a small little house, with three little rooms [and one window]. It ain't hardly fit to live in," for which he paid three dollars a month in rent. Asked the ridiculous question of whether the house was papered, Coldiron answered genuinely, "It is sort of papered. It is patched, too." When work in the onion fields was available, he was paid $1.75 per day, and his two oldest children—aged fourteen and eleven—also worked in the fields and were paid five cents per crate. Asked about his future prospects since the onion harvest was about to begin, he answered, "They won't hardly hire you. They just have got their own men that works for them all the time. You have to just catch a day when you can. That is the way they work. They just take out a bunch of men and they work all the way, and then if we get a day, it is a day they need a hand or two to come in and work, or something like that. I just do the best I can. Sometimes I work in the stores, and sometimes husking corn; just anything I can get to do."[34]

When Leander Tungate of Greenwood, Indiana, was asked why he moved north, he answered, "Well, my wife had a brother up there. He had a tomato crop that he wanted picked. I wanted to help pick the tomatoes. I came up here." Arriving in 1933, he had been in Johnson County for seven years, though occasionally in the winter months he would go back to his Kentucky birthplace for a spell, perhaps trying to escape the cold that often made southerners fair-weather migrants. He and his wife and five children were living in a one-room house with no water or inside toilet (although he told the committee he had built his own "sanitary closet") when he was summoned to Chicago to appear before the Tolan committee. Before coming to Indiana, Tungate had worked as a farm laborer, never owning any land himself. About to begin the picking season, which would last almost three months, he was expecting to earn $3.50 to $4.00 a day. He told the committee that fellow southerners who were coming to the area for the harvest were desperate for housing, and many were living "just in school-bus bodies, tents, or anything they can get to stay in"; most, he said, would go back south after the harvest. Those who decided to stay would have trouble getting any relief because of Indiana's settlement laws. When asked if officials considered him a resident of Indiana, Tungate answered flatly, "They ought to. I voted."[35]

As the committee hearings continued, congressmen were told that migration in the South was caused by a number of things, including the consolidation, mechanization, and seasonal nature of agriculture; drought, especially in 1934 and 1936; the decline of foreign markets; erosion; better transportation; and the exploding southern white population. Rupert B. Vance, the southern sociologist, while pointing out that fertility in some areas of the highlands would double the population every thirty years without migration, testified that migration was a safety valve for the region, "for there is no additional land supply that will not quickly erode if put to the plow." Vance's words were warnings against any legislation that sought to prevent migration, since the first ten hearings of the committee were intended, at least implicitly, to explore ways to halt the migration of destitute people because many, particularly those in the Midwest and California, wanted to keep migrants away. Even though West Virginia, Kentucky, and Tennessee had provided a chunk of the industrial labor force of Illinois, Indiana, Michigan, and Ohio since the rise of the automobile industry, migrants were still largely unwelcome during the late 1930s.[36]

For migrants themselves, however, migration was a temporary attempt to get their hands on some money and then return to their familiar southern life-style; those who migrated were merely trying to remedy the difficult economic conditions in their lives, since many southerners would explain not knowing the difference between the "official" onset of the depression and the period before it. Curtis Stiner, from east Tennessee, spoke for a multitude: "You had food to eat, you just didn't have any money to spend. I've lived in a depression all my life; that's all I ever knowed. I can't tell any difference; not between the twenties and the thirties." Before the depression, said Jesse Martin of his family in western Kentucky, life was tolerable, "and we really done all right through the depression. Of course we lived on the farm, and we had our garden, and we had corn." "It was a good life in a way," he commented, "we didn't know any better." His wife, Emma, concurred: "Life was rough and we didn't know any better—we didn't realize how bad off we were." Sally Etter, who grew up in western Kentucky after her parents returned from Whiting, Indiana, in the 1920s, said her family was not poor, they simply had no money: "Really, I guess we were [poor], and nowadays they would probably say we were underprivileged children. But we didn't feel that way, no. We had a lot of love in our home and we always had plenty to eat." Migrating, the Tolan committee discovered, was substituting underemployment for the risk of unemployment. Those who were fortunate once they moved left behind the old frustrations (and certainly the joys) of southern life, although in the 1930s many migrants simply encountered new frustrations.[37]

Notes

1. O'Harrow, *Preliminary Survey of County Planning Problems in Johnson County, Indiana,* 7–8; *Detroit Free Press,* July 22, 1937, 1.

2. For California migration, see Gregory, *American Exodus.* See also Weisiger, *Land of Plenty;* Westefeld, *Michigan Migrants;* and Tolles, "Survey of Labor Migration between States," 3–16.

3. Webb, *Transient Unemployed,* 1; Hawkins, *New Deal for the Newcomer,* 3–4, 22–79; Taylor and Rowell, "Refugee Labor Migration to California, 1937," 240–50.

4. U.S. Congress, House, Select Committee to Investigate the Interstate Migration of Destitute Citizens, *Interstate Migration: Hearings,* 3: 1200–1201, 880–81, 867–70, 814, 1063; U.S. Congress, House, Select Committee to Investigate the Interstate Migration of Destitute Citizens, *Interstate Migration Report,* 640, 648. On shuttle migration, see Collins, *America's Own Refugees,* 26.

5. Indiana, State Department of Public Welfare, "Summary of Deportation of Indigents from Indiana by Township Trustees during the Months of November 1938 and December 1938," Migration and Transient Activity in Indiana, Indiana Division, Indiana State Library, Indianapolis, Ind.; Indiana, State Department of Public Welfare, "Inter-State Deportation, November 1938," ibid.

6. *Hague v. CIO,* 307 U.S. 469 (1939); *Chirillo v. Lehman,* 312 U.S. 662 (1941); *Edwards v. California,* 314 U.S. 160 (1941); "Depression Migrants and the State," 1031–42; U.S. Congress, House, Select Committee Investigating National Defense Migration, *National Defense Migration: Hearings,* 18:7070, 27:9969, 27:9971–72. Not until the 1960s and 1970s, however, did Supreme Court decisions rule against travel restrictions, vagrancy laws, and discriminatory state settlement laws. See Hawkins, *New Deal for the Newcomer,* 18n3.

7. Pierson, "M-Factor in American History," 275–89; Congress, House, Select Committee to Investigate the Interstate Migration of Destitute Citizens, *Interstate Migration: Hearings,* 3:1072 (Dawson quote).

8. Historians of the New Deal have largely ignored the FTS; the only complete history is Hawkins, *New Deal for the Newcomer.* See also Crouse, *Homeless Transient in the Great Depression.*

9. Akers, "Southern Whites in Detroit," 43–44.

10. Webb, *Transient Unemployed,* 1–2, 117, 118; Anderson, *Men on the Move,* 88 (psychologist's quote). See also Minehan, *Boy and Girl Tramps of America,* 260. Even as late as 1939, studies still found that most migrated to find employment, not the best kinds of relief. See Webb and Westefeld, "Labor Mobility and Relief," 16–24.

11. Webb, *Transient Unemployed,* 117; Webb and Brown, *Migrant Families,* 5, 10, xxvii–xxviii, xxvi.

12. Hawkins, *New Deal for the Newcomer,* 2; Hopkins, *Spending to Save,* 136; Anderson, *Men on the Move,* 310. See also Webb, Northrop, Brown, and Gordon, *Survey of the Transient and Homeless Population in Twelve Cities.*

13. Quoted in McDonald and Muldowny, *TVA and the Dispossessed,* 263. See also Biles, *South and the New Deal,* 36–82.

14. Cox interview; Adams interview, 3; Allen interview, 4. Ironically, some planners thought the WPA prevented migration by providing work at home. See U.S. Congress, House, Select Committee Investigating National Defense Migration, *National Defense Migration: Hearings,* 18:7423.

15. Caudill, *Night Comes to the Cumberlands,* 214–15; Watkins, *Great Depression,* 130 (quote); Hill, *In the Shadow of the Mountain;* Salmond, *Civilian Conservation Corps, 1933–1942.*

16. Thompson interview.

17. Barkley interview.

18. P. Daniel, *Standing at the Crossroads,* 121; U.S. Congress, House, Select Committee to Investigate the Interstate Migration of Destitute Citizens, *Interstate Migration: Hearings,* 2:624; U.S. Congress, House, Select Committee Investigating National Defense Migration, *National Defense Migration: Hearings,* 23:9163 (Snow quote).

19. Thompson interview; U.S. Congress, House, Select Committee to Investigate the Interstate Migration of Destitute Citizens, *Interstate Migration: Hearings,* 2:794–95 (Little quote); Butler interview. See also Kirby, *Rural Worlds Lost,* 195–204, 335–36.

20. Thompson interview; U.S. Congress, House, Select Committee to Investigate the Interstate Migration of Destitute Citizens, *Interstate Migration: Hearings,* 2:627; J. Jones, *Dispossessed,* 225.

21. Quoted in McDonald and Muldowny, *TVA and the Dispossessed,* 58–61.

22. Brummett interview, 19–20. See also Johnson and Schaffer, *Oak Ridge National Laboratory,* 1–52.

23. *Natchez Trace Parkway Survey,* 143, 123–24, 150, 151; *Wayne County (Tenn.) News,* Feb. 9, May 3, 1940.

24. R. G. Hudson, who grew up in northern Georgia's Fannin County, remembered how the damning of the Toccoa River by the Tennessee Power Company, begun in 1929 and completed in 1932, also brought short-lived jobs for the area's men, as contractors hired them and their mules to drag out the thousands of logs that were cleared before the area could be flooded. Lake Blue Ridge was eventually taken over by the Tennessee Valley Authority. Hudson interview.

25. Reeves interview.

26. Williams interview.

27. Reeves interview; Williams interview.

28. James S. Brown to P. F. Ayer, Apr. 20, 1959, Urban Migrant Project, folder 7, box 278, Records of the Council of the Southern Mountains, Southern Appalachian Archives, Hutchins Library, Berea College, Berea, Ky.

29. U.S. Congress, House, Select Committee to Investigate the Interstate Migration of Destitute Citizens, *Interstate Migration: Hearings,* 3:821, 1:50–51, 1:2–3, 2:427; U.S. Congress, House, Select Committee to Investigate the Interstate Migration of Destitute Citizens, *Interstate Migration Report,* 4 (quote).

30. U.S. Congress, House, Select Committee to Investigate the Interstate Migration of Destitute Citizens, *Interstate Migration: Hearings,* 1:65–67, 12:4279.

31. Ibid., 3:961–65.

32. Ibid., 2:797–98.

33. U.S. Congress, House, Select Committee to Investigate the Interstate Migration of Destitute Citizens, *Interstate Migration: Hearings,* 3:1224, 3:1221, 2:500. Berrien County, Michigan, first became popular because residents there sent truck loads of food and clothing to Arkansans who suffered serious crop failure in 1931. The act of kindness allegedly led many to Berrien County after they were forced from their land. Reports of high wages in Michigan orchards lured even more there. See U.S. Congress, House, Select Committee Investigating National Defense Migration, *National Defense Migration: Hearings,* 32:12381; and Lacy interview.

34. U.S. Congress, House, Select Committee to Investigate the Interstate Migration of Destitute Citizens, *Interstate Migration: Hearings,* 3:1216–20.

35. Ibid., 3:993–97.

36. Ibid., 3:1199.

37. McDonald and Muldowny, *TVA and the Dispossessed,* 30 (Stiner quote); Jesse and Emma Martin interview; James and Sally Etter interview, 14.

4 *What a Difference a War Makes*

> Detroit was a good town till da hillbillies come,
> an den Detroit went tu hell.
>
> —Harriette Arnow, *The Dollmaker*

> Over at the Greek's most of the stools at the counter were occupied by men and young girls drinking coffee. The boy behind the counter had an accent akin to the flat, slurred Indiana speech but less harsh. "Him?" said the newspaperman. "He's one of the hill-billies. Haven't you heard that there are only forty-five states left in the Union? Kentucky and Tennessee have gone to Indiana, and Indiana has gone to hell."
>
> —John Bartlow Martin, 1944, Muncie, Ind.

A SHORT TIME BEFORE the bombing of Pearl Harbor, the Tolan committee scrambled to change its investigation to national defense migration. Decision makers looking at the political economy of wartime mobilization not only had discovered migrants but also were planning ways these multitudes of desperate people could be used to win the war against World War II's "isms": totalitarianism, authoritarianism, and fascism. Like the Great Depression, World War II would be a watershed, as the hundreds of thousands who had been forced to return south because of the depression now joined thousands of others and enlisted in the armed forces or traveled back to the Midwest to help make the planes, bombs, and tanks to support their fellow southerners abroad. If the Great

Depression forced migrants back to the South, easing the ambivalence associated with migration, wartime prosperity sucked them northward again. There was great money to be made, and many, though not all, reasoned that they would answer the call of industry, working temporarily and then returning home with their savings, perhaps able to make a down payment on some land. Some undoubtedly stuck to this plan, but many southerners seem to have been unable to resist the wages and benefits and consumer goods that would characterize the postwar industrial economy, spending their working lives in the North but dreaming about one day retiring and returning "down home." A divided heart would continue for most southern white migrants until their last days.

From Resistance to Welcome

On March 31, 1941, over eight months before the bombing of Pearl Harbor, the Seventy-seventh Congress adopted House Resolution 113, extending the interstate migration hearings until January 3, 1943, changing the committee's name to the Committee on National Defense Migration, and authorizing it to investigate migration specifically related to defense mobilization. The change of the committee's focus would suddenly transform it from one designed to prevent people from migrating to one worried that not enough people would migrate to fill the jobs required by defense mobilization. Suddenly, *reemployment migration* demanded by imminent war was added to the *unemployment migration* associated with the Great Depression, and the numbers of those migrating would be massive, forever changing the cultural, social, and economic landscapes of both the South and the North as hopeful job seekers again came north hunting work.

Just before this transformation, however, was a period of intense paranoia about curtailment and the changeover to defense production; during 1941, industry was gearing up for a defense economy, but the nation itself had not begun drafting the massive number of people required to win a war abroad. Northern politicians were consequently frantic about the lay-offs associated with conversion. In Indiana, more than three thousand workers were laid off by mid-September 1941 in nineteen plants because of curtailment; over five thousand more were scheduled to lose their jobs. In the auto and auto parts industries, the backbone of the state's industrial economy, close to two thousand had been laid off, and at least that many more were expected to be let go. In tiny Connersville, for example—population 13,000—800 jobs were lost at Rex Manufacturing and 115 at Stant Manufacturing Company. It was feared that of the half-million people in Michigan's auto industry, one-third would be laid off by January 1942 because of the decline of auto production. Michigan's Governor Murray D. Van Wagoner told the committee that "as far as the state of Michigan is concerned, we do not want any people to come into our State . . . until the people we have here now are fully employed on this defense work."[1]

The problem was the maldistribution of industry, and the historic trend only worsened as the government began awarding defense contracts. The South, with a glut of surplus labor, continued to lose out to an already industrialized Midwest (where labor shortages had been widespread), thus wasting a rare opportunity to change the course of southern social and economic life. Until January 1, 1941, for example, those areas of the country that received only one-fourth of the defense contracts had four-fifths of WPA employment. "The necessity of bringing the worker and the job together," the authors of the committee report reasoned, "will require large-scale migration, whose magnitude is as yet little considered." Harlow S. Person of the Department of Agriculture admitted that "defense migration is coming to be more and more the result of a failure to distribute defense orders widely among the many thousands of plants of the country." Senator Harley M. Kilgore, from the Senate committee investigating the national defense program, was incensed that the Willow Run bomber plant, near Detroit, was placed in such a congested area, especially since most workers received on-the-job training. Faced with a huge housing shortage, he asked a witness from the National Housing Agency if "there [was] any reason why we had to put a plant like this in such a congested area for labor and cause such a tremendous defense migration? Was there any particular reason there?" "No, sir," the witness answered meekly. Sidney Hillman, representing the Office of Production Management, pointed out that this inequity of defense contracts was not policy: "The Labor Division from its inception has urged that contracts be equitably distributed and that they be placed in areas where idle men and idle machines were to be found." Yet he also told the committee that "it has been the policy of the Labor Division from the beginning that every worker should, if possible, be employed locally, be trained locally, and be brought into the defense effort locally," a policy much more idealistic than realistic.[2]

With mounting conversion layoffs and in spite of the change in the Tolan committee's orientation, what followed were several more months of feverish activity—especially at the local level—designed to prevent migrant job seekers from coming northward. As early as 1939, the Social Security Board and state employment agencies had begun disseminating employment information over the radio, but by 1941, the action was increased through speeches, interviews, dramatic sketches, and announcements. W. L. Mitchell, director of the board, testified that "a continuous attempt has been made to influence migration by outright warnings to workers not to travel without prior checking with the local employment office," all because conversion had policymakers worried. The state of Michigan was sending releases to other states informing them that "Michigan does not at the present time need a large influx of new workers."[3] Industry, meanwhile, was probably not cooperating to its fullest extent, since many industries preferred fresh southern migrants who were willing to work for virtually any wage over seasoned northern natives.

In spite of the best efforts to keep potential migrants put, they poured northward during the summer and fall of 1941. Those who came were mostly returnees who had been forced southward during the back-to-the-land movement of the Great Depression and those who were now coming of age (as early as sixteen), ready to make their way into the wage economy they thought was about to explode. Many new arrivals were unable to get assembly line or other manufacturing jobs, but they could often find work in construction—building new factories, housing, and roads. Construction was soon to begin for the mammoth Willow Run plant near Detroit, and with a projected employment of sixty thousand, virtually no policy short of instituting border patrols could keep job seekers away. Already in 1941 estimates placed the in-migration to Detroit at over seventy-five thousand, and the housing shortage there was critical (an official vacancy figure of 0.4 percent). A WPA study of predominantly white workers and their dependents in Detroit found a large number from "Appalachia." Their statistics begin to paint a picture of the migrant job seeker: average distance traveled was 340 miles; 41 percent were from rural areas; 21 percent were last involved in agriculture; 68 percent were in Detroit for the first time; 10 percent were unemployed; more than 50 percent were alone (and thus not yet a burden on area schools); and approximately 33 percent were living in a separate dwelling, over 50 percent were doubling with others, and 10 percent were living in trailers and motels. As before, other popular destinations for migrants included northern Indiana's Calumet region, South Bend, and Indianapolis; Dayton and Cincinnati in southern Ohio; and Toledo, Sandusky, Cleveland, Akron, Ravenna, Canton, and Youngstown in northern Ohio.[4]

The bombing of Pearl Harbor galvanized the wartime mind-set even though the nation had for some time been fervently preparing for war. Once war was declared, midwestern political and economic elites almost instantaneously changed their viewpoint regarding migrant laborers. Howard B. Myers, of the WPA, articulating the differences between depression and wartime migration, said matter-of-factly, "Instead of the border controls and restrictive legislation of the depression period, we now have situations . . . where migration is actively encouraged both through advertising, through various types of local efforts and in a sense through the defense-housing and community-facilities program." Suddenly, he noted, unemployment was very low among most migrants to the Midwest; indeed, he said, it was "exceptionally" low in South Bend. Different now were both the success rate of getting a job and the public reaction to the migrants. Sidney Hillman estimated "conservatively" that three million workers would be needed, but John Tolan was less cautious in February 1942. "Industry, agriculture, and the army will require additional millions of workers during the next year," he said. "It is estimated that in the coming year 10,000,000 additional workers will be needed." In short, he concluded, "it appears that the Nation will face an overall labor shortage problem in 1942." In less than six months, the committee had gone from trying to prevent migrant labor to being frightened about a shortage of (migrant) labor, a fear only aggravated by the unbalanced distribution of economic opportunity throughout the country in which industry was concentrated in the Northeast, Midwest, and West at the expense of the South. By that time, the country was fully involved in the war effort, and southern men and women were again on the move—both northward and abroad.[5]

The Floodgates Open Once Again

Those who describe the migration of southern whites often use metaphors connected to water. Population increases and lack of economic opportunity "dammed" them up in the South since the beginning of the twentieth century. Occasionally, however, increasing opportunity outside and realities inside the South resulted in pressure that forced open the "floodgates," resulting in a "torrent" of migration. The floodgates had been opened during the 1920s, but during World War II they were washed away. Hundreds of thousands of men and women spilled over into the North looking to fill the massive needs of a country at war. The war, of course, also sent many southerners to Europe, Africa, and the Pacific to fight; if they were lucky enough to return home alive, many soldiers saw life differently, for the war and its aftermath—notably the GI Bill that made them attractive to employers and universities—introduced them to a new life filled with many more places to live and work. Like World

War I for an earlier generation, World War II became the benchmark in the lives of those it touched, but even more than the Great War, this war would be one of the crucial factors in the migration of southern whites.

Throughout the South, midwestern employers were placing ads in southern newspapers to lure eager southerners northward. "ASSIST THE WAR EFFORT! TO WIN THE WAR OUR BOYS NEED EQUIPMENT," a Michigan employer advertised in the *Nashville Tennessean.* Another explained, "ARMAMENT AIRCRAFT PROGRAM FOR NAVY WAR WORK. We are one of America's largest automobile manufacturers at present hiring men for our new arsenal at Detroit, Mich. We desire to hire immediately men with the following qualifications. . . ." Ford even sponsored mass meetings in the rural South and patriotically cajoled southerners to come north and work in its bomber plant. As Melvin Profitt recalled of mountaineers, "Now, in World War II the works picked up in Dayton, Cincinnati, and everywhere, and people just moved off and left this country."[6]

Jim Hammittee, the oldest of thirteen children and born on Christmas Day in 1916 in eastern Kentucky's Bell County, was one of thousands who answered the call. He had gone to work in a coal mine at age sixteen to help support the large family. "I worked in a coal mine," he said, "until nineteen and forty-two. At that time World War II had broken out. Detroit, Michigan, was calling for help in the war plants. I left the hills of Kentucky to try working in war plants." He continued, summarizing what is the classic wartime experience of countless white southerners:

> I arrived in Detroit in July of forty-two and found employment in the east side of Detroit in a roller bearing plant. My wife went with me. At that time we had two small children which we left with my mother. . . . We found employment and a place to live, then we brought the two kids along. I immediately liked my work, decided I'd stay till the war was over.
>
> When I first came there, we only planned to stay till the war was over and then we's moving back South, back home—cause it was hard to adjust to living in Detroit, living in the big city after being used to a mountain life, and a small town was such a drastic change, it was hard to adjust to. So to make ourselves feel comfortable, well, we'll go back home as soon as the war's over. So, it was either work there or go into service. We decided to stay with it. But by the time the war's over in 1945, we had pretty well adjusted and accepted that way of life as the way we wanted to live. So we settled down in the city for another five years. Then we decided it was time we bought a home, so we went out in the suburbs (at that time it was farm section), bought property, and started building a home.[7]

Two of the biggest adjustments for the Hammittees concerned the congestion of urban life and the northern dialect:

> When I first came to Detroit, we lived in apartment houses on the east side of Detroit and this was, I guess, one of the hardest things, I'd say, to adjust to because [of] our standard or our style of living in the South and put us in a apartment house all cooped up—that was more than I could almost bear—that was all.
>
> We rented from local people and this created a problem cause the language we talked and the language they spoke was entirely different. Finally in '43 we got government housing, which was wartime housing, and we more or less had a private home and this made it better for us. Then along came the third child which we hadn't planned, so we kept digging in.

Hammittee noted that housing was virtually impossible to find when he first arrived in Detroit; he and his wife "hunted for days" trying to find an apartment suitable for two children. "They wasn't too expensive in comparison today," he explained. "It was a matter of finding one or finding somebody where they accept kids, and this was something we couldn't cope with—why people don't want kids," a concern expressed by other migrants searching for an apartment. "We had one was two and one was four and this we couldn't understand why people don't want kids. But we finally found a place and it was less desirable by any standard, but we made out with it until we got government housing."[8]

Another difference was the mélange of people in Detroit that Hammittee and his family encountered. "By this time," he explained, "there's so many people migrated to Detroit—say from Pennsylvania, Delaware, Virginia, the Carolinas, Georgia, Tennessee and Kentucky, Alabama, Missouri and Arkansas so, it was just by this time really mixed up. Everybody was working war work, working around the clock and it was a mixture of everything by this time." Relations with other southerners in the city were even strained, because everyone was cautious:

> There were a lot of people there came from the South, but it was hard to get acquainted with them because once you moved into the city the friendly atmosphere that we were used to no longer exists. You pass people on the street, they don't talk to you—you don't talk to them. If you tried to smile and talk to somebody, why they thought you's up to something, gonna rob them or something so, and this was another thing that bothered you real bad. You go into a store to shop, there's nobody you could talk to. You could not talk to people and turn and walk off.
>
> They was a lot of discrimination on the job or in the city. As far as promotions, I can't say that. But you had to constant be on your toes, have your guard up, for southern language you used, because if you spilled some of it out, . . . why some northern person grab it and poke fun at you immediately and the ones that could cope with it and roll and joke back

come through all right as far as I'm concerned. The North was as much or more critical of southern people than southern people has ever been of northern people. And to my opinion this still exists.

The kids didn't have a hard time adjusting at that age but kids that come up there in, say, in their early teens, they had a hard time adjusting cause kids will be kids and the northern kids would poke fun at them for some of the slang they used. It would be the same way as a kid from the North coming down here, some of the language they used was the same way, so they had a terrible time, especially once they was school age and started school.

Hammittee's comments go against the notion of southerners' moving northward and taking their prejudices against African Americans with them, pointing out that southern whites often suffered forms of discrimination and even hostility, particularly in Detroit, where they were a fairly large percentage of the population:

Surprisingly, in the North, I don't think public opinion was like this, but the southern whites working in the northern plants with southern blacks, I should say at that time, there was very little problem. In my opinion, it was the northern people prejudiced to the blacks. In my honest opinion, the southern white was only just one step ahead of the blacks as far as the northern people was concerned when I went there, and I felt this real deep, because we suffered a lot by being from the South. I'm talking about for the schools and in public places where you spoke with a Southern accent; I never felt comfortable for a lot of years. I worked hard at overcoming it and ignoring the slurs or gigs. I felt our kids were in school and we lived in one of these government houses. The schools were overcrowded. I felt that our kids were going to a good school but all at once they were overcrowded so they wanted to put kids in another school which they had to go by bus, and it upset a whole lot of people. But the only kids that had to transfer and go to another school by bus was southern people. I spoke my piece to the school principal, but she let it roll right over; she didn't do anything about it. Such a licks as this hurt real deep, took a long time to get over.

Hammittee said that "then we moved out in the suburbs, and we moved into a practically all northern" (and white) neighborhood, as many other successful migrants eventually did. "I'm talking about Germans, Polish, you name it," he elaborated. "But we seemed to dig in there and the southern aspect of it seemed to melt away. But it was a long hard climb as long as we lived in the city."[9]

Although as the oldest, Hammittee often got jobs in Detroit for his siblings, he poignantly explained the difficulty of packing up and leaving behind the social relations of family:

> I was the oldest one of thirteen, and my father got killed in the coal mine when I was twenty-one, so I more or less took the responsibility of the father. So I kept close touch with the family, and as each one got older I helped them prepare and found them a job—helped them get started. So, as they got older, I'd bring them from home up there, help them get started in the plants, or a job, so I was in constant contact with the people back home. And her [his wife's] mother and father was [in the South], too, so we kept close contact. This seemed to be one of the worst things of southern people going north. We's so close in our relation with each other; it was just hard to separate yourself from the family, and going north was one of the worst difficulties you can imagine. Pulling yourself away from the family, you know, church on Sundays, Sunday dinner at one of the houses, and visits two or three times a week, or doing it all the time. I lived in a mining community where I could see my grandmother daily, half-dozen uncles, aunts, and when you move out away from that, moving to a strange city, it was really hard to adjust to.

"I guess," he summed, "I ended up with most of my friends from the South, although I did make friendship—lasting friendship—with some northern people over the years. But the closest ties we had was people from the South."[10]

Other changes associated with city life were difficult for the Hammittees. When his wife became pregnant in Detroit with their third child, she refused to go through delivery with a northern doctor, much less in one of the city's hospitals. Accustomed to births in the coal camp by the mining company's doctor or a "granny midwife," "come time for the third baby to be born," Hammittee remembered, "she wasn't about to go to the hospital in Detroit. She insisted on coming home to her mother and that's where the baby was borned by another company doctor coming in the house." Politics and religion, northern style, were also different, as Hammittee explained, so different that he chose to stay away from both:

> There's so many different denominations. . . . Southern people went to a Baptist or Church of God or Methodist type of church, Church of Christ—there's a whole bunch of them. But so many northern people are Catholic people, an awful lot of them, so there's an awful lot of Polish people in Detroit. They's practically all Catholics. So, it was a real mixed up thing. Far as talking religion and politics, that was two subjects I stayed away from in Detroit. I didn't choose to talk that or express my feeling on it. Very, very rarely would I express my feelings because of so many different people you worked around, you didn't get that close to know them, exactly know their ideas so, I always practiced staying away from politics and religion. Especially after I got into supervision where you had a couple of hundred people working under you what you might say to that one, he'll relate that to someone else and they get a different

meaning out of it and you'll create some problems, either politically or religious ideas, so, I never allowed myself to get into discussions of that.

These early years of migration were not a time of great religious fervor among migrants. Most migrants who came north presumed they were only sojourners working long enough to save money to return home, buy land, and live the agrarian lives of their dreams, and churchgoing in the mountains was not always widespread. Only during the 1950s, when migrants started buying homes and raising families in the North (and new migrants were arriving every day and were thus able to fill congregations) did the great church-building era begin in the North. "I'll speak from my own experience," Hammittee added:

> We were raised in the South with many other people I was raised around and know. We went to church regular—two or three times a week and on Sunday was church and Sunday night was church. Especially when you went in to wartime, to Detroit plants, you was working on a seven-day basis. And by being new up there, more than likely, you'd get on the afternoon shift or the midnight shift. So you's working seven nights a week and you found excuses: your church was inconvenient, you had to drive across town to get with a church of people you knew or something like that, and first thing you know, why, you find yourself getting out of the habit of going and church is like anything else—if you don't participate in it, why, you get lost and you get away from it. So, in my opinion, the people I knew stayed in Detroit and very few of them that I know ever went regular to church. People that we grew up with, an awful lot have settled in Detroit, but for some reason or the other, the most of them settle clean across town, which was probably twenty miles away.[11]

During the economic boom of wartime, churchgoing succumbed to the double time for Sunday work. "I started out at 76 cents an hour" in Detroit, Hammittee said, having made $1.02 an hour in the Kentucky coal mines. But the long work week in the North more than compensated for the inconsistent work days in the mines that rarely brought more than thirty-five dollars. "But 76 cents an hour, I believe, best I remember, brought me about $57.60 for seven days," still an amount vividly remembered after thirty years. He continued:

> The time and a half and double time for Sunday we looked forward to because it boosted our pay. And, as a starter, this is very interesting because we had money we hadn't been used to. So that, changed fast, you know, that was starting pay so it—by nineteen and forty-five I was making $1.76 an hour and I was still working ten, twelve hours a day, seven days a week when the war was over.
>
> You had to like your work, or else you's bored stiff because there was

> no time for anything else much. You worked all the time. You got caught up like that. I worked over thirty-one years in Detroit and I worked more seven days than I did five days a week—by choice. I could have got other jobs or I could have took other jobs that worked five days a week, but I chose to work, I guess.[12]

Other parts of Hammittee's life in the North were not so different from the way it had been in the South. When he first arrived, however, he was forced to rent a sleeping room, which meant that meals were furnished. Speaking about his diet, he said that "at first when we had to rent a room, just a sleeping room, why, it changed because it was hard to find Southern cooking at that time." The food, he said, "was a different type. So, you had to adjust to a different diet; broiled food, you know. Most Southerners, they eat a lot of pork and they eat a lot of fried food, and it changed in that respect. We missed our cornbread and ham and eggs, of course, but it was different entirely." But once they moved into their own quarters, he explained—"by being able to have my own Southern cook with me, it didn't change that much."[13]

Leisure time, too, was not entirely different according to Hammittee. In both the South and the North, he pointed out, "it was built around the kids." In the summers, he and his family spent time in parks picnicking. In the winter, they usually were reluctant to get outside, since like many other southerners, he "could never cope, neither could the wife, with cold weather. We never did adjust to it. The kids enjoyed it most, most of the time. They went ice skating and tobogganing in them days." Overall, he said, "people that wanted to do the things and outside in the North that they done in the South, they were all available for them if you could accept the cold weather or change in weather, which is something to cope with, too. I've seen within eight or ten hours change as much as thirty degrees up there, forty degrees, and this is something else to cope with, something you wasn't used to." One larger difference was professional baseball, which Hammittee came to enjoy very much, having grown up in the South playing ball himself: "In the earlier years, one of the bigger things in Detroit for me was the major league baseball. We enjoyed to see that. We went quite a few times a year to see the great Tigers play. We never were real football fans because where I went to school we did not have a football team, and I wasn't brought up in a football atmosphere, so I never took to it." In later years Hammittee built a cottage in northern Michigan, and they enjoyed it very much.[14]

Like Hammittee, others answered the call to northern cities. Polly Ashley, from Knott County, Kentucky, was fifty-three years old when she moved to Detroit in 1943. "I worked making planes and sorting things to make planes," she said. "You know, bolts and things. They'd get them messed up and we'd have to pick them out, washers, too." The job, Ashley reported, had fringe benefits: "I remember one of the planes. We made planes and when we got one made, if we wanted to we could get in and go try it out." Like virtually every migrant I have interviewed, she received wages that were a permanent part of her memory: "I made fifty-three and fifty-six dollars a week." Dick Fowler, from Wayne County, Tennessee, was forty-five years old when he went to Detroit in 1942 for a three-year stint at factory work. He soon got a job working for the Packard Motor Company and enjoyed his work and the company of fellow southerners up north. Accustomed to the difficult labor of agricultural life ("I didn't work hours," he explained of his Tennessee labors. "They didn't keep the hours. We got up and started at daylight and came in at dark."), Fowler thought factory work was much easier. "Hard work? That wasn't hard work—people'd talk about hard work, hard work. I worked three years, and I worked the time they said and come out with a white card with no marks on it. And I never worked what I call a full day all put together." Clemeth Dixon, also from Wayne County, went to Detroit during the war, traveling north with one of his nephews, but unlike Fowler, Dixon stayed only a week or ten days. "I had all of Detroit I wanted," he said. "You couldn't stick your head out of a night without somebody liable to knock you in the head or something, and I was afraid of it. So I was ready to come home."[15]

Although by far the most popular, Detroit was not the only wartime magnet for southerners eager to work. My own grandparents, Alvin and Ruby Berry, went from Wayne County, Tennessee, to Akron, Ohio, in 1944, when Alvin was thirty years old and already plenty frustrated at trying to "make it" in Tennessee. Their friends and family had already left or were planning to leave when they made the decision to go: Ruby's brother was in Detroit, and Alvin's brother had gone to Akron in 1943 because his brother-in-law was there. At the time, Alvin had gotten a draft deferment and was working in a sawmill for Homer Simms for a dollar a day (ten cents an hour). "I got enough of that and I come in that evening and I told Homer I was quitting. And he said, 'I got you deferred—I'll have to turn you in,' and I said, 'Turn me in—I don't care.' He had to turn me in. And I said, 'Well, I['d] just as soon be in the army as having to work at this sawmill.'" The next day, Alvin was on a bus with Ed Montgomery, another of Ruby's brothers, bound for Akron. Two days later, he was working at Firestone. His next priority was to find housing so that Ruby and their three children, ages eleven, eight, and two, could join him. Housing was nearly impossible to find, but eventually, the owner of the room Alvin and Ed were sleeping in told them that her mother-in-law had a house they would rent to them. They were delighted, even though living in a neighborhood of African Americans was a new experience. After six weeks of working in Akron, Alvin's family joined him; Ruby rode a train with her children and Walter Dial, her brother-in-law, who decided he would try factory work but soon realized it was not for him. They stayed there about four or five weeks, until Alvin got his draft notice. He quit his job, and they went back home. When Alvin was turned down by the army, he and his family returned to Akron, and he got his same job back. He also began working evenings packing semitrailer trucks at Motor Express. After years of frustration in Tennessee, Alvin said he truly enjoyed his job at Firestone: "Why sure I liked it. I had a good job—it wasn't like a sawmill. It was getting the green tires ready to put the air bags in them for them to cure them." Although he did recall having to join the rubber workers' union, he did not have any memories of unions; for him, factory life was pleasant, rewarding, and easier than sawmill or farm work in Tennessee. There were thousands of other southern migrants in Akron, but Alvin and Ruby were cautious socially. "Back then," Alvin said, "I didn't know how to get acquainted with people like I do now."[16]

Soon, they were joined by others from their community. Farm life in Wayne County for Vera and Carmel Lawson, for example, was "hard but good," Vera said, just not good enough. Carmel, like Alvin, had repeatedly gotten deferments, Vera said, because he was married and because Tennessee was a "volunteer state." In the fall of 1944, they decided to go to Akron so that Carmel could "work in a defense plant because it was too hard to make ends meet." In December, the draft board had given him permission to go for three months, which suited them perfectly because they planned to come back in March "to put in a crop." "We didn't know anybody [except the Berrys]," Vera said. "We just went there because we knew" Alvin and Ruby. Without waiting to write them a letter, the Lawsons locked their house and got on a bus. "Oh, we'd never been that far from home in our lives!" Vera said, remembering how panicked they were on the bus that Alvin and Ruby would not be home once they arrived. The next day, Alvin took Carmel to Firestone, and he was hired; later that evening, he also was hired at Motor Express. Both men worked two jobs seven days a week. Although Akron was a difficult adjustment for Vera, especially the snows and living among blacks (Wayne County was virtually all white), her life was made easier because of Alvin and Ruby and because she knew they would eventually return to Tennessee. In March, they returned to Wayne County to plant their crop. "Usually in the spring," Vera explained, "you would go and borrow money to buy your seeds and everything to live on through the summer. And then in the fall you would sell some cotton or whatever and then you'd pay that off, and you'd barely have money to live through the winter." Well," she continued, "that year we had saved enough money that we didn't have to borrow any money. That's what we spent that for."[17]

After the war was over, Ruby was homesick and wanted to go home because her mother was dying. "I never even knowed to turn in two weeks notice," Alvin said, still obviously angry with himself. They returned to Tennessee and used their savings to open a tiny general store, but people in the community had little or no money to spend. Soon, they were going broke. "We went home and put in that little old store," Alvin explained, "and I went back up there and I went to the office and asked them about a job. (I went back to Akron and thought I'd get my job back at Firestone.) And I went to Firestone and told them who I was and they looked up my record and said, 'You got a complete record except one thing'—and I said, 'What's that?' And they said, 'You didn't give no notice.' They wouldn't hire me back." Even more frustrated, he went back to Tennessee and thought about trying another place in the North. "I told Ruby, I said, 'If I ever go off any more I'll never come back down here.' I said, '*I'll stay.*'"[18]

Not only did the war pull southerners to the North, but also it lured them to southern cities, often preparing them for northward migration later. Emma Martin had grown up in western Kentucky's Butler County and had, as she described it, a difficult life after her mother died when Emma was only four years old. In 1941, she became engaged to Jesse Martin, but he was soon drafted, and she would not see him again for forty-five months. Because her father had finally remarried the year before, she was suddenly free "to take out" on her own. She went to Nashville, Tennessee, to be a domestic. "It was a matter of survival," Emma explained. "You didn't have any money on the farm, so I went there . . . and did all the work for a dollar and a half a week." After a few months, she moved to Hickory Hollow, away from the inner city, and got a job looking after six children while their parents worked. "And I didn't get a day off. Back in those days you didn't expect a day off. Seven days you were on duty." Her weekly wage of $1.50 was enough to buy books and bus fare to night school at the Wadkins Institute so she could finish her high school degree. Her teachers, realizing the lure of a nearby Du Pont rayon plant, begged her not to go to work there but to continue school. On a whim, however, she filled out an application at Du Pont and was soon called in for an interview. She went to work on January 3, 1943. She was given a "man's job," she said, because she was so strong:

> In the spinning room, I had to do cake wrapping, they called it. But before that I was in the room [that] was really hot and really steamy and stinky. And I would lift like fifty pounds at a time all day long. This was a man's work—a man's job. Men's jobs is what I did. I had a lady's job to start with and they saw how strong I was—my big hands and feet—and they put me on a man's job because during the war there weren't many men around. And there was some men from down home that went up there and got a job and passed out right on the job. I didn't think anything because I was just trying to get along—trying to live!

Emma remembered fondly, "You don't worry about things. You just do what you have to do. I made fifty cents an hour there and that was such a big switch. That gave me enough to pay for my room and board." She found a boardinghouse across the street from the plant and enjoyed helping the old woman who ran the house. "I came from the farm, and if I saw her dressing chickens, I'd fly in and dress the chickens for her and help her. None of the rest of the girls felt obligated to help anybody." But before long, she was forced to move because her roommate was dating a married man who lived upstairs. "I didn't know that," Emma explained. "It curled my hair, and I thought to myself, I can't take any more of this. So I went down the street to my Sunday school teacher and told her the situation. So she found me a place to stay with some really good people."[19]

Meanwhile, Jess was stationed in San Francisco and on December 7, 1941, was awaiting his departure for the Philippines. He was sent first to Hawaii, then to Australia, and ultimately to New Guinea. Both Jess and Emma recalled their letter writing; suspicious after a time that not all the letters were reaching their destination, they decided to begin numbering each one. About half never made it. Before he came home nearly four years later, he was awarded a Purple Heart and a Silver Star. On May 16, 1945, Jess returned home, and he and Emma were married what must have been three long days later. They decided to spend their honeymoon in Detroit, Michigan, since Jess's sister, Ollie Bell Martin, had gone there in 1939 to help their brother and his wife, who was pregnant. Emma and Ollie were also good friends. "I couldn't see the town for the people," Jess remembered of Detroit.[20]

Because he had accumulated so many military points while abroad, Jess was able to come home early and hence had an easy time finding a job at a cellophane plant next to the factory where Emma was working. Unfortunately, he had contracted malaria while in the military and, suffering repeated bouts of fever and chills, was barely able to work the first year. Emma, however, was still at Du Pont on her "man's job" working eight hours a day, seven days a week. "When you're brought up like we were during the depression, you don't take anything for granted," Emma said, although eventually she was moved out of her position and back to a "woman's position." "Yes," she said, "I had to take a cut in pay, but I didn't mind that because he was working then. And we lived real simply." They eventually moved from their home rented through the Office of Price Administration to another place in the country. Jess got over his malaria, but he was never able to shake his desire to own a farm back home in Butler County, Kentucky. In January 1950, after five-and-a-half years of factory work, they moved back to Kentucky and bought a 281-acre farm, only to go broke because of drought and later be forced into migrating one last time—to Indianapolis.[21]

R. G. Hudson was twenty years old in 1940. Born in Gilmer County, Georgia, but raised in adjacent Fannin County, he received his associate's degree in engineering at North Georgia Military College, where he had a basketball scholarship. He immediately got a job with the Georgia Highway Department, but Eugene Talmadge was running for governor, and he had already warned the voters that if elected he would fire all Republican workers, so Hudson quit to avoid giving Talmadge the pleasure of firing him. He then got a job with the U.S. Geological Survey producing contour maps, first in nearby Rome, Georgia, and then in Maine. On his way back to Maine, he got a bus ticket to Gary, Indiana, to visit Joe and Bill Allen, friends from home who had moved there and were working for U.S. Steel's Gary Works and for Youngstown Sheet and Tube. Hudson was not enthusiastic about spending the winter in Maine, so the Allens easily talked him into staying, assuring him they could get him a job at Youngstown, which they did. Hudson was soon working in a skilled position testing the hardness and tensile strength of steel in the metallurgical lab. "I don't know if I made a decision," he said. "This was a job. I wanted to go to work and this was it. I think in those days I didn't have any plan. This was it." Like most southern migrant men, Hudson bought a new car as soon as he could—a new Ford convertible that he picked up in Detroit. Soon, too, he moved out of a boardinghouse and into an apartment, across from Horace Mann High School, with Joe Allen (Bill had just married). "It was a super town," Hudson remembered, "very clean, real nice. Just a real good town. I had a ball. But I was only there about six months—if that long—before I went into the army. I was the greenest second lieutenant in the army." By late 1941, he was with the 91st Cavalry Reconnaissance Squadron in California, preparing for the North African campaign. Ultimately, he would have a stellar army career, involved in the North African, Sicilian, Italian, and French campaigns. He would lead the first troops into Rome and have a private audience with Pope Pius XII.[22]

Many other southern young men like Jess Martin and R. G. Hudson were sent abroad. Allen Barkley, like Martin, went to the South Pacific. Grady Roberson came out of the CCC and then a few years later helped build the Natchez Trace Parkway. "I drove a little old dump truck. We'd haul things off and dump it. And then while I was doing that I decided, well, the heck with this, and I went and joined the army" in 1941. "They was drafting everybody for a year, they said. So what I did, I said, Well, I'll just go get my year up and then I can get me a job. But before my year was up, they declared war, and I stayed till after the war was over," traveling through Italy. James Shelby, from Hardin County, Tennessee, went to Europe too. Harvey Austin, from Lauderdale County, Alabama, was sent to Germany. James Etter had gone to Louisville to work at Reynolds Research, a defense contractor, after high school but was soon drafted and went to Germany and France. Charles Brummett still vividly remembered his "sisters, you know, crying when we got on the bus to leave." The bus took him to a train that went from east Tennessee to an army base just outside of New York City, quite a change. "You should have seen us. There's a whole train load, you know, came from the South up there." In May 1944, he was in England, and the week after D-Day, he landed at Omaha Beach. In September, he was wounded while in a tree in Germany. Unable to give his family in Tennessee too many details, he said, he had to outwit the censors:

> See, when I got wounded, I couldn't tell them [his family] what had happened. And so, you'd have to just think of things to put in the letter cause a lot of times they would censor it and they would mark it out, you know. I told them, there in Clinton where we lived they were pretty close to a highway and you could get off on the main highway and go down to a big bank down to where my parents lived next to the river there, you know.
>
> So I told them, I said, One of these days, I said, I'll get off a bus and I will come down that hill, you know, running. I said something about my arms, so they knew that I still had my hands and my legs okay. Like I could still move, you know.

Sterlin Reeves, from Wayne County, Tennessee, migrated to Detroit in 1940 during the midst of conversion. He soon got a construction job helping build a veteran's hospital in Dearborn; he made $105 per month and was given room and board. In the spring of 1942, he was drafted into the army and paid $21 per month. "Uncle Sam," he said, "gave me a little pay cut, see." While in the army, he went to Georgia, Texas, New Mexico, California, the Philippines, and later Okinawa and Tokyo. After his stint was over, he went back to Dearborn for construction jobs and even got hired at Ford's River Rouge plant, but he soon decided to return to Tennessee: "Too much city, too many people, for me." Leonard Dodd, who lived just across the creek from Reeves, went to Hawaii and New Guinea. Earl Cox, born in 1929 in Fannin County, Georgia, went into service just at the end of the war but stayed in long enough to see duty with the occupational forces in Korea.[23]

The war years had a tremendous influence on the lives of southern whites, whether they were sent abroad, called north, or stayed in the region. The influence on those who stayed in the South would be particularly significant in the decades to come. Bituminous coal miners, for instance—many of whom virtually starved during the Great Depression—saw their wages skyrocket during the war. In 1939, the average weekly earnings were $23.83; in 1945, $56.84, an increase because of demand and union pay scales. John C. Frazier, a miner from Price, Kentucky, explained. "When I started out, I started at four dollars and something a day, between four and five dollars a day, and when I went in service I [had] worked eighteen months here, at that mine before I went in service. When I quit to join the service I was making five dollars and sixty cents a day. That was in 1942," which "was considered really good wages at that time," he said. "Of course, I was on what most people would call a company wage, a daily wage, and the fellows that loaded the coal loaded by hand and the machine men there made more money than that." But the specter of automation, which had begun in the 1920s, continued. Prior to World War II, the peak years of production were 1918 and 1926, when 542,000 workers in central Appalachia mined 527 million tons of coal; in 1944, the region produced 620 million tons but did so with 65 percent fewer than had been employed in 1926. Soldiers who were returning from the war were soon thwarted when they tried to find a job in a coal mine. Automation and increasing competition from oil and gas made coal miners obsolete. As Laurel Shackelford and Bill Weinberg have written:

> The migration of people from the hills of Central Appalachia to the urban centers of the North . . . following World War II was prompted by the mechanization of the coal mines more than anything else. Mechanization was itself an outgrowth of the Depression years that received a hearty welcome from the officials of large coal companies because, in the long run, machines were more efficient than human beings and less expensive to sustain. . . . The phenomenon of mechanization is of course not unique to an industrial society, but it is ironic that in the United States its origins are found in the coalfields of Central Appalachia, one of the nation's least industrial regions.[24]

McKinley Little spoke for many: "I came back home and, as you know, during the war everybody was working—there was plenty of jobs. When World War II was over they turned out about a million people loose and all these ex-servicemen were looking for jobs and there wasn't any because all the war industries had shut down. So, I dug ditches, fifty cents an hour. That's all I could get."[25]

After the war, mountaineers suddenly were faced with two options—welfare at home or migration—and both were contrary to their culture and society. The temporary, depression-inspired measures of the 1930s would after World War II become a permanent fixture of mountain life, and the decision to stay at home and accept "public help" was not made easily. Similarly, the sojourning of the 1920s and 1930s—that is, going north, getting a job, saving money, and, most important, returning to buy some land—after World War II would be long postponed. Like welfare, migration for many exiles became permanent, at least until retirement in the 1970s and 1980s permitted other options.

Notes

1. U.S. Congress, House, Select Committee Investigating National Defense Migration, *National Defense Migration: Hearings,* 18:7086, 20:8115, 18:7494 (Van Wagoner quote).

2. U.S. Congress, House, Select Committee to Investigate the Interstate Migration of Destitute Citizens, *Interstate Migration Report,* 7; U.S. Congress, House, Select Committee Investigating National Defense Migration, *National Defense Migration: Hearings,* 20:8039 (Person quote), 16:6311 (Hillman quote); U.S. Congress, Senate, Special Committee Investigating the National Defense Program, *Investigation of the National Defense Program,* 12:5270 (Kilgore quote).

3. U.S. Congress, House, Select Committee Investigating National Defense Migration, *National Defense Migration: Hearings,* 20:8182 (Mitchell quote); U.S. Congress, House, Select Committee to Investigate the Interstate Migration of Destitute Citizens, *Interstate Migration: Hearings,* 3:1212 (Michigan quote).

4. U.S. Congress, House, Select Committee Investigating National Defense Migration, *National Defense Migration: Hearings,* 27:10290; U.S. Congress, Senate, Special Committee Investigating the National Defense Program, *Investigation of the National Defense Program,* 22:5253–54, 5270; Hawley, *Population of Michigan, 1840 to 1960,* 73–88, esp. 82.

5. U.S. Congress, House, Select Committee Investigating National Defense Migration, *National Defense Migration: Hearings,* 27:10333–34, 16:6393, 27:10235.

6. *Nashville Tennessean,* July 18, June 22, 1942; Profitt interview, May 30, 1975, 18.

7. Hammittee interview, 1.

8. Ibid., 1–2.

9. Ibid., 2, 4. Others disagreed with Hammittee about southern white attitudes toward African Americans. On June 20, 1943, in Detroit, a two-day race riot be-

gan, and ultimately twenty African Americans were killed. After the calm ensued, southern white migrants were linked to the cause of the riot that began at Belle Isle Park. According to a book published soon after the riot, "The effort to make Detroit conform to Kentucky 'hillbilly' and Georgia 'red neck' notions of white domination is reflected in frequent white comments in buses and street cars and bars, such as: 'It wouldn't have happened down home. We know how to keep niggers in their place.' 'Southern niggers aren't like these bold brassy northern niggers.' As a comment, too on the headline, '20 NEGROES KILLED IN RACE RIOT,' some whites commented, 'Served them right. They were getting too chesty anyway.'" Moreover, a black man interviewed afterward also blamed the migration of southern whites: "I don't think anything that happened Sunday started it. I think it has been started from ten months ago when the migration of southern whites and illiterate Negroes started. . . ." See Lee and Humphrey, *Race Riot,* 91, 89; and J. Jones, *Dispossessed,* 248. More discussion of southern white racism appears in chapter 6 herein.

10. Hammittee interview, 4.

11. Ibid., 5. For more on health care among Detroit migrants, see Stekert, "Focus for Conflict," 95–127. In *The Dollmaker,* few migrants participate in organized religion in Detroit at all.

12. Hammittee interview, 6.

13. Ibid.

14. Ibid., 6–7.

15. Ashley interview, 3; Fowler interview; Dixon interview.

16. Alvin and Ruby Berry interview.

17. Lawson interview.

18. Alvin and Ruby Berry interview.

19. Jesse and Emma Martin interview.

20. Ibid.

21. Ibid.

22. Hudson interview.

23. Barkley interview; Roberson interview; Shelby interview; Austin interview; James and Sally Etter interview; Brummett interview; Reeves interview; Dodd interview; Cox interview.

24. Shackelford and Weinberg, eds., *Our Appalachia,* 297–99.

25. Frazier interview, 3; Little interview, 1.

5 *The Great White Migration, 1945–60*

> That's how come so many southern people [are] in Indiana and Michigan. We was hunting work cause we didn't have it; we had to go somewhere and find work. Well, you don't know the nature of a hog. We raised hogs in here in the wild woods. They run outside. You take an old sow off someplace and she's not satisfied, and if you bring her back home she starts rooting and hunting food.
>
> They's a bee man up in Lawrence County that raises wild bees. And I asked him once, I said, "How far will a bee go to get food?" He said, "They're just like a man—they'd go just the distance it takes to get it; if they've got food close to their hive, that's where they'll get it." Yeah, he said, "A man with ambition, you know, will go till he finds food."
>
> And that's how come with me, now, in South Bend, cause I was hunting something to raise my family on, and I would've went years earlier, way back, . . . but I found a job, and worked at it until I come home.
>
> —Dewey Stults, 1985, Collinwood, Tenn.

IN THE LATE 1940S, Knott County, Kentucky, had a peculiar problem. The county, with plenty of youngsters around, was having a hard time finding teachers to staff its schools. Simeon Fields was only seventeen years old when he "took one of these schools on the emergency basis." As Fields explained, "There were about six schools in the county that were not able to get on their way because they had no teachers. These were the days when young seventeen- and eighteen-year-old boys were finishing high school and buying a coal truck, and some were going to Detroit and Cleveland and Cincinnati—the great out migration was in full swing, 1947, '8, and '9."[1]

By the mid-1950s, nearly three thousand people born in Cocke County, Tennessee, deep in the Smoky Mountains, had settled in Cleveland, Ohio. Jack Shepherd, who edited the county's *Plain Talk-Tribune,* published in Newport, Tennessee, said that he had more than four hundred subscribers who were living in Cleveland who "pass the paper around for other Cocke families up there." One Lorain Avenue furniture store in Cleveland ran advertisements in the Tennessee paper simply to reach migrants in Ohio. "Cleveland," said Cocke County Judge Benton Giles, "gets more people from Cocke County than any other city, but Detroit runs a close second." Alluding to the divided heart of the exiles, he declared, "They'd all rather stay here if they had jobs. I have a nephew who is happier here making half the money he made in Cleveland. They don't like living in a big city." Between 1940 and 1960, the 201 counties of the Tennessee Valley region lost more than 1.3 million people to migration. Out-migration had become such a problem in the state by the mid-1950s that Tennessee proclaimed the annual loss of ten thousand young people its number-one social problem.[2]

These are but two examples of the great white migration that resumed with unprecedented force after World War II. As the northern economy was booming, pockets of the southern economy, particularly mining, were as depressed as ever, and out-migration began again, reaching a peak during the 1950s. In the urban Midwest, industry was beckoning southerners northward, and southerners were arriving by the bus load. The Brooks Bus Line, for example—only one of a number of small bus lines that serviced people moving between the North and South—made daily round-trips between Detroit and Paducah, Mayfield, and Fulton, in western Kentucky. Since for many years throughout the South, particularly in depressed regions, what occurred outside determined whether, in the sociologist James S. Brown's words, "there will be a great or a greater movement out," southern whites responded to the calls in droves. In the late 1940s, Brown had studied the Beech Creek community in Clay County, Kentucky, for his doctoral dissertation. In 1961, Brown returned to Beech Creek, which had become something of the Middletown of southern Appalachia, to reinterview residents and was stunned by the extent of migration: more than half had relocated outside Appalachia, and of these, almost two-thirds had moved to southern Ohio and the rest elsewhere in Ohio and Indiana. "You are just thunderstruck," he said, "by how many people have left that part of the country. There are many more people . . . that I knew 15 years ago on Beech Creek in Clay County now in South Lebanon, Ohio, than there are on Beech Creek itself today." When he asked Beech Creek members whether they would want their children to stay in the community or move away, the answer was "*outside* for more *opportunity.*"[3]

The period of upland southern out-migration between 1945 and 1960—one of the largest internal migrations in the history of the United States—has four important characteristics. First, although the migration has been portrayed as a hegira from the hills, in reality people from throughout the Upland South left the region for the Midwest between 1945 and 1960. It is incorrect, in short, to speak of this migration as exclusively "Appalachian." Second, census data show the extraordinary numbers involved in what previous scholars have called the "invisible minority" of migrants in the Midwest. Considering such stunning numbers, one wonders how such a horde of people could remain invisible, the focus of chapter 6. Third, kinship determinism often characterized this migration. People from the Appalachian Mountains, for example, have long been (mis)understood as being too cemented to kindred relationships to search out a better place to live. Those who migrated disproved this view often by making sure that kin came along with them. Finally, even during this period, upland southerners were beginning to find economic success, again debunking the idea that those who did leave the South remained mired in poverty in the Midwest.

Cheap Labor to Sustain the Boom

Economically, of course, one of the most important results of massive southern white out-migration was that the biggest economic boom in U.S. history was sustained, in part, by the sweat, muscles, and backs of southern migrants, many of them young, thus ensuring years of labor for their employers. The boom in the economy and the subsequent need for cheap labor were the primary reasons the "migrant problem" ceased after World War II. Indeed, a personnel manager for the Randall Company in Cincinnati, which employed about eight hundred people, more than half of whom were migrants, said that "they're proving they can be adaptable and can be a worthwhile addition to the community and to labor." "Industry," he summed, is "better off with them." Journalists in several cities began writing series on southern migration that actually attempted to revise commonly held stereotypes about southerners. By the 1960s, for example, a survey of hourly workers in Columbus, Ohio, discovered that a third were from "Appalachia" and that almost half of these workers had been at their current jobs for more than six years; two-thirds of those from the South had lived in Columbus longer than ten years. Others estimated that for Ohio as a whole, one in three workers had been born in southern Appalachian counties.[4]

The demand for workers in the Midwest strengthened the migration between the North and the South. When times were good, the flow of people went northward, and when times were bad, the flow often reversed, as it had in the Great Depression; the needle that indicated northerly or southerly flows of people was very sensitive. Take, for example, Harlan County, Kentucky, and Detroit. In the 1950s, the county was losing as many as one thousand people annually; the majority, it seemed, were headed to Detroit, since a bus line ran daily departures for Detroit. In the recession of 1957–58, however, the northward flow of people reversed, as laid-off autoworking southerners assumed they could make a better living in the South. Requests for surplus food, for example, in Black Mountain, near Harlan, soared by 30 percent the month after auto industry layoffs in 1957. A report in Chicago, too, noted:

> Former coal miners and farmers from the South are the most visible evidence of shuttle migration: when jobs are available in Chicago, the streets of the Uptown area are lined with cars bearing licenses from Kentucky, Tennessee, West Virginia, Alabama, etc. Conversely, when jobs are very limited, the roads in these home states are filled with cars carrying Illinois, Indiana, and Michigan licenses. Nothing has yet improved the job situation at home, so the southern whites continue to move restlessly from town to town and home again.[5]

In 1950, a West Virginian traveled to Chicago to find work, thinking he would return once he saved up some money or if conditions back home improved. When things in West Virginia began to look promising, he quickly returned. His sojourning continued for ten years, until September 1960, when he moved his family permanently to Chicago, realizing that things would never again look promising in West Virginia. While many southerners made return trips to avoid harsh winters, especially during winter slowdowns, others from rural areas returned in April to plant a crop and then came north in October once the harvest was in. In Chicago's Uptown in the 1950s, for example, school attendance among migrant children was highest in November and lowest in April.[6]

Hundreds of white migrants flocked to both agricultural and industrial areas to fuel the economy. Southwestern Michigan, south-central and east-central Indiana, and western Ohio continued to see large numbers of white farm migrants, though by the 1950s farm owners began looking farther south to Texas and Mexico for their labor needs, particularly in Ohio, where Kentuckians who struck the Scioto Marsh's onion fields in the 1930s had left a pungent memory among landowners. Many migrants who began as agricultural workers, of course, moved into factory work.[7]

Take, for example, the case of Adolph Lacy, who grew up in Cleburne County, in north-central Arkansas, the child of farmers. In 1942, Adolph, his three siblings, his parents, Clarence Lackey, Gyle Lacy, and Luther Vance and his wife piled in a pickup truck "like a bunch of cattle" and traveled to Milburg, Michigan, in Berrien County, to harvest fruit. The families returned to Arkansas after the harvest and used the money earned to send their children to school. "Michigan farmers loved to hire southern people," Adolph explained, "because they would work." Each of his family members was paid fifteen cents an hour. Just after World War II, he said, large numbers of Arkansans migrated northward because all there was to do in Arkansas was farm or work in timber, and by the end of the war most of the timber had been cut. In Berrien County, they worked for Wesley Miller picking cherries, apples, strawberries, and peaches and planting tomatoes. They were housed in little "huts"; chicken coops and cow pens were common homes for the migrants. Initially, migrants were happy to harvest fruit, but the Whirlpool Corporation's giant plant in nearby Benton Harbor became the employment dream of many migrant pickers. Whirlpool, Adolph said, would "rather hire a southerner than their own. The only problem they had is most of the time they'd get a little money in their pocket and they'd want to go back south."[8]

On August 21, 1949, Adolph, now married with two children, left Cleburne County for Benton Harbor with a friend. "This is the God's truth: When I left Arkansas," he said, "I had thirty-seven dollars and a half in my pocket. I had two pairs of blue overalls, two blue denim shirts, and my underwear—the wife had made them out of V.C. fertilizer sacks. It had the *V.C.* still on the hip back there." It took them two days to get to Michigan. Once they arrived, Adolph and his friend stayed in a chicken house near his parents, who had been there since the early summer picking fruit. By the end of the first week, he had a job working the night shift at Kaywood Corporation in Benton Harbor making venetian blinds for $1.04 an hour. It was Adolph's first factory job. During the day, he picked fruit for 75 cents an hour. Even with his parents nearby, he said, "I got so homesick I thought I couldn't stay there. But I didn't have no other choice." In October, his wife, Jemae, arrived with their children. She had come with her brother, who was moving to Mishawaka, Indiana, about forty miles south, to do carpentry work. She also longed for home, but not nearly as badly as Adolph. They were living in a furnished three-room apartment in adjacent St. Joseph for seven dollars a week and were able to laugh about their northern "home" when interviewed. In January, Adolph was laid off, but he found a job in St. Joseph at Leeco Platers. After four consecutive days of nosebleeds, he quit and found a job at Auto Specialists, pouring crankshafts for $1.25 an hour. "Of course, they had piece work there," he said:

> They were pouring crankshafts then. They'd make four at a time. And them guys there on them core machines, it was piece work. And I asked somebody about them coremakers if they made any money. They said, Yeah. They was making a hundred bucks a week. And I said, "Boy, that's for me!" And the foreman happened to hear me, and that's all he wanted to hear, you know. The next day I went in and he said, "How would you like to have one of them machines over there?" And I said, "Man, you're looking at the guy that would like to have one of them." And I went to work on that thing and I'll tell you what: I'm no coremaker. I'd work myself to death. I'd get up in the morning and my hand—I had a pound-and-a-half hammer; you had to beat that machine to pack that thing. She'd have to soak my hand in hot salt water to get it back where I could use it the next day. And I think the most I ever made was fifty-eight dollars a week.

Frustrated, Adolph went to Whirlpool in Benton Harbor to complete an application, and on April 8, 1950, he went to work, much more comfortable around the many southern transplants working there. "It was full of them," he said, most of whom had gone first to pick fruit and ended up in a factory job.[9]

Elements of associational life often eased the adjustments of the exiles. One of the strongest examples was union activity. As more southerners migrated, they filled the ranks of union rolls, duping industrialists, many of whom looked favorably upon southern whites because they were thought to be "independent" enough to resist unionization. Few migrants became labor radicals; most seem to have been typical postwar bread-and-butter unionists, eager primarily to gain higher wages and more benefits. Southern migrants were not only active rank and filers but also leaders, again not so much because they were radicals but because they were willing to answer the call of fellow workers. Earl Cox was active at TRW, Daymon Morgan in the UAW at Chrysler, Joe Clardy was a union steward at Studebaker, as was Adolph Lacy at Whirlpool, while Grady Roberson, who began work at Dodge Brothers in Mishawaka in 1959 as a lathe operator, soon became the shopwide set-up man. Eventually, he was elected president of the Steelworkers' local there, though he emphasized modestly that it was others in the plant who forced him into becoming a steward and then ultimately voted him president. John Weatherford also worked at Dodge during the Korean War but says he was never greatly involved with the union because of the "family" atmosphere at Dodge—a feeling of separation between management and labor did not exist, according to him. In 1952, he went to Bendix, and six years later was asked to run for steward. Although also nominated without wanting the job, he won and remained in the position for eleven years, at which time he was "talked into" running for the bargaining committee. Since that time, he has served the UAW as committee member, vice-president, and most recently as president. Clardy, Roberson, and Weatherford pointed out that it was others in the plant (including natives and ethnics) who pushed them into union leadership, mostly because of their social qualities, not their militancy. Roberson and Weatherford, for example, said they socialized with everyone after arriving in the North. Weatherford maintained that his base was much larger than southern whites; native whites, Poles, Hungarians, and African Americans often voted for him more often than southerners did.[10]

My research reveals little of the coolness toward unions that previous scholars have ascribed to migrants. Roscoe Giffin and William W. Philliber, for example, maintain that southern newcomers were not active in unions because of their independence. The sociologist Harry Schwarzweller writes that "Appalachian people just aren't good joiners," feeling "uncomfortable in formal gatherings, and their participation in union activities is in most cases minimal. A general behavioral apathy prevails." He continues:

> Participation in union meetings and activities outside of the immediate job situation are seen as interfering with home life and most migrants are unwilling to allow this to happen. They accept union membership in much the same way as they accept other, more discomfiting aspects of factory work life, and they obey union dictums in much the same way that they obey shop regulations or the orders of a foreman. Further involvement demands a social commitment over and above that for which the familistically-oriented mountaineer is prepared.

Not every migrant became an avid unionist (some may have seen themselves as only temporary sojourners, not permanent employees), but many did, even among the agricultural workers. Although many mountaineers and western Kentuckians came to northern urban areas believing John L. Lewis stood on the right side of God, some southerners, particularly from undeveloped areas outside the Appalachian South, undoubtedly came north with little if any understanding of labor unions. Many, however, were soon converted, as Grady Roberson pointed out: "Well, after you get into a place and you get to working and you understand the jobs and know that the company's really making a lot of money and you're not getting much, you're going to go fighting for more money; that's just all there is to it." Frank Plemons agreed: "Of course, down South, even today there's a lot of places down there that's nonunion. These companies today, they don't want no unions. But I can see what the union's done for the people, you know, over the years. I mean, the things that the company give me, there's no way they'd give it to me if they didn't have to. The company is just common sense." "The company," he concluded, "don't give you nothing if they don't have to, I don't think."[11]

The Upland Southern Hegira

The coalfields continued to transform southerners into exiles following World War II. Although coal mining enjoyed prosperity during World War II, by the 1950s coal mining operations, using their profits from the war, were scrambling to buy automated equipment, and thousands of miners, whose existence had always been precarious, were expelled from the mines. Company stores closed, movie theaters shut their doors, and train and bus services stopped. Ironically, many ex-miners were going to such places as Columbus, Ohio, and getting jobs with the Joy Company, which manufactured much of the equipment that was replacing miners. "It was kind of like watching the place die around me," the novelist Denise Giardina recalled of her youth in West Virginia's coalfields. "The older I got the more things left," including people. "Mostly I remember people leaving and not coming back, or they might have come back to another place where they had relatives. It seemed like everybody left at the same time," she said. "People did try to stay around—sometimes they moved to another coal camp like we did for a while. Sometimes they moved to the next county or something, but probably just as many left for good." When the mine that employed her father closed, the family moved to a nearby coal camp when she was twelve; a year later they moved to Charleston, West Virginia.[12]

The statistics speak for themselves. Between 1950 and 1955, for example, the number of miners in Kentucky fell by almost one-half, hemorrhaging 22,000 people. In McDowell County, West Virginia, 30,000 miners were employed in 1945; ten years later less than half that number were still mining coal. Farther south, Campbell County, Tennessee, was suffering a similar fate. In 1946, 6,000 people were employed in the mines;

by 1955, the figure had dropped to 4,000, and by 1958, said C. J. Daniels, editor of the *LaFollette Press,* "I doubt if there are a thousand miners working today." Some of the mines, he explained, were played out, "but the chief reason for the great decline in the industry is automation in the mines." Many of the people were leaving Tennessee for Cleveland and Dayton. Frank Bradburn, pastor of the local Baptist church, said 47 of his 200-member congregation left for northern jobs in 1957 alone. A Bluefield, West Virginia, bus line was selling a hundred tickets each week for Cleveland. Between 1950 and 1960, over half a million people left West Virginia; more than 67,000 people left the state for Cleveland alone between 1955 and 1960. Estimates on the number of ex-miners and other southern whites in Cleveland ranged between 35,000 and 50,000—as many as one in every eighteen people—clustered mainly on the west side.[13]

The zenith years of upland southern white migration to the Midwest were dawning. In the southern Appalachian region alone, 704,000 people left between 1940 and 1950 compared with a paltry 81,000 between 1935 and 1940. Between 1950 and 1957, another 784,000 fled; between 1940 and 1970, a total of 3.2 million mountaineers bolted. Although the southern Appalachian birthrate had actually begun to fall, out-migration was significant enough to produce losses through interstate migration for each southern state.[14]

Kentucky, always one of the big suppliers of migrants northward, lost almost 400,000 people through migration during the 1940s; during the 1950s, thirteen out of every one hundred people—from western areas and eastern areas—were leaving the state. The high birthrate and limited opportunity left many Kentuckians with little choice but to leave. Harlan County alone lost more than 23,000 people between 1940 and 1950, almost a third of its population, and Leslie County, long having the dubious distinction of the nation's highest birthrate, lost almost a third of its population the following decade. Seven other eastern Kentucky county counties (Breathitt, Elliott, Jackson, Magoffin, Owsley, Rockcastle, and Wolfe) between 1940 and 1950 lost 40 or more percent of their populations to migration. While demographers seemed to focus on eastern counties, western and central counties were also losing people to migration: nine western and south-central counties lost more than 30 percent of their 1940 population figures, proving that migration was a *southern,* not exclusively an *Appalachian,* phenomenon—not a hegira from the hills but rather from the Upland South. Data indicate that more western than eastern Kentuckians were leaving the state.[15]

But it was the southern Appalachian person who was getting all of the attention in the media, beginning in the late 1950s. Census data, however, reveal that almost twice the number of people left western Tennessee than eastern Tennessee between 1955 and 1960, most of whom were bound for Chicago. More western Kentuckians migrated to Indiana than eastern Kentuckians during the same period, although twice as many Tennesseans bound for Indiana left middle and eastern areas than western areas. Of white migrants from Kentucky to Illinois, a little more than half of whom were bound for Chicago, more than twice the number came from western counties than from eastern ones, although slightly more eastern Kentuckians and Tennesseans went to Detroit than did their western counterparts. In spite of these data, Lewis Killian writes that "the stereotype of the hillbilly definitely includes the notion that he is a mountaineer, a white southerner whose caricature is to be seen in Snuffy Smith of the comic strip."[16]

The story of southern white out-migration during these years, then, must include flatlanders as well as highlanders. The experience of Daymon Morgan, born in eastern Kentucky's Leslie County, must be balanced with that of Buddy Lee and Anita Ford, from western Kentucky. Morgan, born in 1926 on Camp Creek, was the first of twelve children. "It was a hard life," Morgan said, "but I guess we enjoyed it." His family was forced to rent land because theirs was too steep even by eastern Kentucky standards. "We learned to save and we learned to take advantage of things growing in the mountains to eat," he explained. "I never went hungry. We got pretty low sometimes, but we didn't go hungry. We could always find something, you know." During the depression, his father worked on the WPA helping build roads that would funnel off the excess population.[17]

In 1942, at the age of sixteen, Morgan went to Detroit and then to Dayton to find a job, because he had two aunts who had recently moved there. Plenty of people, he said, were moving to Dayton, Akron, Cleveland, and Cincinnati, Ohio; Indianapolis and Connersville, Indiana; and Detroit, Michigan. "Well," he explained of wartime mobilization, "some people, you know, just like it is right now, some people tried to take advantage of it. Well, it was an opportunity. We can go to the North and get all of these good jobs and this big money." But the only job he could find in Dayton was cleaning oil drums, so he soon returned to Kentucky. At the age of eighteen, Morgan entered the army air force and was sent to Okinawa for thirteen months. When he returned in 1946, there were no jobs in Kentucky, so he used his GI bill to go to a vocational school to learn to be a welder and a mechanic; he also worked in the area's coal mines.[18]

In 1953, Morgan went back to Detroit. Although he quickly got a job as a mechanic for Greyhound and then later at GM testing diesel engines, he said, "I didn't like it. It was just a big city, and I didn't much like it." He returned to Kentucky and met his wife, Betty, who was born in West Virginia but was raised in Ohio. Her father had moved the family to Mansfield, Ohio, when she was eleven to work for Globe Steel. They later moved to Lexington, Ohio, where she graduated from high school in 1952. She had moved to Kentucky with some friends and met Morgan there. In 1955, they married, and three days later, they moved to Dayton. Morgan quickly found a job with Trailmobile welding and then was hired at Chrysler's heater and air-conditioning plant, joining the ranks of transplanted southerners working there; well over half of the four thousand employees were southerners, he estimated. His plan was to work a short time and then open up a garage. "I needed to go somewhere," he said, "and get a job, and I didn't know any other place. I had some people there and I didn't have too much money. I knew my aunt would keep us there until we got a place."[19]

As a welder on the assembly line, the work "was boring, hard work," Morgan said. "It was a lot different than a farm. You didn't have no freedom," echoing many a migrant. In addition to the monotony, layoffs were also a persistent problem in the early years because he did not have seniority. On one particular layoff, Daymon and Betty decided that they would move out of the house they were renting in New Lebanon, east of Dayton in rural Montgomery County (Daymon always refused to live in the inner city), and return to Kentucky, since they thought it would be cheaper to live there on Daymon's unemployment wages. As soon as they arrived in Kentucky, Daymon received a telegram calling him back to work. He returned, but Betty and their three children stayed in Kentucky for almost a year. Eventually, things improved, and after ten years of living and working in Ohio, the Morgans had saved enough money to buy five acres in Brookville, twenty-two miles east of Dayton. With his family in Kentucky, Daymon began building their home, where they would live for the next twenty years, to the exact day.[20]

Having grown up in the mountains of eastern Kentucky, Daymon found the restrictive, overcrowded, and noisy northern life-style—their five-acre farm outside of Dayton notwithstanding—loathsome. He liked to hunt raccoons, squirrels, and rabbits and to fish, not to discuss who won the ball game or who was starring in the latest Hollywood film. Their youngest child, Sally, who was born in Ohio, explained that "we never went to ball games when I was growing up and stuff like that. We stayed around the house and worked and listened to Daddy always talk about the mountains. When we come down here, we loved it, me and my brothers did. We stayed in the mountains and they never seen us." "Oh, yes," she concluded, "we had freedom. They didn't have that up there. They didn't have woods or mountains like they had here. And we liked it better." Asked about her identity as a Kentuckian or an Ohioan, Sally said she cultivated her Kentuckyness while she was growing up. "We were different, and we liked it. We knew things that they didn't know. We knew that tomatoes grew on a vine. They thought Daddy went out to pick potatoes—you *dig* potatoes. We knew the difference." Growing up, she always "said I would come back here," referring to her father's eastern Kentucky home. Betty, however, enjoyed living in Ohio, particularly since she had practically grown up there, and, unlike Daymon, was not intent on leaving as soon as retirement came.[21]

Eventually, retirement did come, and in 1986, after thirty years of working at Chrysler, Daymon retired. But their youngest son, who at the time was a junior in high school, wanted to graduate from the school in which he began, so they waited another year before putting their house on the market. After his graduation, they sold their place and returned to Leslie County, where they bought property deep in the hollows of Kentucky.[22]

Conditions in the western Kentucky coalfields were little better than those farther east. In 1951, Buddy Lee Ford went to Milwaukee after he graduated from high school because his cousin was working there on a chicken farm. After his cousin returned to Kentucky, Ford got a job with Harley Davidson and worked for a short time until he, too, returned. After serving a year in the service, Ford married in December 1954, about the same time that a cousin came home from Pontiac, Michigan, bragging that "General Motors is hiring every able-bodied man that walks into the factory." That clinched Ford's decision to leave Morganfield, Kentucky, with a friend for Detroit in February of the following year. He assumed his experience from Milwaukee would land him a job. His friend, however, had never worked with machinery. "So I told him," Ford said, "Just put down that you worked at Harley Davidson in Milwaukee. They're not going to question you. Because they were looking for workers, you know. And he got the job, and I didn't. I didn't get a job for about thirty days!" The problem was that GM was not hiring in Pontiac, although eventually he was hired at GM's huge Willow Run transmission plant. "It was a hell of an operation, I'll tell you," he said.[23]

Soon after Ford got the job, his wife, Anita, came to Detroit for what amounted to the second time, having lived there as a child. Her father, also from western Kentucky, was an ironworker who traveled where the work was, and he had gone to Detroit to work on Tiger Stadium after a stint in Oak Ridge. But, Anita said, "it was a different Detroit when we lived there—when we were a child—than when I moved back there with Buddy. It had grown into an ugly city by that time. When we lived there [before], it was fun." One of the reasons for Detroit's ugliness was undoubtedly Anita's homesickness. "When we first moved to Detroit right after we were married," she said, "I was seventeen years old and I had never been away from my mother. And oh, I was terrible. I don't see how he lived with me. All I did was lay in bed and cry." Homesickness did not infect Buddy, who had already been away from home.[24]

As months went by, they moved progressively farther out of the city, first to Ypsilanti (by then just becoming known as "Ypsitucky" because of the growing number of migrants) and then to Ann Arbor, all the while living in apartments. Anita had gotten a job in a restaurant as a waitress but was then hired by the phone company as an operator. "I worked at the telephone company for most of the time we was up there," she said. "Back then you had operators for everything. I was a long distance operator. But I definitely had an accent because I would say '*Operayter.*' And they'd say, '*What are weee all doin' todayyyy?*' They'd make fun of me—they'd just laugh." Some customers who were also migrants would ask her, however, "What part of the South are you from?" which made her work more enjoyable.[25]

Buddy, meanwhile, who was working third shift, was paid a thirty dollar premium just for working a shift few people wanted, which was more than the twenty-five dollars a week he had been making in Kentucky working for his uncle before he left. Before long, however, they returned to Kentucky because Buddy, now having made enough money to buy a television and a new car, was looking for an excuse to leave Detroit and was given one. At GM, the foreman told him he would be switched to days. When Buddy resisted, he was told there would not be a job for him if he refused:

> And I said, "Well, I'll just quit and go back to Kentucky." The next day he said, "Now don't forget, come in on day shift Monday morning." I said, "I told you I'm not coming in on day shift. I said I'd quit." He said, "Oh, you're not going to do that." And I said, "Yes I will." So Saturday morning I got off, and right before quitting time he come in and told me again, and I said, "No, I'm going to go rent me a trailer tomorrow and I'm headed for Kentucky." And that's what we did. I went out and rented a trailer. We had a TV and a brand new automobile—a brand new '55 Chevrolet. I paid $1,975 for it. Brand spanking new with six miles on it.
>
> And we came with our TV and clothes and a new car. I went back to work for my uncle, but he doubled my salary! Fifty bucks a week! And I worked for him for about three months, and my cousin had just gotten out of the service, and he came down from Milwaukee. And he said,

> "Buddy, let's go back to Milwaukee." And I said, "Okay." So we packed up and went to Milwaukee. I went to work for Ambrosia Chocolate Company, and I was making a dollar and five cents an hour, but I was making a forty-five-cent bonus on the shipping floor. . . .
>
> So they put me in the press room, and I was making [a] thirty-five-cent bonus, and I could work four-and-a-half or five hours and I had my twelve hours done, because I learned a lot of shortcuts of how to make the cocoa faster with the presses than what the time study men said they could be made (lot of times they would really screw you). I stayed there for right at ten years; just a little under ten years, I think.

Later he was hired at Evinrude.[26]

On Labor Day in 1957, Anita's sister and brother-in-law, Charis and Charlie Crooks, came to Milwaukee. Charlie's father had owned some of the fertile farmland of Union County, Kentucky, but the government had displaced the owners of thirty thousand acres for Camp Breckinridge, which was later reopened for the Korean War. When the government no longer needed the land, original owners were not given a chance to buy it back. Without land to farm, Charlie looked for other options. He was immediately hired at Ambrosia, and he and Charis stayed for three years, until his father suffered a heart attack in Kentucky. They stayed in Kentucky for five years and returned to Milwaukee in 1965. Charlie worked for a small machine shop for ten years and then at Custom Products, where he retired in 1990 after fourteen years, at which time they returned to Kentucky, in part to avoid Wisconsin taxes.[27]

Buddy, Anita, Charlie, and Charis all liked Milwaukee. Because southerners were a much smaller percentage of the total population than, say, in Detroit, there was less persecution. Instead of the taunts the Fords received in Detroit, Charis said, "You'd say something in a store in Milwaukee and they'd say, 'Oh I love the way you talk! Say something!' People are much nicer in Milwaukee than they are in Detroit," a characteristic she attributed to Milwaukee's being "a big city full of small towns." Besides, Charis said, "what was so great about being up there" was that in Kentucky, "you couldn't get a job. If you got one you didn't make any wages. You went up there, they needed you worse than you needed them, and it was nice to have them need you worse than you needed them." Two sisters in the same northern city also made adjustment much easier. By 1960, the Fords had purchased a three-bedroom home in the Milwaukee suburbs.[28]

Demographic data for these years show not only that whites were leaving the South but that they were headed for the North. Between 1940 and 1950, West Virginia lost 300,000 native whites, Kentucky almost

800,000, Tennessee over 300,000, and Arkansas more than 500,000. Conversely, Ohio gained 175,000 native whites; Michigan added just under 500,000. In 1950, almost 10 percent of the native white males living in Ohio, 7 percent in Indiana, and slightly more than 4 percent in Michigan had been born in West Virginia, Kentucky, Tennessee, Alabama, or Arkansas. Southern whites were building sizable communities in midwestern states, including towns in Ohio's Miami Valley, Cleveland's west side, Indianapolis's south side, Chicago's Uptown, and Detroit's Cass Corridor.[29]

Because more attention has been given to southern Appalachian out-migration, we know more about where migrants from this region of the South were going. For example, Detroit, Canton, and, Chicago were, in descending order, the most common destinations of migrants from north Georgia; the most popular midwestern destination for western North Carolinians was Canton, followed by Detroit, Chicago, and Akron. Among those going to Chicago, the majority came from eastern Tennessee, followed by West Virginia and eastern Kentucky; eastern Kentucky sent half as many as Tennessee did. In Detroit, more migrants came from eastern Tennessee, followed by eastern Kentucky and West Virginia. Cleveland and Columbus received the majority of its southern Appalachian migrants from West Virginia, but many more eastern Tennesseans went to Cleveland than to Columbus; conversely, more eastern Kentuckians went to Columbus than to Cleveland. The overwhelming majority of those going to Akron were from West Virginia.[30]

Kinship at Work

Kinship was a crucial part of southern white out-migration, just as it usually is whenever anyone packs bags and lights out for new territory. Migrants who were attracted to friends and family in the North or attracted friends and family once in the North refute the stereotype of dumb southerners too attached to family to better their situation by moving. In short, kinship among upland southerners did not usually retard migration; it often fostered it.

Because of the efforts of industrial managers who recruited a southern white labor force, many southerners knew more about a factory in a particular town than about the town itself. "I'm going to Champion" must have been an oft-heard refrain, for example, in eastern Kentucky among migrants headed for the Miami Valley. During the 1950s, a joke circulated through Mishawaka, Indiana (and local variants in other cities, such as Muncie and Detroit, with large southern migrant populations), in which a bus loaded with southerners stops and the driver says, "South Bend!" No one gets off the bus. He drives to Mishawaka and announces the stop, but again no one gets off. He drives a few blocks to the Ball-Band plant, which employed many southerners, and once the driver announced it, every passenger scurried off the bus.[31]

Plenty of industries in the North were dominated by southern migrants because they were more willing than native whites to work (at least initially) in difficult conditions and for low wages. John Weatherford said his decision to apply at Ball-Band was easy because half of his friends were employed there, as well as "all of Waterloo and Florence [Alabama]," he added, half-jokingly, an allusion to the common story that southerners answered "Waterloo" or "Florence" when natives asked them where they were from, even if they lived across the state line in Wayne County or Hardin County in Tennessee. As Harvey Austin explained, "The last time I [worked at Ball-Band] a guy said, 'How many people live in Waterloo?' And I said, 'About fifty thousand!' See, why he asked that is because probably 50 percent of the people [who] worked at Ball-Band [were] from Waterloo or Florence." (Waterloo's actual population was about 250, Florence, about 12,000.) Many narrators estimated that of the six thousand employees Ball-Band had in the 1950s, at least half were southern migrants. Certainly desperation drove many southerners to Ball-Band, even though many said Studebaker and Bendix were the "best" companies because of high wages. Ball-Band's low wages and the difficult working conditions—such as the infamous auto mat department—made it low on the desirability list, especially among Hoosier natives. Southerners in South Bend and Mishawaka were hungry for work and for wages—even Ball-Band's low pay was much higher than southern wages—and since many could not produce the connections that gave them preference at Studebaker and, to a lesser extent, Bendix, southerners flocked to Ball-Band out of a combination of kinship (they knew many employees) and desperation.[32]

Among personnel managers, kinship could produce unpredictable results, stocking one's company with either sojourning southerners or those who stayed and attracted family and friends. Turnover at United States Rubber plants (of which Ball-Band was a part), for example, ranged from a low of 50 percent to a peak of 200 percent a year in the 1950s. Turnover may have been the thorn in the side of many personnel managers who hired large numbers of southern whites, but most turnover was undoubtedly due to southerners' simply trying to find a better job, made possible by a labor shortage that, according to R. G. Hudson, allowed one to "quit by ten o'clock [and] . . . have a job by noon with another company." "In East Chicago in those years," he continued, "you'd hired a guy, and if he worked two weeks you were lucky cause he'd look around and find a better job, or somebody'd say something he didn't like, he'd just quit." Max Green agreed: "Everything was in such a hectic deal—they were crying for manpower. They didn't question us much." Daymon Morgan said that managers used to joke about southerners in Dayton: "Lots of times they used to say that they couldn't read one line except U.S. 25 on Friday." Another joke circulating through many migrant towns told of a visitor getting a tour of heaven by St. Peter. Seeing a large group of angels chained to some poles, the visitor inquired about the reason, and St. Peter answered, "This is Friday, and those people are from the South. If we don't chain them, they go home for the weekend." Again, however, turnover seems to be associated more with the type of job and less with the person who held it.[33]

Other companies were savvy in their exploitation of the kinship factor; by exploiting kinship, some companies stabilized personnel and kept waves of cheap labor coming. Until the 1950s, the "big four" employers of the Miami Valley region—Procter and Gamble in Cincinnati, Champion Paper and Fiber in Hamilton, Armco Steel in Middletown, and National Cash Register in Dayton—had had serene labor relations, partly because they had embraced paternalism and had cultivated the "family idea" by hiring family and friends of employees who were once migrants themselves. For example, Inland Container, in Middletown, had 220 Kentuckians on its payroll, 117 of whom were from Wolfe County alone (a supervisor was also from Wolfe County). Above the doorway between two Armco departments was a sign that read "LEAVE MORGAN COUNTY AND ENTER WOLFE COUNTY," because of the number of employees from the two counties. At least a few of the officials John Leslie Thompson interviewed for his dissertation intimated that the reason for labor peace was due in part to southern migrants who were willing to work, at least initially, for less money than the area average because they were simply happy to have a job, which was common in American labor history.[34]

Personnel managers may have been willing to accept high turnover rates to ensure a steady stream of workers. James Shelby, for example, was told to avoid Ball-Band when he came to Indiana in 1948 because the work was hard and the pay low. Consequently, he applied at Bendix but was given "the run-around." To be safe, he completed an application at Ball-Band and was hired by Ed Cavanaugh, the hiring officer who, Shelby believed, had a fondness for southern employees. He began working midnight shifts in the heater room on the vulcanizers, and although he thought the work was hard, he said the eighty-five cents an hour was "good money" even for Ball-Band. After several weeks, he compared his paycheck with his boardinghouse chums' paychecks and found that with overtime, he was making as much money as those who worked at Bendix. He decided to stay and build some seniority, and he eventually retired after thirty-eight years. He detailed the method by which Ball-Band had stabilized its labor force:

> I went home pretty often from there. You know, we was all single, maybe four or five of us guys would get in a car and drive down there [Tennessee] over a weekend, because back then we'd swap up driving. We didn't get much sleep, but we was young. So people'd see me down there, and they'd want to know if they could get a job up there. And I'd say, "Yeah, they're hiring everywhere." So the first thing you know there'd be some of them coming up; they'd go back and tell somebody else. Word of mouth—that's what it all amounted to. A lot of people'd come up here and call me and I'd get them in down there. Some of them'd quit and go back. If they was good workers, they'd come back, and I could get them back in. I've done that. A lot of them, they'd work there two or three weeks and go to Bendix or somewhere else to work.[35]

Throughout northern industrial towns, there were Whirlpools and Ball-Bands that were all too eager to keep the flow of southern newcomers unchecked.

Nonetheless, cities were important in migrant patterns. Hamilton and Middletown, located in Ohio's Miami Valley, are a case in point. The valley's economy was robust after World War II, with 23 percent of Ohio's manufacturing jobs; 49 percent of the paper jobs, 41 percent of printing and publishing; and 33 percent of the machinery jobs in 1947. The number of production workers there grew by almost two-thirds between 1939 and 1947, compared with one-half for the nation as a whole.[36]

The selective nature of migration was much at work. Although only fifteen miles apart in the same county, Hamilton and Middletown received Kentucky migrants from different places of origin. John Leslie Thompson was able to survey half of all industrial workers in Butler County in the early 1950s, and he tabulated the Kentucky counties of origin for both cities. Middletown attracted workers from five eastern Kentucky counties, while Hamilton attracted workers from five other eastern Kentucky counties. Thompson's research also indicated that perhaps a third of Ohio-born employees were descendants of Kentucky migrants, and after Kentucky, five of the next eight most frequently cited birthplaces of Butler County employees were southern states. By 1960,

Hamilton, with a population of over 78,000, had more Kentuckians residing there than Ohioans; the year before, a Kentucky Mountain Folk Festival debuted in Hamilton.[37]

For their part, southerners defined kinship very broadly, including not only kindred but also friends—even distant acquaintances—whom they could call, and usually depend, on for support once in the North. Kinship determined a host of decisions in the migration process, including, of course, where one would go, as well as where one would live and work once there.

Take the case of Joe and Lucille Clardy, whose migration experience is woven with kinship ties and decisions. Both grew up near the banks of the Tennessee River in Waterloo, Alabama, just before the river turns northward to make its meandering way to the Ohio River. Lucille's parents were farmers, and Joe's father owned a sawmill until the depression wiped him out. In 1940, Joe visited some friends in South Bend, Indiana. Although he returned to Alabama, he thought about trying to find a job there in the future. Everyone in Waterloo was talking about South Bend and Mishawaka, Joe recalled, but Lucille clinched his decision to migrate, having come north to South Bend herself during Christmas 1940 to take care of her sister's children.[38]

Lucille babysat for several months but soon grew tired of working for no pay. In Alabama, she had been working for a doctor's family and had been paid a dollar a week plus room and board. She answered an ad in the newspaper for a babysitting position that paid seven dollars a week. "I thought I was getting rich," she said. She soon found an even better job as a car hop at Bonnie Doon, a local drive-in, making fifteen cents an hour—fifteen dollars a week. After their marriage in 1941, she went to Ball-Band, in Mishawaka, as many southerners did, and was hired. She enjoyed Ball-Band because there were plenty of women and plenty of southerners, but her adjustment to factory work was difficult because she was so used to farm life.[39]

When Joe decided to join his girlfriend, Lucille, he met a woman on the Greyhound bus he took to South Bend whose husband owned a construction company. When they arrived, she suggested to her husband that he hire Joe, which he did, for fifty cents an hour. Not yet married, Joe was boarding with Lucille's first cousin, who was a secretary to the personnel manager at Studebaker. Soon, he was working at "Stude's" and making $1.15 an hour doing inspection and assembly work. Joe enjoyed his job very much, partly because people on the shop floor helped each other: "If you goofed up, they would tell you. That's what they called *fami-*

ly." Nine months later, he would be drafted and would not return to South Bend until 1946. When he returned, he became a supervisor.[40]

The dynamics of chain migration were much at work between northern Indiana and Waterloo. Joe estimated that 60 percent of his schoolmates from Waterloo either live or have lived in South Bend–Mishawaka. Even the mayor of Waterloo migrated for a time. As more members of Joe's and Lucille's families came north (all of their siblings eventually left Waterloo for northern Indiana), Joe's parents moved in 1960, officially to take care of their grandchildren, although Joe's father got a job at Armco Steel and later retired there and returned to Alabama.[41]

Hollye Ward, born in 1910 in Knott County, Kentucky, had had her fill of rural life in the South. She and her husband had moved to Buckhorn, Kentucky, so that her husband could manage a farm and the timber operations owned by a boarding school that employed Hollye's brother-in-law. Ward despised the isolated living in Letcher County; there was, she said, no way "to get out or get in." She was particularly peeved at her husband for not taking a job that was offered him when they were visiting his parents, who were living in Hamilton, Ohio. Her husband had refused to move because, in Ward's words, "he was as happy as a coon in a log! He loved that life. He got out a lot, you see, and once in a while I'd go down and catch the mail truck and go to Hazard to my sister-in-law's and spend the day." So she decided to do something about it. While her husband was out hauling grain for the hogs, she hired a driver to pack their belongings and move her and the four children to her in-laws' home in Hamilton. Once her husband came home and found all their belongings and his family gone, he quit his job in Kentucky and came to Hamilton, accepting the painting job that had been offered earlier. "He was glad to see us," she said understatedly. Loving Ohio living, she explained that the difference between living in Buckhorn and Hamilton was like "being in jail and being out footloose and fancy free." The Wards stayed on with Hollye's in-laws until she had saved enough money to buy the Sears, Roebuck, house she had been eying on Hunt Avenue for some time, surrounded by "hillbillies." "The kitchen wasn't big enough to thrash a cat in, but still, it was a kitchen—it was mine," she remembered, quite proud of her decision to leave. In this case, a determined woman combined with kin already in the North to make migration happen.[42]

In 1947, Alvin Berry, my grandfather, was also frustrated with his life. At age thirty-three, he was frustrated that he had not left Wayne County, Tennessee, earlier. "I missed by staying down there so long," he said. "I should've got out whenever we first married" in 1932. He was also frustrated that he went home from Akron, Ohio, and tried one last time to make it in the South. Vowing never to return should he ever leave in the future, he disregarded his father-in-law's warning about living in exile in the North: "He said we'd find it would be different eating out of a paper sack—having to buy everything to eat." Alvin chose Mishawaka because his wife, Ruby, had a nephew who was working there, and Alvin left on a bus with another of her nephews and a cousin. "Whenever I came up here in '47," he explained, "you couldn't hardly find a job. Studebaker's was hiring, but you" had to have a lead to get hired. He was hired, however, at Hygrades, a slaughterhouse, on June 11. Alvin liked the job, not minding the stench and the messy conditions. Several weeks later, he called Ruby. "I got a call," she said, "was it the fifth of July? And I locked up and got to Florence [Alabama] and left that evening" by bus. Alvin had rented an apartment on Wells Street for eighteen dollars a week, but they had to carry water upstairs with which to cook and bathe. One Saturday morning, when they were planning on looking for another apartment, the landlord came up and told them she was cutting their rent to twelve dollars because they were not "like" other southern tenants. They stood by their plans and moved.[43]

In 1950, Alvin was finally hired at Studebaker, and the next year he bought a new 1951 Studebaker automobile. But soon he was laid off, and in 1952, he and Ruby were hired at the local Pepsi bottling plant. They were given the same job on the line, but Alvin's wage—eighty cents an hour—was a nickel more than Ruby's. Both were hired the same day, worked the same job, retired the same day in 1976, and, after the plant was organized by the Teamsters, made the same wage.[44]

Kinship continued to be woven through their lives in northern Indiana. The Berrys soon were able to buy a small house for eight hundred dollars and, after several more years of frugality, overtime wages, and a trash route that Alvin did on the side, a larger house in a middle-class neighborhood. Their first home in particular welcomed many a southerner to the North. Two of Ruby's brothers came to Mishawaka and stayed for a time, but both were homesick and returned south, "like a lot of southerners," Alvin remarked. Four people actually boarded with them upon their arrival. Done more out of a desire to accommodate than a wish to make money, they stopped taking in boarders because it was too much work for Ruby. For ten dollars, boarders got two meals a day and their clothes washed and ironed. Alvin's brother, Homer, also came north, first working in the fruit orchards of southwestern Michigan and eventually getting a job at the same Pepsi plant.

Ruby remembered one story in particular about newly arrived exiles searching out their home upon their arrival. "We'd been to Elkhart that day. Alvin had his teeth pulled. And Alvin says, 'There's a Alabama car in front of us.' We didn't know it was them. And we was coming down Lincoln Way and turned off and went to Logan Street and they went on and missed the road. And they came back." In the car were Vera and Carmel Lawson, who had gone to find them in Akron during the war, and Carmel's half-brother, Grady Roberson, and his wife, Neg. "I cooked dinner for them," Ruby remembered, "and Neg said she'd never seen so many damned pork chops fried in her life! I cooked dinner and they eat." Later in the day, they helped them find an apartment.[45]

On weekends, the Berrys "stayed home and cooked for a bunch of company." "There wasn't no place [else] to hang out," Alvin said. "Not for me—I didn't drink or nothing. I didn't hang out" at the Blue Flame, a notorious tavern for southerners in Mishawaka, "cause I didn't drink. They was just people to come to our house on Sunday, all the time. Every Sunday." In the summers, the Berrys, like many southern transplants, traveled to the Buck Lake Ranch, near Angola, Indiana, to hear *Grand Ole Opry* entertainment that was spreading throughout the Midwest.[46]

The only thing Frank Plemons, born in 1929 in east Tennessee, had his mind set on was finding a job when he grew up. "All I wanted to do," he said, "was get a job and make some money, because I never had no money." Both Frank and his wife, Joyce, born in 1938, grew up in large southern families that demographers often stereotyped. Although born in the middle, in many ways Frank was the pioneer migrant for his family, having moved to northwest Indiana in 1949 to try his luck at finding a job. He found nothing, so he returned home, ready to try again, which he did two months later. On that trip, he was hired at the famed Gary Works of U.S. Steel, which then employed twenty-six thousand people. "And I came here, which, it was pretty good money back then. When I first went to work," he said, "I made forty-nine dollars a week—$1.21 an hour—that's what the steel mill paid at that time. And down South you didn't make nothing like that, even if you could find a job." Through thirty-five years of employment until his retirement in 1984, he worked his way up from a laborer to a craneman. Eventually, all but one brother would move to northwest Indiana; on one block in Whiting, there are four houses that belong to the Plemonses. In the late 1950s, even his father, who had previously worked at Oak Ridge, came to Whiting and worked for about ten years at Inland Steel and then returned south; in 1990, his father, then eighty-eight, left Tennessee again to spend the rest of his days in Indiana. In Joyce's family, only one sibling still remains in Tennessee; the others have moved to Whiting, fascinating examples of the funneling off of upland southern population to the North and the intricacies of chain migration.[47]

For southern migrants who could not lure their families northward with them, the migration experience was difficult. Although Joyce came to accept and to adjust to her northern home, she was greatly saddened to leave her family in east Tennessee. "Of course," she said, "I never stayed here in the summertime when our kid was small, because when school was out, we went south, me and him, and stayed for the summer months." Frank "stayed here and worked and then he would come down late on vacation and pick us up and bring us back." Her parents, she said, "were still living and I wanted to spend time with them." Knowing that it was soon time to leave her parents in the summer would begin a week of crying. "I just never did like that," she said. "And I never got over it, either. Not of leaving my family. Because like I said, I was real close to my mom and dad. Real close to them. And I just never liked to leave."[48]

Some southern women who came north (about four in ten according to census data) with a spouse worked, but the majority chose not to work. Attachment to family usually dictated the choices women made; in addition, husbands frequently "allowed" their wives to work or "prohibited" them from doing so. In Joyce's case, both her attachment to her family and her husband's wishes prevented her from getting a job. "Well," Frank said, "she had a kid; I think you should be home. These people, sometimes I think that's a lot of the problem today, house kids. I know a lot of times they have to work to make a living, this and that, but some people just tries to live too high on the hog, I think. And they get theirself in trouble and then the wife has to go work then to pay bills and stuff." Most people, Frank said, in criticism of twentieth-century consumer culture, "have got to have two cars and a camper and all that crap, you know. I don't try to stay up with the Joneses myself."[49]

But just as migrants struggled to retain their former selves once they migrated, kinship ties were sometimes changed in the process of migrating. Both Joyce and Frank miss people visiting—a loss they believed characteristic of northern culture. Frank noted with amazement that when their next-door neighbor died, they were not even told. "Sometimes you come out, and sometimes they speak to you, sometimes they won't," Frank said of the neighbors who live around them in their neat working-class neighborhood. "Down south, they speak to you, whether they know you or not." In the South, "especially on Sunday," Joyce added, "usually somebody came home with you from church or something like that, you know. Here they don't do that. Everybody goes back to their own home."

Even Joyce and Frank do not socialize very much with their brothers and sisters who live in the area. "I have two brothers that live here," Joyce said. "We don't visit each other like, you know, it would've been I think when we lived in the South. Because usually on every Sunday we went to our grandparents' house, and usually to family there. My mother's brothers and sisters and their children usually came on a Sunday afternoon, you know, to our grandpa's place, you know, because he lived on a big farm. That was usually every Sunday we went to see our grandparents, you know. Of course, we saw all of our aunts and uncles and cousins because they all came, too, you know."[50]

While Daymon Morgan was thankful he was able to find work to support his family in Dayton, he, too, regretted that kinship ties were changed by migration:

> See they heard about it there. They was a lot of work in the factories going up north. And I think that had a very bad effect on people down here. Well, there's a lot of people, you know, they wasn't living too good, but they said, 'Boy there's big money up there. Let's go up there. We can get two dollars an hour. Let's get up there and we'll go up there and work a while and get some money saved up and we'll come down here and fix this old place up.' Well what they do—they go up there and then this factory thing was so much different. The children and everything would be so homesick and everything, they couldn't stand it for maybe two or three weeks. And then they'd get used to it and then the dad and mother'd both get jobs and the children were neglected. They'd meet with other children that was done the same way, and they didn't have no supervision. And then this old place they was going to come back and fix up, why, after they got up there a while, they just let it run down worse, and never come back. I think it had a bad effect. The family values broke down. There's no communication between the parents and the children. It was different. People down here were raised poor but they had a certain amount of respect, a certain amount of family ties. And whenever that started, that broke that up to a great extent. And I seen some very bad effects of it. In my own people.[51]

Interestingly, the changes in familial relationships that the Plemons and Daymon Morgan detail are attributed to migration—another example of divided hearts—and less to the impact of modernization: increasing privacy, wives having to work, and the primacy of the nuclear family. Exiles imply that had they remained in their homeland, these changes would not have affected their families.

Overall, southerners who chose to come to the Midwest loosened their kinship ties in the South. But in so doing, migrants sought to transplant in the North the social relationships that they had so valued in the South, although many migrants would still always lament having to leave the place they grew up, extended family and friends notwithstanding. In many ways, then, the great white migration was kin determined; upland southerners were willing to forego, to a limited extent, kin in the South as long as some kin could be brought to the North. The cultural components they brought with them are the subject of chapter 6.

Success or Failure?

One of the crucial issues any study of migration should address is whether migrants to a particular area were bettering themselves economically. This question is particularly important for the story of southern white out-migration for two main reasons. First, this migration, like most migration streams, was based heavily on kinship, and the question arises whether migrants were merely following friends and family to a particular northern city or whether they were using kinship as a way to increase their standard of living. A second point concerns the stereotypes of white southern migrants, which maintained that they were quiescent victims unable to adjust to their northern urban environments, living lives amid poverty and welfare, crime and alcoholism, educational dropout and delinquency, underachievement and overabundant fertility. These stereotypes became even more entrenched in the mind-set of many Americans after 1960 and are explored more fully in chapter 7, but it is important to test their validity to the extent possible.

Qualitatively, it is not difficult to find migrant testimony that argues that economically, at least, southerners achieved the material gains they were seeking. Recall Lucille Clardy's amazement at her salary in the North. Will Pennington, born in 1941 in Clay County, Kentucky, moved with his divorced mother to Cincinnati, the destination of a host of relatives since the 1930s. He eloquently testified about his family's reasons for leaving the South:

> The biggest migration, I think of people in my family, of people I'm related to, was in the late '40s and early '50s. The biggest majority of them came up then. There's many different reasons for it. I think one of the biggest reasons is they were wanting to do better from what they were doing down there and it was getting to be such a task down there to survive on the same type of cash crop that they were growing prior to the War, and that was the tobacco. Especially, you know, they cut down on "baccer" allotments on some of the farms, and a lot of my relatives, my dad in particular, were renters, so, you know, you only got a part of what you were growing anyway. And then if you had a bad year, and that did come about sometimes—sometimes it would be a disease or something like that would hit your cash crop of tobacco and you didn't have that

income coming in and you already owed the store man because he was carrying you for a year—so sometimes that meant you had to sell your milk cow.[52]

Migrating to Cincinnati as a youngster entailed a host of difficult adjustments for Pennington, but, remembering his citified relatives returning to Kentucky for visits when he was young, he sympathized with those who left the South for northern cities. Of his uncle who had left in the 1940s, he said:

> When they left they left with nothing. They left with a bag with practically nothing in it, they caught a bus to the city, and when they came back he was driving his own car, he had a nice suit on, and he had *money.* That's the thing about it: he had money. He would pull out money, give it to his mom [and say], Go down and get you this. And surely the other people were envious of him to an extent. They'd say, Well, if he can do it, I can do it; he's got more than I've got. Like I say, it was a treat to go out with him, because he'd stop at a store and buy you an ice cream. You just didn't have money to buy ice cream. When I was coming up I remember the most money I ever had until I was twelve years old. I used to trap animals and sell their hides, and that's where I used to make my money, because I never got any money from the tobacco, we never got any money from that. The kids didn't. You'd get a pair of shoes or some clothing, or one little toy for Christmas or something like that, an apple or an orange, or something like that, but you never got any money. I liked to hunt so I trapped, and I trapped a big old opossum. This guy gave me a dollar and a quarter for it. I will never forget that, I kept that dollar for a long, long time. Spent the quarter, but kept the dollar. That was the most money I ever had in my life. It's things like that. Then one person goes and another person went and like I said, finally six out of eight of the members of the family are in the city now.

Thirteen of fifteen in his father's family moved northward. Like many from preindustrial societies, they did not want material goods until they were exposed to them—the we-didn't-know-any-better excuse of many migrants. Pennington continued:

> I don't think it really mattered to them until they got exposed to it. Then when they got exposed to it, especially when one of their own was the one who had it, and especially when that one [would] say: Hey, this is really nice to have this and to have that; it's nice to have a dollar in your pocket instead of having nothing in your pocket; I can get this and I can get that. I think it's just from exposure. Before you wasn't exposed to it, nobody had it. Everybody had the same thing and I don't think it really crossed their mind too much. Because like when they went to town, there you'd see people who did have things, but Them are other folks, them

> are other folks, and that's where the difference is. But now, This is one of our folks. He can do it. Look at the money he's flashing. Man, I work all year long and I don't have this much left over when I get finished. I think that's what changes it, because we did see other people but that was "other" folks, they were different from us and stuff like that.[53]

Other qualitative evidence points to the success of migrants who ventured northward. One example in particular was that those who remained in the South resented those who left—both because they were making money and because sometimes they were perceived as having sold out. The attitudes of those who stay behind are often neglected in migration studies, but they can be very revealing. As the historian Jeanette Keith writes of her childhood in the east Tennessee's Cumberland Plateau, "I lived in a place that was losing population, in a community that was losing its locus." The novelist Denise Giardina concurred. "I can remember somebody going to Indiana actually," Giardina explained, "and coming back and having a job in a factory and saying, Well, I'm getting so much an hour. People were envious of the money but maybe not envious that the person was homesick." Homesickness was not an ailment of those who remained, of course, but there was resentment of those who left, as Giardina detailed:

> I think there were strong feelings of rejection or betrayal sometimes, which is not fair, because people did what they had to do. But I can remember as a kid thinking, Why don't they just stay and tough it out, you know? If people would just stay and fight for something, then maybe we'd make somebody listen to us or something. I mean, I didn't think that when I was five, but I can remember when I was like thirteen or fourteen and going through it myself feeling that way. Although we didn't leave the state, so in a sense that wasn't so bad. It's like seeing limbs amputated, I think it really was devastating for people who stayed. But there's a sort of survivor mentality, and I think it makes you more resentful of criticism, too, because you're sort of saying well, the place you've created—your home and all of that—is not good enough, so people have to leave it.[54]

Quantitatively, the national census is the way to compare southern white migrants with other white midwestern and southern natives. Extracting information on those southern whites who were living in 1960 in the five states of the Old Northwest from the Integrated Public Use Microdata Sample (IPUMS) from the census produces a revealing socioeconomic picture.[55]

We see that southern white out-migration (at least in 1960) was *upland* southern out-migration: almost four out of ten southerners leaving their region were from Kentucky, and almost eight out of ten were from Kentucky, Tennessee, and West Virginia. Arkansans were the next significant group leaving for the Midwest. The data also reveal that Ohio was the overwhelming destination, receiving twice as many southerners as Illinois, Indiana, and Michigan did. But that Michigan received one-fifth of all southern whites to the Midwest disproves distance determinism; industry and agriculture across the Lower Peninsula attracted the second-highest number of migrants from the South. In contrast, Wisconsin was never a significant destination among white southerners; it received less than 2 percent of southern whites bound for the Midwest. The Fords and the Crooks must have been rather exotic in Milwaukee.[56]

One of the most important revelations from the data concerns the employment status of southern white migrants in the Midwest. Data show how similar southern white migrants and midwestern whites were. Migrants who were working compare favorably with midwesterners who were working; indeed, southern white migrants had an unemployment rate only a percentage point higher than midwestern whites, indicating that southern migrants were having little difficulty finding jobs in 1960. One of the most significant figures concerns average wages. White male migrants from the South had average wages that were only $246 lower than those for white midwestern males, and southern migrant women's wages were even closer to white midwestern women's average wages, with a difference of only $81. When the average wage of white migrants is compared with that of whites in the South, there are striking differences. Southern white men in the South were earning, on average, $1,037 less than those southerners living in the Midwest. Women's wages were closer, with a difference of $249. (Interestingly, roughly the same proportion of migrant women and southern women were working; migration did not seem to lure southern white women into the midwestern labor market, a significant continuity with life in the South.) The data also indicate that relatively equal numbers of southern whites were employed both in the South and the Midwest; thus, the significant difference in 1960 was earning power. Since most southerners seemed to be employed in 1960, the reason for migrating was to earn more, not just to find a job, as was the case in earlier decades. Southern migrants were acting on their knowledge that they could earn more in the Midwest, on average 21 percent more than they could earn in the South, evidence refuting the stereotype of the lazy, welfare-grabbing migrant.[57]

The IPUMS data also reveal that southern white migrants in the Midwest in 1960 were overwhelmingly blue collar, more so than other white midwesterners or native white southerners. One in four migrants was an operative; slightly more migrants were involved in manual labor and service jobs (particularly women). A significant number of operatives were truck drivers; large numbers of migrant laborers were carpenters, foremen, machinists, and auto and machine repairmen; and many of the women migrants were cashiers, secretaries, telephone operators, domestic servants, hospital attendants, public cooks, and waitresses. Because the percentages in other categories, such as professional and technical, managers, and sales, were lower for southern white migrants than for either midwestern native whites or southern native whites, the great white migration was one predominantly of working-class people, or at least one in which people were intent on becoming working class and perhaps even middle class.

The data indicate that southerners were assuming blue-collar jobs that required little prior education; most jobs allowed migrants to be trained on the spot in just a few hours. Migrants to the Midwest appear to have had less education than either midwestern or southern natives had. Many more migrants terminated their education in the eighth grade, suggesting that migration may have occurred in place of education or because of lack of education.[58] In any case, midwestern jobs that southerners were filling did not require twelve years of education.

Finally, the IPUMS data also seem to discredit the notion that migration induced the breakup of southern families once in the North. For example, among midwestern white households in 1960, 17 percent were headed by women; among southern white migrant households in 1960, 13 percent were headed by women. Complex kinship networks and processes kept families together in spite of migrant families' sometimes difficult adjustment.[59]

Overall data from the peak years of the great white migration—1945 to 1960—suggest the volume and types of people involved, the ways kinship ties directed migrant decision making, and the extent to which migration economically improved their lives. Already by 1960, after only a little more than a decade of heavy settlement in the North, the economic status of southern white exiles was becoming indistinguishable from that of their blue-collar white midwestern neighbors. Memories of those involved in the exile confirm their growing characteristic of an "invisible minority," but migrant testimony also reveals the ways that southerners transplanted southern white culture in the Midwest, the focus of the following chapter.

Notes

1. Fields interview, 2.

2. Shepherd and Giles quoted in "Cocke County Boasts Scenery and Moonshine," mimeographed clipping (from *Harlan Daily Enterprise*), Urban Migrant Project, folder 3, box 278, Records of the Council of the Southern Mountains (hereafter CSM Collection), Southern Appalachian Archives, Hutchins Library, Berea College, Berea, Ky.; Tennessee Valley Authority, *Tennessee Valley Region,* n.p.; Norma Lee Browning, "Poverty Spurs Hill Folk on Road to North," *Chicago Daily Tribune,* May 11, 1957. For more on Cleveland's migrants, see Julian Krawcheck, "Smile When You Say 'Hillbilly!'" *Cleveland Press,* Jan. 29–Feb. 4, 1958.

3. James S. Brown, "Migration within, to, and from the Southern Appalachians, 1935–1939," 18, 20, Urban Migrant Project, folder 3, box 278, CSM Collection. For the original study, see Brown, "Social Organization of an Isolated Kentucky Mountain Neighborhood."

4. William Collins, "Your Neighbor!" clipping (from *Cincinnati Enquirer*), Migrants II folder, CSM Collection (quote); Roscoe Giffin, "Newcomers from the Southern Mountains," 3, Southern Appalachia—General, folder 8, box 3, Roscoe Giffin Collection, Southern Appalachian Archives; "Appalachian Workers in Columbus Surveyed," 37. For journalistic revisionism, see the series by Krawcheck, "Smile When You Say 'Hillbilly.'" There were exceptions, of course, particularly in Chicago, such as Norma Lee Browning's series on "Otter Hollow, Appalachia, U.S.A.," the first of which was printed in the *Chicago Daily Tribune* on May 5, 1957. The complete collection of articles is in Newspaper Clippings, folder 15, box 293, CSM Collection. See also one of the most notorious articles: Votaw, "Hillbillies Invade Chicago," 64–67. Not surprisingly, when the economic boom slowed in the 1960s, voices once again began to clamor about the migrant problem, a focus of chapter 7.

5. Drake, "Recession Is Far from Over in the Southern Mountains," 36–37; Chicago Commission on Human Relations, *1960 Annual Report of the Migration Services Department,* 3, 6 (quotation), Urban Migrant Project, folder 2, box 283, CSM Collection.

6. Lake View Newcomer Committee, *Summary of Visits to Southern White Families,* 4; Killian, *White Southerners,* 106.

7. Mary Ellen Wolfe, "Migrants Loyal, Easily Adjust to Jobs," *Dayton Journal Herald,* Feb. 26, 1960; Hundley, "Mountain Man in Northern Industry," 34–38.

8. Lacy interview.

9. Ibid.

10. Roberson interview; Weatherford interview.

11. Giffin, "Appalachian Newcomers to Cincinnati," 79–84; Philliber, *Appalachian Migrants in Urban America,* 89; Schwarzweller, "Occupational Patterns of Appalachian Migrants," 136; Roberson interview; Plemons and Collins interview, 22. James Gregory found "little reluctance" and "considerable enthusiasm for workplace organization" among "Okies" in California. See Gregory, *American Exodus,* 163.

12. Stroud interview; Giardina interview.

13. Daniels quoted in Browning, "Poverty Spurs Hill Folk on Road to North"; "Industry Comes, but Workers Quit Tennessee," clipping, Urban Migrant Project,

folder 3, box 278, CSM Collection; "'Bloody Harlan' Hit Hard by Strike," clipping, Urban Migrant Project, folder 3, box 278, CSM Collection; Krawcheck, "Smile When You Say 'Hillbilly'"; Julian Krawcheck, "Coal Industry Decline Sends Southerners Here," *Cleveland Press,* July 20, 1959; Schweiker, "Some Facts and a Theory of Migration." Many ex-miners, of course, also traveled to Chicago. See Chicago Fact Book Consortium, *Local Community Fact Book,* 6.

14. Brown, "Migration within, to, and from the Southern Appalachians," 10. Southern-born people constituted ever increasing percentages in midwestern states, including 12 percent of Ohio's total population, 11 percent of Indiana's, 10 percent of Michigan's, and 9 percent of Illinois's. See U.S. Bureau of the Census, *U.S. Census of Population: 1950,* vol. 4, *Special Reports,* part 4, chap. A, State of Birth, tables 4, 8, 9, and 14. See also U.S. Bureau of the Census, "Estimates of the Population of States and Selected Outlying Areas of the United States, July 1, 1957 and 1956."

15. James S. Brown and Paul D. Richardson, "Changes in Kentucky's Population by Counties: Natural Increase and Net Migration," 1–4, manuscript, Southern Appalachian Studies—Roscoe Giffin, folder 7, box 3, Faculty and Staff Collection, Berea College Archives; "Exodus from the Hills," *Hazard (Ky.) Herald,* Feb. 28, 1963; Jim Hampton, "Exodus," *Louisville Courier-Journal,* June 16, 1962; "Area Still Gets Steady Stream from South," *Dayton Journal Herald,* July 22, 1961; Mary Ellen Wolfe, "Daytonians Accept South's Migrants," *Dayton Journal Herald,* Feb. 22, 1960. For exact out-migration numbers, contact author.

16. U.S. Bureau of the Census, *U.S. Census of Population: 1960, Subject Reports, Mobility for State Economic Areas,* Final Report PC (2)-2B, tables 33–36; Donald Janson, "30,000 Hill People Now Cluster in Chicago," *New York Times,* Aug. 31, 1963; Killian, *White Southerners,* 103.

17. Morgan interview.

18. Ibid.

19. Ibid.

20. Ibid.

21. Ibid.

22. Ibid.

23. Ford interview.

24. Ibid.

25. Ibid. Anita continued to work after they moved to Milwaukee, first at Briggs and Stratton and later at Globe Union.

26. Ibid.

27. Crooks interview. Of those five years in Kentucky, Charis said, "I'm glad we brought the kids home to have five years of rural life. They had those when they were young. And I think that's very good. But I'm glad we went back to the city for them to get an education then. Schools I think are better up there, and I'm glad we did that." Ibid.

28. Ibid.

29. Brown, "Migration within, to, and from the Southern Appalachians," 10; U.S. Bureau of the Census, *U.S. Census of Population: 1950,* vol. 4, *Special Reports,* part 4, chap. A, State of Birth, tables 9, 14. Schools in urban areas with growing numbers of southerners also began acquiring majorities of children born in the South. In Lake View (Chicago), almost three-quarters of the children were born

in southern states in 1960. Columbus, Ohio, and Detroit also had sizable numbers of southern migrant children. See Lake View Citizens' Council, "The Southern White Migrant to Lake View," 4, Cities—Chicago, Ill., folder 2, box 283, CSM Collection; "Area Still Gets Steady Stream from South"; and Richard A. Anderson, "Detroit Population Mobility, as Reflected by School Census Data: 1949 to 1959," Workshops—Urban Migrant, folder 2, box 281, CSM Collection.

30. Southern Appalachian Studies, folder 6, box 3, Roscoe Giffin Collection.

31. A variant of the story is found in Montell, *Killings,* 130. See also J. R. Williams, "Appalachian Migrants in Cincinnati, Ohio," 127; and Worley, "Social Characteristics and Participation Patterns of Rural Migrants in an Industrial Community," 49.

32. Weatherford interview; Austin interview.

33. Babcock, *History of United States Rubber Company,* 158–59; R. G. Hudson quoted in Green interview; D. Montgomery, *Workers' Control in America,* 140; D. Nelson, *American Rubberworkers and Organized Labor, 1900–1941,* 90; Crowe, "Occupational Adaptation of a Selected Group of Eastern Kentuckians in Southern Ohio"; Morgan interview; Mayor's Friendly Relations Committee of Cincinnati, *When Cultures Meet,* 2; Ora Spaid, "Southerners Shuttle North, Back," *Louisville Courier-Journal,* Oct. 21, 1959; Flynt, *Dixie's Forgotten People,* 98; and J. Jones, *Dispossessed,* 243.

34. Thompson, "Industrialization in the Miami Valley," 19, 132–35, 148.

35. Shelby interview. See also Clive, *State of War.*

36. Thompson, "Industrialization in the Miami Valley," 13; Alexander, "Industrial Expansion in the United States, 1939–1947," 133. Up the Miami River, Montgomery and Greene counties, in the Dayton metropolitan area, grew at a 98 percent rate and not surprisingly attracted many southerners. Cincinnati grew at only 51 percent.

37. Thompson, "Industrialization in the Miami Valley," 109; Worley, "Social Characteristics and Participation Patterns of Rural Migrants in an Industrial Community," 50; McCoy, Brown, and Watkins, "Migration Stream System of Southwest Ohio and Its Relation to Southern Appalachian Migration."

38. Clardy interview.

39. Ibid.

40. Ibid.

41. Ibid.

42. Ward interview.

43. Alvin and Ruby Berry interview.

44. Ibid.

45. Ibid.

46. Ibid.

47. Plemons and Collins interview, 1–6, 19, 25, 44.

48. Ibid., 9–10.

49. Ibid., 32–33. According to the census in 1960, 63 percent of migrant white women were not in the labor force. 1960 Integrated Public Use Microdata Samples, One Percent Sample.

50. Plemons and Collins interview, 15, 28.

51. Morgan interview.

52. Pennington interview, Nov. 14, 1975, 2–3.

53. Ibid., 7–8. See J. Jones, *Dispossessed,* 216.

54. Keith, *Country People in the New South,* 211; Giardina interview.

55. Several data sets exist; the following data are from the Integrated Public Use Microdata Sample (IPUMS) compiled by the Social History Research Laboratory at the University of Minnesota. I thank Jim Palmieri for his assistance.

56. 1960 Integrated Public Use Microdata Sample: One Percent Sample. Percentages are more significant than actual numbers.

57. Ibid.

58. The percentages are 43.9 percent for migrants, contrasted with only 23.3 percent for midwesterners and 37.7 percent for southerners. Ibid.

59. Ibid.

6 *South by Midwest: Transplanted Southern White Culture*

> It was the thousands of Southern Baptists intermingled with these mobile multitudes that initiated Southern Baptist churches in every new area.
>
> —Robert A. Baker, *The Southern Baptist Convention and Its People, 1607–1972*

> There is a practice among recording companies, and those who are inclined to speak slightingly of the mountain songs, to call them Hilly Billy songs. When they say Hilly Billy songs they generally mean bum songs and jail songs. . . . [These] are not characteristic of mountain songs, and I hope . . . you will come to distinguish between these fine old folk songs of the mountains, and the so-called Hilly Billy songs.
>
> —Bradley Kincaid, Kentucky folksinger, 1930

WHITE UPLAND SOUTHERNERS who migrated northward, of course, left behind neither their way of life nor their cultural baggage. Even those migrants who were most "assimilated" never completely ceased to be, in some sense of the word, *southern.* Many more migrants, in the process of moving to northern communities where their welcome ranged from mildly friendly to openly hostile, fell back on the standards and values of their southern upbringing, which is not to imply that there was any one, monolithic southern white response to the perils experienced in moving to a new and different place. Indeed, there was tremendous diversity in the places from which migrants came (where the common push was poverty) and the responses that occurred in the North (where the common pull was work). In spite of the debates in the scholarly literature about whether, for example, Appalachian migrants constituted an ethnic group (since most social scientists have ignored the fact that whites from throughout the South left in massive numbers), there are some patterns that seem to be significant.[1]

In postmodern scholarship, readers are often reminded that regionalism is still an important element in American culture. The idea here is not to quibble about the levels of regional distinctiveness in the southern migrant experience but to highlight some patterns of that distinctiveness. One of the strongest indications that southern migrants called on their past once in the North (and hence demonstrated a type of minority group behavior) was group formation once in the North, as argued in chapter 5. There was another important component: cultural retention. Migrants from eastern Kentucky who moved to Chicago, for example, often stopped thinking in terms of a worldview based on their small communities. In the North, migrants expanded their concept of kith to include someone from the next county over in Kentucky who was working adjacent on the shop floor. Moreover, according to oral testimony, people from, say, Perry County, began seeing migrants from Arkansas as members of their community. In the face of prejudice and persecution in the Midwest, many southern white migrants began to see themselves as a *people* with a common history and a common ancestry—their diversity notwithstanding—and their responses after this recognition began to show common patterns of thought and behavior. Recall, for example, how Gertie Nevels in *The Dollmaker* nervously tells her child's principal, "My country is Kentucky." James N. Gregory, who studied Dust Bowl migrants to California, discovered a set of sociopolitical ideologies that he calls plain-folk Americanism. Being an Okie—or, for that matter, a white migrant from the South—was a matter of experiences, standards, and values.[2]

My grandfather, for example, who migrated to northern Indiana from middle Tennessee, loves nothing more than to come across a southerner in the North. To him, most southern migrants, whether they are from West Virginia or Georgia or Arkansas (Maryland probably does not figure in his definition), have something in common with him. Whenever he meets a southerner, he never fails to "test" the person with a question such as, "Do you know what a muscadine is?" If the answer is something like, "Lord yes. We went out and picked muscadines every summer, and it's a wonder we never got snake-bit, too . . . ," my grandfather knows that the person really *is* a southerner. He often follows up with a question such as, "When you were growing up did you get a lot of toys for Christmas?" If the response is, "Shoot no. We were lucky to get an orange for Christmas and were happier with that orange than kids are today who get all these toys . . . ," my grandfather has found a southerner whose experiences, standards, and values are much like his own.

In this chapter, I examine some of the cultural results of southern white migration to the Midwest. After a more general discussion of associational customs, I concentrate on two notables: religion and music. It should be clear, however, that some of the transplanted aspects of southern culture in the Midwest took on different characteristics, just as a transplanted plant will not necessarily grow the same in a different climate zone. Country music in the Midwest, for example, seems to be a new hybrid, although religion seems to maintain itself in ways largely unchanged by transplantation.

Plain Folk of the New North

Southerners who came to the Great Lakes states of Illinois, Indiana, Michigan, Ohio, and Wisconsin infrequently followed the political and associational paths of other immigrants to these states, such as the German, Irish, and Central Europeans, much to the apparent chagrin of many scholars who have bemoaned the absence of political activity among southern migrants. An article in *Time* magazine reported in the early 1960s that southern migrants "are the despair of law-enforcement, welfare, health and academic officials who try to help them become assimilated in the city." Unfortunately, there was no NAACP (National Association for the Advancement of Colored People) or Urban League or B'nai B'rith or Hibernian Society or Polish Workers Alliance to welcome southern newcomers or help them in times of need. Instead, smaller, more local organizations emerged in many cities. The Southern Club, organized in the mid-1950s by Jake Winslow, a barber who came to Chicago from Martin, Tennessee, in 1936, was much like a fraternal association for southern men. In 1959, the club had a mailing list of two thousand. "We try to help the Southern men find a job and a place to live," Winslow said. "And we try to get him in with decent people." Migrants from the South often did not end up as precinct committee chairs or as ward bosses or even as candidates for public office. One of the most important reasons for what many have labeled political apathy is that many migrants saw themselves as sojourners who were coming north long enough to make money and return south. Since those who stayed in the North generally moved out of port-of-entry neighborhoods as time went on, many migrants were not often together in one place. Others undoubtedly saw their new lives as successful and therefore believed political change was unnecessary, while still others came home after their shift and were too exhausted for political activity. But the impact of their migration northward was felt in other ways. In addition to participating in unions, some, such as Joe Clardy, were deeply involved in and committed to veterans' organizations, such as the Veterans of Foreign Wars and the American Legion, while others were active in fraternal organizations, such as the Eastern Star and the Masons. Many migrants—men and women—showed the most associational activity in the churches that they began creating after World War II.[3]

Many migrants' political involvement (or lack of) in the Midwest was consistent with what it had been in the South. As Daymon Morgan explained, many southerners did not think or talk much about politics in the South. Joyce Plemons recounted that she "really didn't know" about the political orientation of her neighbors "because really I didn't hear politics talked a lot when I was growing up." Her husband, Frank, agreed. "I didn't either. They voted and everything, but they didn't discuss politics an awful lot. You know, now they might have when it was like, Mom and Dad talking, but with us I didn't hear a lot." Frank did recall how his father, as a survivor of the Great Depression, would occasionally rail against Republicans. "The only thing I heard my father say, 'Republicans starve you to death.' He remembered back during the depression when Hoover was in and they were going to put a chick in every pot and all that, and he used to tell us boys when we was small, 'When you get big enough to vote, you better vote a Democrat.'" Frank, as a citizen, listened to his father's admonition. Asked if he had ever voted Republican, he replied, "No sir, which sometimes you put them in the same barrel and they all come out black. But to me, I still think that a Democrat is better for the working class of people. The Republicans don't want to give you nothing, I believe. They want to keep it all for theirselves. And I like to see people live and let live."[4]

Quietness, however, did not mean acquiescence, particularly given the nature of southern politics. Earl Cox, for example, was disgusted that in order to work in his north Georgia community, he would have "had to go through a damn lawyer-politician . . . that didn't know me from Adam" and pay him off for a recommendation that would lead to employment. Buddy Lee Ford was angry over having to go before a local bank president to get hired at a western Kentucky coal mine. Daymon Morgan also found the same practice repugnant in Leslie County, Kentucky. To get hired at a coal mine, you had to go to the county judge, who, for a promised vote presumably, would recommend your name. "I don't like these political cliques that they have in the county where it's kind of like one of these old-fashioned handkerchief games—you drop behind me and I'll drop behind you." Morgan, for one, helped Kentuckians for the Commonwealth sponsor candidate forums in which office-seekers responded to questions from members of the community, which, he said, has helped lessen the influence of county judges.[5]

Southern migrants did seem to have an impact on northern political culture, in much the same way that southwesterners influenced California culture. James Gregory saw in migrants to California a plain-folk Americanism that derived logically from southern plain-folk culture, a worldview common to many rural and working-class white southerners, as John Shelton Reed has shown. Gregory writes that southern white plain folk, since the days of the Farmers' Alliance through Huey Long, "responded best to shirt-sleeved campaigners who talked about the dignity of hard work and plain living and promised deliverance from the forces of power, privilege, and moral pollution, near and far."[6]

As former rural plain folk living in the urban North, southerners brought their worldviews with them. One of the elements of this worldview was honor, which a typical southern migrant—male or female—would go to great lengths to preserve. Don Edward Merten, who studied migrants in Chicago, found honor to be extremely important to them. My grandmother often came dangerously close to blows to preserve her family's honor—as well as that of southern white folk generally—in the North. Many other migrants did come to blows. As a young school-age migrant, Will Pennington would fight to the end to preserve his mother's reputation on the playground. Max Green remembered vividly the rowdy culture that southerners brought with them to Detroit in the 1940s, and his explanation reveals, on the one hand, a fear of the fighting but, on the other, a pride that was not easily trounced upon. "It was kind of a wild place with all the crazy hillbillies," Max recalled. "I never did go to them [honky-tonks]. I guess I was chicken or something, but a lot of guys would go to the big nightclubs. Hell, it wasn't nothing on a weekend to have fights. Guys would get cut up and everything else." All southerners, he said, "are known for the knife business. They all carry knives. They were known for that. They were rowdy." "Most of the hillbillies did not like Yankees to start with," he said revealingly. "We were true southerners even though we worked in Detroit. We still had to stick together even though we worked in Yankeeland and worked for Yankees, we didn't like Yankees. That's our heritage." On the weekends, he would go to a "local bar or something" owned by native whites but virtually the exclusive domain of southerners. "They just start gathering—the word gets around, you know. Country bands and that sort of thing. Most of them worked in the automobile business, but they had their band for the weekend or whatever. I didn't think that was a lot of fun: sitting around and drink beer and watch your back—afraid somebody was going to knock your head off." Many southerners, he said, "didn't have a successful weekend if they hadn't been in a brawl or two. I never did understand it. That wasn't a part of my makeup. I think I was too much of a coward or liked myself too well for that." Almost every city that hosted a sizable southern migrant population saw an increase in direct aggression crime, including fighting, but also less serious offenses, such as weapons charges, since some migrants apparently saw little difference in carrying their gun with them in the rural South and in the urban North.[7]

James Shelby explained why southerners acquired their reputation as drunken brawlers. "I'll tell you—you take a lot of the guys from down home that come up here from Savannah [Tennessee]. Savannah was always [in] a dry county, and they'd get up here and they wasn't used to drinking that beer and they'd get drunk on that beer and they'd get to wanting to fight." Florence, Alabama, the closest wet town from Hardin County, was fifty miles away, and even its county—Lauderdale—was dry. "See," he continued, "it was plentiful for them to go to a tavern to drink when they wasn't used to that there." Even young migrants that never touched bootleg whiskey would readily drink beer in the North. "They got away from their parents that didn't know they sipped a little now and then; they was away from there and they had their freedom and they could do what they wanted to without a lot of people knowing about it," Shelby noted.[8]

Southerners also brought with them a certain amount of toughness that gave them strength, identity, and a great deal of appeal to northern employers. Almost every migrant I have interviewed has said something to the effect that "southerners were not afraid of hard work, and that's why a factory would rather hire a southerner over anybody else." Max Green explained that "they liked us hillbillies because most of us would work, and didn't give them a lot of trouble compared to the native Detroit people. Hell, we went in and didn't give them the lip. They tell us to do something, we'd do it."[9]

But along with toughness, many southerners' worldviews included nativism and racism. Southerners who came north—like those who went to coal camps in the early twentieth century—often encountered resistance and prejudice from European immigrants, and the southern response was often one of Americanism—that southern whites were in fact more "American" than the Poles, Hungarians, and Italians, against whom they were often competing in the workplace. Many southerners interviewed would share their dislike (often *after* the tape recorder was turned off), even in the 1980s and 1990s, of several immigrant groups that teased and taunted them. Poles and Slovaks in Whiting, Indiana, Joyce Plemons said, in agreement with Earl Cox, who went to Detroit, "weren't friendly to people from the South" at all. She explained:

> And we rented from a Polish lady. She liked him [Frank, her husband], she didn't like me, you know. And she never said anything to him, but every time, when I'd go out the door she was always on to me about something. I left the light on (which we paid the light bill, but yet I left it on). And I would go down in the basement to do laundry, every time I went down I had done something.
>
> I just didn't do it right. I guess they had their ways and we had ours. But she never said anything to him, it was always me. And then when we rented the place she said, you know, she wanted no children, she didn't want any children. So when I got pregnant then of course we knew we would have to move, so we went down, or he did, to tell her, you know, and then she didn't want us to move. But we did anyway.

Those southerners who moved to such cities as Chicago, East Chicago, Hammond, South Bend, Detroit, Flint, and Cleveland frequently complained that Poles gave them the most trouble in the North. Although the southerner frequently thought of a Slovene, Slovak, or Hungarian as a Pole, the ill feelings between southerners and Poles were probably because Central Europeans had long experienced persecution. As the next wave of newcomers to the urban North, southern whites (along with African Americans and Mexicans) were next in line for prejudice. "I guess they felt like we were invading when we came," Joyce Plemons reasoned. "I don't mind being called a hillbilly. If that suits them, it's okay with me, because I think a lot of them have never been south and they don't know anything about the South. We've always been I guess classified as a low class of people, dirty—you know—a lot of times you see on television a little hut, you know, that sets on a hill, everything. And I guess that's what they think everybody is." Pauline Mayberry, who grew up in Tennessee, explained how in Detroit, "I had this one lady—she was my next-door neighbor—and I just think she was Polish. But she said to me one day, she said, 'You know, Pauline, you could go back to school and learn to speak better English if you wanted to.'" Mayberry explained laughingly, "I told her that I didn't think I needed to learn to speak any better English (cause I had the accent—that's what the reason that she said it)."[10]

Southern whites who migrated also brought the racism of their homeland with them. As early as 1943, just after the Detroit race riot, southern white migrants were blamed for the crisis that began at Belle Isle Park. In an editorial in the *Detroit News,* a writer opined:

> The present fracas is due to the fact that the immensity of the war work here has brought scores of thousands of people to Detroit who have encountered new conditions to which they apply old standards. Southern whites have come here in vast numbers, bringing with them their Jim Crow notions of the Negro. Southern Negroes have come here to take jobs which give them for the first time in the lives of many of them a decent wage, and a sense of freedom they have never known before. Some of them have become, in white opinion, too "uppity." The embers smoldered a long time, and at last a slight incident caused them to burst into flame.

Isaac Frank, a Detroit social worker, agreed: "There has been a large influx of southern white[s]. They are ignorant and hold traditional southern attitudes toward the Negroes. Socially . . . they are in great need for compensation—to look down upon other groups." "The Negroes," he concluded, "made a convenient target." If reports were true that white southerners convinced some employers to make them supervisors because they knew how to "handle" African Americans, then the resentment of blacks, who clearly and repeatedly lost out to southern whites in the northern workplace because of prejudice, would be even greater.[11]

Several southerners argued candidly that northern cities, such as Gary and Detroit, were nice cities until African Americans moved in. After Max Green was discharged from the army in January 1953, he chose not to go back to the job that was waiting for him at the Detroit Chrysler plant. "The work was fine," he said, "but I hated living in Detroit." He was unaccustomed to living among African Americans. "I wasn't used to that—even in Atlanta when I lived there and went to school in Atlanta. What colored people I saw were very few. At the time, maybe one family or two" were living in Blue Ridge when he was growing up. "I could've gone back [to Detroit] and gone to work after I got out of the service, but I just couldn't stand the thoughts of living in Detroit. They was really moving in then. This was in the early fifties." Detroit, he concluded, "was a terrible city—at least I thought it was. I just never did adapt to the city living by growing up in the country. There's just something about it that you're accustomed to."[12]

Evidence also suggests that southerners, at least those who came north before the 1960s, brought with them their independent spirit that resisted public aid. Daymon Morgan, who grew up in Leslie County, Kentucky, was still cool toward relief sixty years after its introduction: "Well, they [people in eastern Kentucky] had mixed feelings about it. There's a lot of people you know that didn't draw. Criticize or make fun of people that did. I guess it was all right. It helped a lot of people, but maybe some people that drawed it maybe didn't need it." Migrating southerners who were not successful on a particular trip north generally returned south instead of applying for relief, such as the Alabama man interviewed by a Cleveland journalist: "If I lost my job here, I'd head for Alabama first thing." Many migrants even kept their southern homes as an added measure of security in case of layoff, such as Elbert and Ellen Humphrey. Elbert, a former coal miner from Caryville, Tennessee, kept their nine-room home so that, in his words, "If I get hurt or laid off and can't pay rent here, we can always go back to Tennessee and have a place to stay." One former textile worker from Gastonia, North Carolina, who moved to Cleveland said, "All I ask is a steady job and a reasonable rent. Give me those things and I won't need anybody's help. I'll make out all right." Will Pennington spoke for many when he said his mother would never have taken welfare in Cincinnati because for her, like for many other southerners, it was a matter of pride:

> There is no way, even today, that they'll accept welfare in any form or fashion. As a matter of fact, she's like me or I'm like her. It burns you up to go to the food market and they ask you whether it's going to be cash or food stamps. I guess it's not a fault on the part of the people who are asking you—they got a job to do—but I think it just rakes her wrong. Because when she was working up here, I guess what rubbed a little salt into the wound, when we lived on Walnut Street there was a fellow who lived on the third floor (we lived on the second floor) and he was as able bodied as my mom was to work, but he lived on welfare and he used to laugh and make fun: You're a fool for working. You got three kids, why don't you go on welfare and you'll make more than you will working (and she would). She would have made more on welfare than she would working for thirty-five dollars a week, but she wouldn't do it. She said, No, no, what I get is going to be from me and not from somebody else. They're mine. I brought them into the world and I'm going to feed them. If they get what they need it's going to be me that provides for them. I'm not going to set back on my can and let somebody else provide for them. When we lived back there I don't remember anybody, anywhere, that I came into contact with that was on welfare. They shared things within the group, they didn't accept things from somebody outside. They just didn't do it.

A journalist interviewed a group of southern migrants for an early newspaper article on migrants in Cincinnati. One by one they were commenting on the hardships they were experiencing when a boy quipped, "You could always go on welfare." "Everybody laughed," the journalist wrote, "as if at some long-standing private joke." "'Yeah, but welfare don't pay your bills, do they?'" asked one migrant. Nonetheless, the stereotype and perhaps even the prevalence of southern migrants on welfare would increase in the 1960s as migrants kept coming after the economy contracted.[13]

The Church and the Saloon

Scholars of southern white culture have documented how alcohol and religion, two seemingly polarized elements in Protestant life, are so intimately connected. James Gregory, for example, notes how drinking in the South was often an act of defiance, but, he writes, "it was a kind of ritualized, guilt-ridden defiance which in the end reinforced the religious-based moral codes." Southern white men, especially young men, were almost expected to lead Augustinian life-styles based not so much on the pursuit of women but on the intake of alcohol, which, paradoxically, was one of the most deplorable yet forgivable of "sins" in southern society. This, Gregory continues, "was all part of growing up and the larger rhythm of sin and repentance that tied together this culture of moral opposites." Denise Giardina knew well the male culture in eastern Kentucky:

> I knew a kid in eastern Kentucky whose father was like a lay preacher kind of person, and this kid would go out and drink a case of beer a weekend. Every weekend. (He lived in the coal camp where I lived a couple years ago.) And I said he was on his way to being an alcoholic. And he said, "Oh, I'm not worried. My dad did this too. And when he was thirty he got converted. That's what I'm going to do. You get old enough, and you get saved, and then you stop doing it." I said, "What happens if you die before you get saved?" And he said, "Well, I'll go to hell then! But I'm just too young to get saved right now. I'm going to do this and I'm going to do that, you know, and eventually I'll get saved and settle down like he did, you know."[14]

Beer and liquor were part of the same society in which the blood of Christ, once represented as red wine, became re-symbolized as grape juice. Those who were religious knew those who were "wild," and vice versa; the hope was that eventually the latter would come around to the ways of the former.

In the South, religious-minded guardians of culture had managed to create a society in which there were many more opportunities to find religion than opportunities to find drink. Throughout the South, there were thousands of churches, and the majority of them were small, rural congregations that may have had no more than several families: belief was always more significant than attendance. Meanwhile, the crusade against alcoholic consumption was feverish in many areas. Even after the repeal of national Prohibition, evangelical Protestants in many areas invoked the local option plan that they knew would mean the continued prohibition of alcohol for decades to come.[15]

In the North, however, things were reversed. Southern migrants, particularly those in larger cities populated by ethnic groups whose cultural and even religious lives were rooted firmly in the freedom to consume alcohol, found a bar on virtually every street corner. As a critical mass of southerners—particularly single men and those whose wives or girlfriends were in the South waiting for the call to come north—developed in the cities, bars and nightclubs exclusively for southern whites began to emerge, such as the three bars in the 3000 block of Madison Street in Chicago—La Conga, the 3022 Club, and the Casanova—that advertised "LIVE HILLBILLY MUSIC" in neon signs; those near Uptown known as New Southern Inn, Jim's Country Place, and Mountain Tavern; or Cat's Corner in Dayton, Ohio. In midwestern cities, the tavern became the social substitute for the church. Pauline Mayberry remembered the availability of beer and liquor in the North: "It was awful when we first came. I don't know, the southern people, it seemed like all they did was drink up here. Just like if they had the money they had to drink. My [first] husband didn't have the money to drink down there [in the South] like he did up here. It wasn't available down there. They didn't have the beer gardens and things down there back then—it was all bootleg. And I guess when they come up here, and you could go to the grocery stores and buy it back then too up here. So I guess it was just convenient to them." "There was bars for anybody that wanted to go," Earl Cox said of Detroit. "They was a bunch of bars up there. And I enjoyed them on the weekends—during the week I worked. But the weekends, I spent a lot of time in the bars. And when I first went up there there was a place where a lot of people that didn't drink went dancing on the weekends. But it closed. They used to have big name bands come in." One of the freedoms that came with migration, of course, was the ability to consume liquor as one pleased. Cox recounted that "in the North, you can stand right on the sidewalk and drink a beer and there ain't nobody going to say nothing." This was very different from Blue Ridge, Georgia: "You could get out here on the sidewalk and start drinking a beer and they'll put you in jail," Cox declared.[16]

In spite of crusading southern preachers who were active in larger cities such as Detroit and Akron since the Great Depression, the southern Protestant evangelical church, which was the definer of morality in the South, was conspicuously absent in the North. This may have been another reason for more alcoholic consumption by southern migrants—men and women. Although the media probably exaggerated the stereotype of the beer- and whiskey-drinking, honky-tonk southern (male) migrant, there probably was a kernel of truth to the charges, particularly among newcomers.[17] In the postwar years, however, religious-minded southern migrants, having rejected the northern churches, scurried to transplant the southern church in the North, thereby changing the northern religious landscape.

In the South, of course, there were two types of patterns regarding churchgoing, patterns that would influence a migrant once in the North. One type of southern migrant seldom went to church in the South, or at least rarely went inside the church "house." Instead, this southerner stayed outside and talked, exchanging the spiritual for the purely social, or rejected religion completely. Once this type of migrant came north, he or she found very few social outlets of the variety that existed in the South. There was no "country store thing" in northern Indiana, John Weatherford said. "When I came here you went to a candy store they had in Mishawaka on the south side; that's where the younger people went. You went in the pool hall, you could set in there, [but] there was no place like swapping pocket knives here like there was in the South." Reuben Tune also missed the lack of social places. "The people that's born and raised here," he said of northern natives, "if he runs a station, whenever you pull up and get a tank of gas and you pay him, he'd just as soon you be on your way, where the southerner is not that way." "He had something to say to you and talk to you and carry on a conversation," he continued, "where the real true Indiana born-and-raised, they [are] just not gifted for that. That's one of the things that really got me. I was always used to hanging around this store, see, and you might go in there and talk—just drink a Coke or what have you." The nonchurchgoing type who did not drink alcohol had an even harder time socializing, since, along with the church, the other important social outlet for migrants, the tavern, was off-limits. In Mishawaka in the 1950s and 1960s, for example, the Blue Flame tavern was directly across the St. Joseph River from the Ball-Band, later Uniroyal, plant that was a magnet for southern job seekers. "At the time," said Reuben Tune, who did not drink, "that I lived over on Broadway on a Friday night I'd go by there and they'd have a bluegrass band about eleven o'clock and I'd get out of [work], and I'd be so homesick whenever I got home that I couldn't hardly stand it."[18] Plenty of other southerners, however, found themselves in midwestern taverns and honky-tonks trying to overcome the loneliness of migration.

Loneliness was not the only thing that drove men to bars. Some men were distressed about the changing social patterns within their own families. Southern culture was patriarchal. When rural families migrated northward to urban areas, the household situation changed. Women were in charge during the initial period of migration when men left families for weeks or months searching for a job in the North and while men were gone from the home for their eight- or ten-hour factory days. Once they came home, men accustomed to the openness of farm life had difficulty adjusting to the cramped surroundings of a small apartment. Women's adjustment was facilitated by conveniences they had often lacked in the South. Running water—cold and hot—meant no more backbreaking trips to the well or springhouse. A gas or electric stove made cooking easier, and instead of preserving food, a woman was able to go to the grocery and buy most of the items her family needed. Moreover, schoolchildren spent much of the day outside the home, further freeing a woman's day and allowing time for socializing with other southern women living in the same building or next door. As in migration to coal camps, migration to urban areas often made life easier and more pleasant for women, which may be a prime reason why many of the men interviewed were much more homesick than women. This change in men's lives may also, of course, have been another reason why tavern company became so popular.[19]

Jim Hensley's parents, who moved from Clover Bend, Arkansas, to Anderson, Indiana, in 1947, when Hensley was eleven, are a case in point. Hensley's mother got a job at National Tile along with her husband, and she enjoyed very much her new life in Anderson, Indiana. Hensley's father, however, was like many of the men interviewed who came northward. He did not like the northern life-style, and he may have seen his authority weakened after his wife became employed; he soon began longing for his Arkansas home. When Hensley's father was fired at National Tile for helping organize a union, the family returned to Arkansas. "My father," Hensley said, "he liked that area and that type [of] lifestyle better and my mother liked this one better, so we went back for about six months, and my older brother liked it better back there also." "But my mother, myself, and the three younger ones," he added, "we liked it here better. So, at the end of six months my mother told my father that we were coming back to Anderson, and [said] If you want to stay in Arkansas, why, you can stay, but we were going. So he came. And when we came back, why, they got different jobs. That's when he got on at the [New York Central] railroad and she got on at Ward Stilson Company, made clothing and this type of thing."[20]

The other group of southern migrants—those who were regular churchgoers—began looking for a church as soon as they had secured housing and perhaps before they even had a job. "Right away we began going to church, and you meet up with so many people there," explained Vera Lawson, a migrant from Tennessee to northern Indiana. These migrants had been churchgoers in the South, not only for spiritual fulfillment but also for social opportunities, as Mary Tune explained: "When you were growing up in the South at the time we did, church was really the only place you had to go. That's where you met your friends; well, you went to church for the good of it, you know, but that was the thing."[21]

Upon migrating, however, southerners accustomed to churchgoing found very different congregations in the Midwest. For example, those who went to the ubiquitous Southern Baptist church in the South were in for an awakening of the nonreligious sort when they entered churches belonging to the Northern Baptist Convention (NBC). Northern churches, particularly those in urban areas, were often of a higher social class than that of migrants and were more formal, with robed clergy and regular choirs that sang rehearsed anthems. The closely knit rural character of southern churches was often missing: no family atmosphere, no Sunday evening "meetings," no gospel "singings"—even the quarterlies were from a different publishing house and had a different perspective. Moreover, those migrants who in the South had been Sunday school superintendents, deacons, and teachers were doubtless denied or at least delayed in attaining such positions in northern churches. Northern Baptists seem to have made no significant attempt to welcome Southern Baptist newcomers. As one historian writes, "Somewhat like exiles of an earlier time, they hung their harps away and lamented that they could not sing the Lord's song in a strange land."[22]

The legacy of antebellum sectionalism that had spilled over into religion was not to be overcome among the Baptists, even one hundred years later, and the Southern and Northern Baptist conventions that, along with every major Protestant faith, had split in the 1850s, continued many years of competition, some of which was hostile. The Fortress Monroe agreement between the northern and southern conventions was finally signed in 1894. The NBC, in an offensive posture, was, in theory, not to go south of the Mason-Dixon line, and the Southern Baptist Convention (SBC), on the defensive, was to stay out of the North. Although comity agreements were never strictly followed, the 1894 agreement was reaffirmed in 1912. Denominational committees, however, could do little about the increasing number of Southern Baptists migrating north of the Ohio River after 1920. Suddenly, as the church historian Leon McBeth explained, "Northern Baptists had ample occasion to complain of southern encroachment upon their territory." Northern Baptists found themselves making the same complaints that Southern Baptists had voiced a half-century earlier. In 1944 and again in 1949, with the southern white exile (composed of many Southern Baptists, of course) not only continuing but growing to mammoth numbers, the SBC voted to disregard territorial limitations; in 1950, it held its national convention in Chicago, a significant policy switch. For its part, the NBC changed its name in 1950 to the American Baptist Convention, perhaps in a defensive yet purely symbolic exercise, since few NBC churches were being organized in the South anyway. Southern Baptist organization in the Midwest soon followed; state conventions, the ultimate recognition of Southern Baptist association, were organized in Ohio in 1954, in Michigan in 1957, and in Indiana in 1958. As the historian Tom Nettles writes, "In Ohio, Southern Baptists gained a foothold when southern people with Baptist convictions journeyed into the state. Michigan saw large numbers of Southerners converge upon its cities to find work during the periods of depression and war." These transplanted Baptists formed "missions," or proto-congregations, which eventually joined the Southern Baptist Convention. By the early 1960s, the fifty-two Southern Baptist churches in Dayton were sending aid to the poor in eastern Kentucky.[23]

The spread of Southern Baptist churches in the Midwest and the country as a whole was no doubt due to southerners wanting to create their own churches in their new communities. Jesse and Emma Martin were Southern Baptists in their native Butler County, Kentucky, and their religious experiences as migrants are revealing. Having been avid churchgoers, they were looking for an established church in Indianapolis to attend. When Jess first arrived in the early 1950s, he began attending the Garfield Baptist Church, a Northern Baptist church. The people, Jess said, were friendly, but the differences in style made him miss the small, Southern Baptist congregations he had always known. When the rest of the family arrived in Indianapolis, the children came down with the mumps, and then Emma became ill. For three weeks, Jess had to wait to attend church with his family. One Saturday, they were visiting with a friend from Kentucky who had been their neighbor but was also living in Indianapolis. "We went to see him," Jess said, "and [said] well, we was going to get started to church the next morning." "Well," his friend asked, "where're you going Jess?" "I imagine I'll go to Garfield Park," he answered, "I know that, I've been there." "Well Jess, they've got Southern Baptist churches here." "I said, 'They have?'" "Yeah," he said. Jess got out the newspaper intending to find the address of the Southern Baptist church but noticed that a new Southern Baptist "mission," or church, was forming the next morning. Eager to attend the new church, "we got up and we got all dolled up in the Sunday best, you know," Jess explained, "and drove around":

> We drove up at 1133 Gilbert. I stopped on the other side of the street, and she [Emma] said, "Let's go on to Garfield—that's somebody's house." Well, I started off going to Garfield, I guess. And something happened—I found myself going around the block and back again. She says, "Somebody lives there—that's somebody's house!" By that time the pastor drove up [and said] "Yeah, this is the place. Come on in!" If I'd a drove off before he got up (we was a little early—I always am early when I go to church or anywhere else as far as that's concerned), we'd never helped start Arlington Avenue.[24]

The house belonged to Carlton Oliver, who was originally from Glasgow, in south-central Kentucky. The minister was a cousin of Oliver's wife. Eventually, the members of the new church were able to rent a building on Madison Avenue, and they named their Southern Baptist church the Edgewood Baptist Church. A short time later, they bought a plot of land southeast of the city on Arlington Avenue and, all with volunteer labor (except for heating), built a new church: the Arlington Avenue Baptist Church. A migrant from Somerset, Kentucky, even donated the lumber for the new building. Jess remembered fondly one Thanksgiving when he and Oliver were at the church until 2 A.M. trying to put on a roof. The Martins were only one example of many southern migrants who transplanted their southern churches in the North. After their church was built, it seemed to cement the Martins—like many southern migrants—in the North.[25]

Not all southerners, of course, were comfortable in Southern Baptist churches. Other conservative Protestant evangelical congregations blossomed in the North after World War II. Many became avid supporters of transplanted southern evangelists, such as Rex Humbard and his Cathedral of Tomorrow, located near Akron. Others, however, formed smaller churches—Pentecostal, Holiness, and a host of other Baptist denominations, such as the General Baptists.

David L. Kimbrough, for example, in his study of snake handling among eastern Kentuckians, documented the religious expression of the Saylor family—originally from Straight Creek, Kentucky—in Fort Wayne,

Indiana. After having moved north with his parents in the 1950s, Arnold Saylor founded the Highway Holiness Church of God in Riverhaven, near Fort Wayne, in 1968, and, in Kimbrough's words, began preaching "snake handling the eastern Kentucky style" to what is now a 150-member congregation. Their snake handling elicited Hoosier hostility and stereotyping, so much so that Saylor organized his own school in 1991 for children of his congregation. In spite of such difficulties, Saylor, something of a religious patriarch, managed to transplant the mountain Holiness church—complete with snake handlings, foot washings, and annual homecomings—north of the Ohio River. "By keeping close ties with family and friends in the mountains," Kimbrough summarizes, "the Holiness churches in places like Fort Wayne have preserved their lay religion and heritage."[26]

Adolph and Jemae Lacy, after undergoing their own conversion, were instrumental in nurturing the General Baptist tradition in the Midwest. In 1949, Adolph and Jemae, who were originally from Arkansas, migrated to southwestern Michigan, where Adolph picked fruit and eventually landed a job in a factory. In 1952, they began attending a General Baptist church in Dowagiac, Michigan, which had been established several years earlier by "Uncle" Frank Shearer, who had moved to nearby St. Joseph, Michigan, from Arkansas in 1946. Neither Adolph nor Jemae had ever been churchgoers, but the pastor of the church was Lesley Henderson, someone Adolph knew well because they used to "drink and run around" together. Most of the congregation were from north-central and northeastern Arkansas. By 1957, Adolph, who had been one of nine "called" to preach from the congregation, was preaching at the Dowagiac church. Meanwhile, three General Baptist churches were forming nearby in St. Joseph County, Indiana—two in Mishawaka and one in Osceola. When one of the congregations in Mishawaka asked Adolph to be its minister, he and Jemae moved there on June 1, 1957. A man of God on Sunday, Adolph continued to be a man of Whirlpool through the week, until the following year when he was laid off in the recession. Jemae took her first factory job at Burcliff Industries, making electronic parts at a dollar an hour. She enjoyed her job and the many women who worked there. Adolph bounced between several jobs until one of the members of the congregation got him hired at Fabricated Steel in 1963 in South Bend. In 1979, he quit Fabricated to pursue "full-time pastoring."[27]

There were plenty of other "religious pioneers" who were converted and called to preach among those in the northern "wilderness." Olus Baldridge, from eastern Kentucky, for example, in only several minutes of audiotape encapsulated his religious experience in his life history.

Religious conversion, hard times, and migration are represented in what seems to be a classic story:

> I was born in this section within four or five miles of here in 1913 on September 3. I grew up here until I was nine or ten years old. Then we moved to Floyd County for thirty-four years. After the depression came I went to work when I was sixteen years old. I completed the eighth grade and I intended to continue my education. The depression came and made it so hard people just couldn't make it. That's all there was to it.
>
> Later on things opened up a little bit, and I had some pretty good jobs. I got married. I lived around here for quite a while. I thought I wanted to be an automobile mechanic so I started working in garages. Finally I felt the Lord was working with me. I know he has worked with several people on this earth. I prayed to the Lord and asked him to forgive me of my sins. Meantime, I was running the garage. After that I felt the Lord call me to preach.
>
> I have tried to carry out my faith as much as I can. I've went almost everywhere I have been called. I went to different sections. I went to Virginia and West Virginia. Finally I moved to Indiana and I preached up there. I went up to the northern part of Indiana and established a church [Old Regular Baptist] or two up there. I established one in the eastern part of Indiana and one in the northwestern part. We had three or four churches up there. I went to Ohio and visited churches over there which were just barely established. I made one trip to Washington state about church ministry. Then we came back to Indiana. I stayed and hurried up my ministry the best I could.
>
> After that I had a stroke, paralysis. I was knocked out for quite a while. My speech was very bad, rugged you might say. I had to overcome that. It gradually took about five or six years before I could speak good. After that we moved back here. I've been here ten or twelve years, and I carried out my last years [of] obligation as much as I could. Then after that I had blood trouble. I don't know what you call it. It was the same thing that caused my stroke, and I lost my leg. That has not kept me down too much yet. I've taken two trips to Indiana and two or three to Ohio. I went to Virginia and West Virginia a time or two. I try to do my ministerial duty as much as I can without using my legs. I guess that about covers it in a brief outline.[28]

Information on Protestant church membership in the United States indicates that the types of churches in which southerners would be comfortable were increasing; especially significant was the growing Protestant character of many northern ethnic cities dominated by Roman Catholicism. On November 5, 1951, eight southwestern Michigan Southern Baptist congregations met in Roseville and voted to form the Motor Cities Association of Southern Baptists in Michigan. Chicago in 1950 had nine SBC churches; just nine years later, there were more than seventy.

In the 1950s and 1960s, the fastest growing denomination in Ohio was Southern Baptist.[29] By 1971, an astonishing 169 Southern Baptist churches had been recorded in Michigan, 230 in Indiana, and 380 in Ohio. Illinois, with 893, had always had an active Southern Baptist tradition in the southern portions of the state; the first state convention was organized there in 1907. In twenty years, Southern Baptists had almost equaled their Northern Baptist rivals in Ohio and Michigan (again Illinois is different). Church membership data show the extraordinary gains the SBC made in two decades, particularly in Lake County, Indiana, and Macomb County, Michigan (where they exceeded Northern Baptists threefold); Berrien County, Michigan (twice as many); Butler County, Ohio (where Southern Baptists constituted 11 percent of total adherents compared with 5 percent for Northern Baptists), as well as in Franklin County (Columbus), Hamilton County (Cincinnati), and Lorain County in Ohio. In Detroit's Wayne County in 1971, there were thirty-three recorded Southern Baptist churches, with a total membership of almost twelve thousand. Many small congregations founded by and for southerners—from storefront churches in large cities to those meeting in the homes of migrants—were not necessarily included in the national surveys, perhaps by choice (some southerners resisted any and all kinds of national association) or simply by churchgoers' failure to complete a questionnaire, since in many smaller churches ministers were present only on Sundays. South Bend, Indiana, for example, in 1971 had three General Baptist churches that were almost exclusively attended by southern white migrants, yet they do not appear in national survey data.[30]

Those who have done research on transplanted southern churches in the Midwest have found that the congregations differed little from their southern counterparts. Generally, southern churchgoers in the Midwest, like those in the South, continued to have an emotional religious style ("Amen!" is frequently heard by men in the congregation to emphasize a song lyric or a preacher's point; other congregants liked to "shout") and to believe in the authority of the Bible, in judgment by God, in salvation by grace, and in a pietism that always forbade drinking, occasionally dancing, and sometimes even cosmetics. Earl Cunningham studied migrant religious concerns in Cleveland in the 1960s and found no widespread evidence of stereotypical sectlike attitudes, such as extreme fundamentalism. Most conservative southern churches, such as the Southern Baptists, were for the most part religious separatists in the North, as they were in the South; new midwestern congregations, for example, were not interested in ecumenical participation in the wider religious community. Instead, each congregation was the fundamental unit, a tiny island of southern exile culture surrounded by a sea of northern diversity. Some congregations, however, looked to the South for direction and activities, relying on ministers through diaspora movements and even hosting traveling singing quartets from the South.[31]

Southern migrants who created churches in the North not only changed the northern religious landscape but also had an impact on the religious lives of many southern migrants who had previously not attended church, such as the Lacys. Once opportunities in the Midwest for worshipping in a southern manner began to rival another common migrant pastime—drinking in taverns—some southerners who had not been churchgoers began attending these fledgling congregations, as southern migrants who had created churches in the North began evangelizing to fellow migrants to help fill church pews. Although some may have attended for spiritual reasons, the fellowship of meeting other southerners was undoubtedly attractive to otherwise homesick southerners. Church activities and socializing apparently bound the sojourning-prone migrants to the North because the churches, perhaps more than taverns, nurtured a more permanent type of bond, as the preacher Ledford Stults explained: "If you leave what has always been home for economic reasons, no matter how good the economy is, and how good it is for you in the area, if you don't reach out and get a hold of something else, you're just never going to be satisfied, and eventually most people are going to end up going back home. So that's what most people done, because they never put their roots into anything else."[32]

James Shelby, who had migrated from Hardin County, Tennessee, to Mishawaka in the late 1940s, articulated what he thought was a typical male migrant's life pattern: "I think the majority of the younger generation that came up here when I did, they didn't go to church. This more or less settled them down when they got married. And if they married a girl that their family went to church, that's how they got into going to church." Male leisure activity was replaced with a more family-based associational activity in these churches. Adolph Lacy, while reluctant to talk extensively about drinking, concurred, admitting that he "spent quite a bit of time in a bar the first couple of years. You could meet a lot of southerners there." As a young migrant, Lacy lived out the Augustinian role that cultural historians and anthropologists of southern life say was almost expected before their religious conversion. Lacy also believed that 75 percent of southerners did not go to church when they first arrived in the North; it was something they eventually joined out of homesickness and loneliness. Leon McBeth writes that "the socio-economic diaspora, not missionary programs, first transplanted Southern Baptists into non-southern areas." "Many Baptists," he continues, "do not like to acknowledge it, but the fact remains that in those areas their original ministry was mostly to displaced and disheartened Southerners. 'Dixie Clubs in the North' may be too harsh a description of these early southern churches, but they did provide a haven for lonely exiles."[33]

Religious life, then, once southerners managed to transplant it to the North, became one of the most common associational outlets for southern men and women. Although southern white migrants are said to be the "invisible minority," this hardly seems the case; if one looks in any midwestern urban yellow-page listing for southern Protestant churches, one finds evidence of plenty of migrants. These churches also kept migrants in the North; indeed, even when retirement neared in the 1970s and 1980s, some migrants refused to return to the South because they wanted to stay near their family and friends at church. Men socialized before and after services in parking lots; women, through their auxiliaries, helped raise money for the congregation through quilting parties and the like; and all members joined together for the numerous church dinners of fried chicken, biscuits and cornbread, green beans and salt pork, chicken and dumplings, and red velvet cakes.[34]

Music of and for the Migrants

Long before southerners in the North helped create what has come to be known as country and western music, the music of the American South was formed by migrants. In the Upland South, migrants from different areas with different tastes in music were creating new sounds in new cultural borderlands. Railroad and mining camps were especially important in bringing the white folk tradition in contact with African American work and social music. But others had a hand in this creation—even traveling circuses and quacks. As the folklorist D. K. Wilgus notes, "Loggers brought in music; young natives rafted logs to cities and brought back music." In a culture typified by the extremes of, in Wilgus's words, "sobriety and drunkenness, piety and hellraising, daily stoicism and orgiastic religious revivals," sacred music would have a great influence on the new secular music that was forming by the late nineteenth century. By World War I, there were "hillbilly" musicians who were roaming throughout the southern diaspora—which stretched from Florida to Ohio, Indiana, and Illinois—playing their music to white audiences. The notion that southern "folk" musicians were living in isolation (as were, so the perception went, their southern Appalachian counterparts who migrated to northern cities) dies hard; hillbilly performers, Wilgus writes, had had experiences that ranged from railroads and coal mines to northern industries and western oil fields. "They were musicians looking for audiences, paying audiences," he explains. "The acceptance of music as a career for a healthy adult—a violation of folk taboo—is but one of the tensions of the urban hillbilly."[35]

Discussion of the diffusion of hillbilly music and southern migrants in the twentieth century often centers on chicken and egg scenarios. Most agree that there were plenty of ears well north of the Ohio River eager for the new sound of hillbilly music. But as hundreds of thousands of southern whites flowed into the North, there were even more ears, and music lyrics, as the rest of this chapter details, began reflecting the experiences of southern white transplants in midwestern areas.[36]

The barn dance was the key to propagating a southern sound in the North. The first successful radio barn dance began in 1924 in, of all places, Chicago at WLS. Although it included, almost by accident, a strong dose of Kentucky style and sound, the program featured mainly a hillbilly-rural sound, since the key to early success was based on not only the horde of southern whites in the North who tuned in but also the wide appeal to countless rural midwesterners who were within WLS's extensive reach. "We must admit," writes Wilgus, "that the early fare of WLS was 'bland' compared with many of the southern recordings and that the few national hits in the 1920s were not strictly 'southern.'" Migration had helped create a new music style in the South, and migration northward had refined the new sound.[37]

WLS is an interesting example of the new sound. Although the first program that aired on the *National Barn Dance* included a group of country-style fiddlers and was followed during the next week with hundreds of letters requesting fiddle tunes, throughout the next decades the *National Barn Dance* became less hillbilly just as more southerners were entering Chicago. Three groups made up the components of the program's loyal audience: city folk, who always formed block-long lines waiting to get into one of two tapings at the Eighth Street Theater; rural midwesterners, who, with a radio ownership rate higher than the national average in 1930, tuned in each Saturday night for "down home" entertainment sponsored by the likes of Red Brand farm fence, Murphy's feed and seed corn, and Warp Brothers' flexible glass for chicken coops and barns; and, of course, the thousands of transplanted southern whites, including not only those in Chicago and northwestern Indiana but also those who doubtless tuned in in such cities as South Bend, Indianapolis, Detroit, and Dayton. The *National Barn Dance* producers, however, chose what they called "uptown hillbilly" over the more southern "hungry hillbilly" style and sound. Jethro, a member of the cast in the 1950s, explained that the northern style favored "educated hillbilly." "You can educate this Northern audience to anything," he said, "but you can't change the Southern audience." Other members of the cast were hardly hillbilly themselves, a pattern dating back to at least 1932, and by the 1940s and 1950s the cast already epitomized commercialized country-western packaging. Bob Atcher, the "top hand of the cowhands," was born in Hardin County, Kentucky, but got his radio experience among "educated hillbillies" at the University of Kentucky's radio station. He also spent more time at his father's North Dakota ranch than in Kentucky. Scarcely a reflection of the southern job-seeking migrant, his embroidered shirts and pants cost $250 each. Lulu Belle and Scotty were genuine North Carolinians, but Scotty in the 1950s had earned a master's degree in English; Red Blanchard, from Wisconsin, was the show's "Texas Yodeler." Woody Mercer came to Chicago via Phoenix, the University of Arizona, and a successful law practice because he wanted to pursue his true love: singing cowboy songs. Finally, the square dance caller, John Dolce, hailed from Palermo, Italy.[38]

The Chicago *National Barn Dance* differed significantly from the more southern—yet still very much commercialized—*Grand Ole Opry;* its success was due to its hybridization of hillbilly with popular music, seen and heard by a rural but not necessarily southern audience. Yet it is important not to discount the presence of a sizable number of southerners in Chicago having at least some kind of influence on the WLS producers. In Des Moines, Iowa, a city with virtually no southerners, fifty-thousand watt WHO began its *Iowa Barn Dance Frolic* in 1932, and its character was markedly less southern and more rural midwestern than the format at WLS. Timothy Patterson, in discussing midwestern radio barn dances, placed the early barn dances on a spectrum identified by their "southernness": from WSB/WBAP (Atlanta), as the most southern, to WSM (Nashville), WLS, and WHO.[39]

Southern migrants had an impact on music in the North in less visible ways. One of the most famous southern musicians of all time, Bill Monroe, got his start as a migrant musician in Hammond, Indiana. Born in 1911 in western Kentucky, where, he said, music was one of life's few enjoyments and therefore a *way* of life, he found himself alone after his parents died in the late 1920s. "It was kindly sad there, you know, after my folks had passed away—my father and mother," he said.

> But I was raised on the farm, and I liked that kind of work, and I liked to live there. So, I'd never been in the cities, you see, and I didn't know what it would be like. I was really scared of it. But there were a lot of country

> people there, of course. A lot of them wanted to get off the farm, you know, because that was hard work, and they wanted to come into the city, where they'd make so much each week. My brothers, they was already up North, and they was moving from Detroit down to Indiana, and they all wanted me to come up there, so I decided to go.

Like many other factory-working southerners, Monroe got his first "break" from the new opportunities for weekend musicians. "We got on some stations up there in the northern part of Indiana," Bill continued. "The Monroe Brothers, you know, Charlie and me, worked hard at it as a duet, you see. Our first station we went on was WAE in Hammond in 1930." From there, they went to Gary's WJKS—call letters that stood for WHERE JOY KILLS SORROW, showing the close proximity in the early years of the sacred and the secular. After Gary, the Monroe Brothers were a hit, and they eventually made it to the *Grand Ole Opry.* Monroe's new music—bluegrass, according to the film *High Lonesome*—a blend of sacred and secular, urban and rural, hill and ragtime, sentimental and blue, may have been born in the South, but it was nurtured in the North.[40]

Southern white migrants living in Chicago and other places knew where to find the songs in the style of those heard in the South, for they blared from jukeboxes and from their taverns and nightclubs. The ABC Music Service Corporation, for example, was Chicago's largest jukebox operator in the 1950s. Of twelve different "routes" of jukebox service people, two used predominantly country and western records. One was in the Uptown neighborhood, which after the war had become the most popular port of entry for southern white newcomers; the other was between California and Kedzie streets. Moreover, Hudson-Ross, the largest record chain in the city, reported that in the 1950s Wil-Ken Music store at Wilson and Kenmore, in the heart of Uptown, sold 30 percent of its volume in country and western records, compared with 2 percent citywide. Explained George Topper, the store's owner, "This area is loaded with Southerners. They come up here to get factory and construction jobs at higher pay. They come to this neighborhood until they get settled permanently. Wherever you find furnished rooms and low priced hotels, you find country-and-western music." Topper added that the recession in 1954 stifled new jobs. "A lot of my customers come in to say good-bye. They're going back south to help Dad put in the crops. If conditions pick up, they'll come back." Joe Sipiora, who owned a wholesale record business for jukebox owners, explained, "Wherever transient populations exist, we sell a lot of C&W records." His volume was highest in the Uptown neighborhood, but he noted that other strong markets existed in Rockford, Illinois, and in Gary, Hammond, East Chicago, and South Bend, Indiana.[41]

By 1940, hillbilly—now increasingly known as country and western music because of the pejorative nature of the word *hillbilly*—was poised to become one of the country's most popular styles of music. Shapers had carefully melded a rural image with working-class appeal; southern migrants were particularly attracted to this new style because they, of course, were previously rural and currently working class. Country music made its most impressive gains during World War II. The extraordinary number of southerners who moved out of the South as well as the wartime economic boom were two major reasons: southerners who had an ear for this new music moved to urban areas, and wartime jobs gave fans enough money to support the music industry. D. K. Wilgus also notes that country music became the standard music after people in the armed forces with different musical tastes were integrated. A GI "could not always silence a company radio tuned to the armed forces network," he writes, nor could a soldier "always silence the guitar of the boy on the next bunk." Country music, which had long been shaped by varieties of urban music, not only survived the upheaval of the war years but also grew stronger, appealing to the emotional temper of the time with such songs as "I'll Be Back in a Year, Little Darlin.'"[42]

After the war, country and western music searched for stars, resulting in the Tin Pan Alley of country music. The growth of AM radio was largely responsible. In the mid-1950s, when barn dance programs were declining (only the *Grand Ole Opry*, the *National Barn Dance*, and the *WWVA Jamboree* were still on the air), all–country music radio stations began supplanting older formats. By 1971, there were 525 such stations across the country, making up 12.3 percent of all AM stations. By 1974, there were 856 all-country stations, 20 percent of all AM stations. As a testimony to the number of southern migrants, California, Washington, Indiana, Illinois, and Michigan led the states outside the South in the number of new stations devoted entirely to country music.[43]

Home Folks Think I'm Big in Detroit City

To the nonaficionado and especially to the academic critic, the lyrics in country music may be known more for their sentimental simplicity than anything else. But to the southerner hearing them away from home, whether in Chicago's Uptown, Detroit's Hamtramck, Cincinnati's Lower Price Hill, or, for that matter, Korea in the 1950s, the songs hit home. Even though country music songwriters (who were not necessarily southerners) were producing songs they hoped would appeal to migrant ears and thus become commercial hits, D. K. Wilgus says more than anything else, songs had to be meaningful. Because of a new environment, songs about mules and farms transformed into songs about trucks and factories; farms, especially, were relegated to sacred corners of songwriters' memories. As time passed and as more southerners moved to the North, the songs included more anti-urban themes and became even more nostalgic, with references to mom and dad, the old homeplace, and a way of life that no longer was. The music of migration was thus both old and new. To a migrant struggling to overcome aching loneliness as well as trying to obtain the jobs and the wages in the North that were beyond reach in the South, country music was clearly the voice—commercialism notwithstanding—of southern migrant subculture.[44]

Those who were separated from their roots predominated in the lyrics of country music, and many songs detailed the comfort, security, and love that were key memories of home. One of the early songs that epitomized homesickness was "Daddy and Home," sung by Jimmie Rodgers. The song was written by Rodgers and his sister-in-law late in 1928 as the two were en route to a recording session in New York, but it later became the classic song of homesickness. John Lair, originally from Kentucky, was a musical director at WLS when he "went home on vacation and was so depressed by the changes that, upon my return, I put it all into this song." "The more I heard it sung," he said, "the more homesick I got, and the more determined I became to go back and make it more like it had been in my boyhood."[45] The first result of this homesickness was "Take Me Back to the Renfro Valley"; the second was the *Renfro Valley Barn Dance,* in many ways the *Grand Ole Opry* of Kentucky. Lair's lyrics deal with the common theme of days gone by, further conditioned by distance.

Gene Autry's "That Silver-Haired Daddy of Mine," which was Autry's first million-record seller, would have struck a chord for migrants who had missed out on the last years of their parents' lives. The last stanza of the song deals openly with death and a troublesome child's guilt after his mother died and death seems imminent for his father. Another song that doubtless made many migrants from the southern Appalachians think about leaving the North for home was Carson Robison's "Carry Me Back to the Mountains," in which the singer longs for the mountains of home and his sweetheart, whom he left because he was "a wild, careless youngster" who had wanderlust from the beginning. After he received a letter that "told me my sweetheart had died," guilt is added to homesickness, a potent combination.[46]

In many of the songs that deal with parents and home, guilt is often as common as loneliness. Even though rural poverty frequently forced migrants to go north to seek a better livelihood, many still felt the guilt of leaving family—particularly aged parents—behind. This is one of the strongest manifestations of the divided heart. Nellie Austin cried all the way from Waterloo, Alabama, to Nashville, Tennessee, each time she and her husband drove away from home, heading for South Bend. Joyce Plemons dearly missed her parents in the South. Ruby Berry felt terrible guilt for leaving her widower father behind in Tennessee, and after his death her siblings, she believed, slighted her when it came time to divide her parents' possessions, because, they maintained, she was up north while they were taking care of her father. Songwriters also felt guilty for leaving home to seek fame, and writing a song for Ma or Pa may have eased the guilt of forsaking their parents. Tom T. Hall's "Homecoming" is a perfect example, a song about a son who tells his father he's sorry for not writing and who tries to explain what he does for a living as a musician ("No, we don't ever call them beer joints," the singer explains, nightclubs are the preferred name for his place of employment). Guilt is brought to an extreme in Curley Putnam Jr.'s "Green, Green Grass of Home" when the singer realizes that the fond memories of home are only a dream. Other songs expressed longings not only for parents and mountains but actually for childhood homes, many of them, of course, log cabins. B. L. Shook had his Mississippi boyhood cabin in mind when he wrote "Cabin on the Hill," but the song's motifs of a cabin standing on a hill beneath a shade tree were universal across the South.[47]

One of the classic songs of the migrant experience, however, is Danny Dill and Mel Tillis's "Detroit City," which touches on the guilt of foolish pride. Danny Dill, when asked about the song, explained its real-life origins:

> About three years before we wrote this, I played a little old club in Detroit—me and Annie Lou—and I saw these people that are in this song. They did go North. When I was a kid, they'd say, "Where's John now?" "Well, he's gone off up to De-troit." I sat there and talked to these people. They were from Alabama, West Tennessee, Kentucky, and they'd go to Detroit to work in the car factories. Now, they had more cash money in their pockets than they'd ever seen in their lives, but they were homesick. And to keep from being so lonely, they'd go sit in a bar and drink. And when they did get home, they'd get home with no money. . . . They wanted to go home all the time. They'd think they were rich, but they'd spend it. Then, eventually, they'd dovetail and catch that Southbound freight and ride back home where they came from.[48]

The epitome of the southern migrant classic admitted:

Home folks think I'm big in Detroit City
From the letters that I write they think I'm fine
But by day I make the cars, by night I make the bars
If only they could read between the lines.[49]

All of these songs were performed by big-name country artists in the commercial world. Some of the more popular songs, such as "Detroit City," have been sung by several artists. Even though the songs doubtless spoke to thousands of migrants in the North, they were not necessarily written by migrants or created out of the migrant experience. *South on 23,* an album by Curly Dan, Wilma Ann, and the Danville Mountain Boys, however, is significant because it was. The songs were all written by Wilma Ann Holcomb, who, along with her husband Curly Dan, left Clay, West Virginia, for the factories of Detroit, Michigan, in the 1950s. Their success on Homestead Records, a southeastern Michigan label founded by John Morris, himself a Kentucky migrant, owes to both the local success of smaller country and bluegrass musicians and the migration of southern music northward. Their first album, *Sleep Darling,* was recorded in 1956, and "My Little Rose" was number one on the "tri-state" (Indiana, Ohio, and Michigan) country charts for eight weeks. As part-time musicians, the Holcombs held on more tightly to the more traditional, bluegrasslike sound than most Nashville recordings did. *South on 23* was cut in 1973 and in many ways is the classic country music album produced by migrants for migrants.[50]

Songs from *South on 23* deal with leitmotifs of southern migrant culture: lost lovers, adultery, truck driving (which the 1960 microdata census samples prove was a popular migrant occupation), mother and dad, migration, homeplaces, eschatology, and taverns. Songs about the hereafter and taverns (and the inevitable sorrow over a broken relationship) in particular reflect the dualities with which many migrants struggled. For example, in "Mixed Up Life," the singer apologizes for cheating on his lover and, while drowning his sorrows in taverns, wonders how many others have lives as "mixed up" as his: "Pretend that I'm happy / And everything is just fine / I wonder just how many lives are mixed up like mine?" In "Drink Up and Go," the singer has spent the night "in this tavern / Just crying the blues in my beer," while "The couples around me are dancing / Oh Lord how I wish you were here." The singer admits that "I'll make it all right when I'm working," but "Tonight I'll be back in some tavern / Just crying the blues in my beer."[51]

Tavern and "cheatin' songs" are in stark contrast to those with religious themes in which the singers yearn for the heavenly hereafter. In "I Want to Live in Glory," the singers implore the listener to "Make things right with your Jesus," since "While living in this world of sorrow / And you find no peace within." The refrain speaks of returning not to one's southern home but to a heavenly one with which migrants were no doubt familiar. In "Family Altar," the Holcombs give advice to migrants who were struggling with life:

> There's many little children that's raised in homes today
> That never seen a Bible or heard their parents pray
> If they go wrong in later years they'll be the one to blame
> Just learn then now together at the family altar prayer.[52]

But it is the songs about Detroit that are particularly revealing about the migration experience. "Up in Detroit City" captures the variety of jobs that wandering migrants held before they settled on a particular place:

> I remember when I come to Detroit City
> Back in the year of '52
> Went up to the man and asked him for a job
> He looked at me and said, What can you do?
>
> I been in every state in the Union
> Some of them two or three times
> Dressed tools on an oil rig and chopped cotton in Mississippi
> I've even loaded coal down in the mines

Interestingly, the singer notes that although the wandering has paid off—suburban, working-class life has been attained after two decades in Detroit—still the hills and the freedom there are missed, the classic divided heart:

> Went to work in an automobile factory
> Detroit, the city of wheels
> Now I live a quiet suburban life
> Still miss the deep rolling hills
>
> I've been in every town, every city
> For I was born free as the wind
> I've been here going on twenty years
> Don't I wish I could turn the time back again.

Homesickness and memories of parents send the singer in "South on 23" heading back to the West Virginia homeplace on the main north-south artery between Flint, Ypsilanti, Columbus, and the Big Sandy Valley of Kentucky and West Virginia. Hundreds of thousands of migrants in the North began their sojourning on U.S. 23:

Down in West Virginia near the little town of Clay
Nestled in the shade of the pines
I know my dad and mom with open arms will welcome me
I'm heading south tonight on 23

You can hear the old folks singing
You can hear the banjos ringing
I'm heading south tonight on 23

There's a little homestead natural there among the trees
You smell the honeysuckle in the breeze
And the birds sing so gaily to a lovely melody
I'm heading south tonight on 23

Realizing that his parents will not be around much longer makes the migrant more eager to get back:

Someday the Lord will call them to their home beyond the sky
The homestead won't be the same to me
As they ride that big highway made of gold up in the sky
It'll be like going south on 23.[53]

One of the biggest fears and deepest sources of guilt for migrants was missing the funeral of a family member; even being gone and coming back to see the changes in the home brought guilt and homesickness to many migrants. "The Home Still Stands on the Hill" epitomizes that guilt. As a migrant of "only seventeen" from "down in the hills of Tennessee," the singer "left Mother and Dad and the friends that I had" "to stake out my claim." But on a visit to the "house that still stands on the hill," the singer regrets the years that "swiftly flew," and later, "forgetting the ones I left behind / Today the letter that came put me to shame / Said Mother and Dad had done been gone." In "A Visit Back Home," the singer reflects on his life in the South and the years that took him away, painfully seeing the changes that have occurred:

Well I just came back from a visit down home
The coal mines was all closed down
And the coal camps where I stayed when I was just a boy
Now is just an old ghost town
And my old flame, Molly
She was married to a little guy we called Pee Wee
But the things that I seen on the old homeplace
Left me with a sad memory
I took a stroll down by the family cemetery
And two new graves had been added there
On Dad's it said, Rest in Peace

And on Mama's, there was a prayer
Oh I know they waited, thinking that I'd be back
But I was gone, too long, you see
But the light was still shining out the front-room window
Just like they left it for me
And on the front porch was Mama's old rocking chair
And I could see her as she'd rocked every day
And down by the barn was a pitchfork and a wagon
That Dad used when he'd haul in his hay
And in the parlor set Mama's old spinning wheel
Setting there to be used no more
And there was an old faded-out sunbonnet
She'd left on a peg behind the door.[54]

County songs spoke to migrants in deep and meaningful ways, but occasionally, migrants themselves communicated to those who played the songs that touched their lives. In 1974, William Lynwood Montell and Atelia Clarkson published an article about letters written to John Morris, host of a four-hour Saturday afternoon radio program of bluegrass, gospel, and mountain music at WNRS/WNRZ in Ann Arbor and Saline, Michigan. Himself a migrant from Breathitt County, Kentucky, who was trained as a pharmacist, Morris was a southern music buff who founded the Old Homestead Recording Company in southeastern Michigan, a regional label for the music of transplanted southerners. Montell and Clarkson point out that the "eight A&P grocery sacks full of letters" collected over ten years were not only an indication of traditional music's importance in migrants' lives but also "a concrete demonstration of the old-timey radio program evoking sentiment and nostalgia" from a culture that was essentially oral. Throughout the four hours of airtime each week, migrants found a personal connection in the North that evoked down-home social relationships; the phone rang constantly as listeners called in to request a favorite but obscure song for their birthday or anniversary, and listeners drove to the station to bring Morris cookies, blueberry cobblers, and homemade preserves to show their appreciation. Others wrote in hesitantly to invite themselves into the station: "If it's OK with you, we would like to stop by the radio station to meet you. We won't have much time, but we can at least say hello. I don't know if there are any rules against coming to the station or not. I guess it would be about five o'clock." At the end of the four hours, the authors observed, one "has the feeling of having witnessed an important cultural and traditional event."[55]

Memories were evoked each time migrants tuned in to Morris's show:

> Hello John Morris—I thought I'd drop you a line to let you know I really enjoy your program. I'm an old Kentuckian, Murray, Kentucky, Calloway County. I've been in Michigan since 1937. But as a boy *at home* I used to buy all of the Carter Family and Jimmie Rodgers records, and I love to hear them all again after so long.
>
> Dear friend: Will drop you a few lines to let you know I still listen to your program every Saturday and think it is great—*one Hill Billie to another. ha ha.* Shore is good to hear your voice. Hope to meet you some day.

One listener wrote that he was "on the verge of tears and about ready to shout some" after listening to Brother Tommy Crank's singing on the program. Listening to his songs recalled memories of home and religion in Arkansas: "I could almost see my Mama's reaction if she could just hear Brother Tommy's singing back up there in the Ozark mountains, in Batesville, Arkansas, my hometown. She would probably just about tear up the kitchen shouting and that little bun of hair rolled up on the back of her head would probably be unrolled down to the waist before you'd know it . . . I just love the way Brother Tommy puts all of his feelings into his singing, and I will welcome the privilege to set in one of his services if I ever get the chance."[56]

Country music, then, including bluegrass and gospel music, was one of the most visible symbols of southern migrant culture in the North. While country music was not always created exclusively by and for southern migrants, their presence in the North profoundly influenced the messages and the medium. Commercial songwriters knew they had a guaranteed audience for songs that celebrated mother and dad, home, and the romantic view of the way things used to be. Even the southerners who tuned in to John Morris's radio program had influence, both on what he played over the radio and to whom he gave a record contract. Listeners like Morris's—throughout the Midwest—appreciated local migrant talent, whether they performed a honky-tonk song at a "hillbilly beer joint" or sang four-part harmony as a gospel group at a Sunday evening service of a Southern Baptist church.

Southern migrants seem to be not so much an invisible minority as a visible one. They were hardly meek migrants who encountered a host population and left it unaffected. Whether it was through their shop-floor life or their associational, religious, or musical activity, the culture they brought with them was visible and pronounced.

Notes

A version of this chapter appeared in the *Register of the Kentucky Historical Society* 94 (Summer 1996): 265–96.

1. See, for example, Myadze, "Rethinking Urban Appalachian Ethnicity," 243–52; Tucker, "Toward a New Ethnicity," 225–47; Killian, *White Southerners;* Reed, *Enduring South;* Reed, *Southern Folk, Plain and Fancy;* Merten, "Up Here and Down Home"; Philliber, *Appalachian Migrants in Urban America;* and Ford, ed., *Southern Appalachian Region.*

2. Arnow, *Dollmaker,* 183; Gregory, *American Exodus,* 140–41. Gregory's work has been very influential in the writing of this chapter.

3. "Okies of the '60s," 31; Schwarzweller, "Parental Family Ties and Social Integration of Rural to Urban Migrants," 410–16; J. Jones, *Dispossessed,* 257; Sam S. King, "Southern Whites Too Proud to Ask Help Here," *Chicago Daily News,* Aug. 13, 1959 (Winslow quote). See also Julian Krawcheck, "Southern Whites Ask Only a Job, Fair Rent," Newspaper Clippings, folder 15, box 293, Records of the Council of the Southern Mountains (hereafter CSM Collection), Southern Appalachian Archives, Hutchins Library, Berea College, Berea, Ky. Part of the problem is that many sociologists have described the experiences of southerners who came to northern urban ghettos and remained poor, never escaping the grip of poverty, as the essence of southern white migration. As my study shows, white migrants came to the Midwest from all areas of the South—not just from the southern Appalachians—and most saw their migration as a successful economic move, allowing them access to the northern working class. I discuss this more in chapter 7.

4. Plemons and Collins interview, 18.

5. Cox interview; Ford interview; Morgan interview.

6. Gregory, *American Exodus,* 141–42; Reed, *Southern Folk, Plain and Fancy,* esp. 23; Brinkley, *Voices of Protest.*

7. Merten, "Up Here and Down Home," 142–79; Pennington interview, Nov. 14, 1975; Green interview; William Collins, "Code of the Hills Fails in City," clipping (from *Cincinnati Enquirer*), Migrant Folder II, CSM Collection. See also Gregory, *American Exodus,* 146–49; Wyatt-Brown, *Southern Honor;* and Votaw, "Hillbillies Invade Chicago," 64–67.

8. Shelby interview.

9. Green interview.

10. Plemons and Collins interview, 7–8; Mayberry interview. On landlords who refused to rent to southerners with children and on prejudice against southerners by ethnics, particularly Poles, see Alvin and Ruby Berry interview.

11. "Midsummer Madness," *Detroit News,* June 22, 1943. See also Lee and Humphrey, *Race Riot,* 92; Denby, *Indignant Heart,* 87–89; Gitlin and Hollander, *Uptown,* 70; and J. Jones, *Dispossessed,* 234–38.

12. Green interview. Green worked for Lockheed in Marietta, Georgia, after his military service. He went on to work for NASA and returned permanently to Blue Ridge, Georgia, in 1974.

13. Morgan interview; Krawcheck, "Southern Whites Ask Only a Job, Fair Rent"; Pennington interview, Nov. 14, 1975, 10–11; William Collins, "Migrants

Battle Poverty," clipping (from *Cincinnati Enquirer*), Migrant Folder II, CSM Collection. A Chicago study in 1959 found that migrants from the southern Appalachians receiving public aid were only 0.15 percent of the public aid recipients, hardly a significant number. See Hilliard and Brooks, *Study of Families from the Southern Appalachian Region Receiving Public Assistance,* 3. For more on welfare, see chapter 7.

14. Gregory, *American Exodus,* 193; Giardina interview.

15. Franklin, *Born Sober;* Cash, *Mind of the South.* A study in the 1930s in the southern Appalachians found spotty and inconsistent church participation. See U.S. Department of Agriculture, *Economic and Social Problems and Conditions of the Southern Appalachians.* Compare Cunningham, "Religious Concerns of Southern Appalachian Migrants in a North Central City," 132. Low church attendance should not be taken to mean a lack of religious belief, however. Thomas Ford surveyed 1,450 people in ninety mountain counties in the 1950s and found that 99.1 percent said they believed in God; 97.8 percent declared God answers prayer; 90.9 percent believed in life after death; 76.9 percent thought they would be punished in the hereafter; 43.5 percent contended that God sends misfortune and illness to sinners; 85.1 percent believed church teaching over science; 84.8 percent asserted that gambling was always wrong; 76.8 percent claimed that drinking was always wrong, 95.8 percent insisted that moonshining was always wrong, and 24.1 percent were against tobacco. Reported in *Detroit Free Press,* July 28, 1959, sec. A, 1, 24.

16. Lake View Citizens' Council, "The Southern White Migrant to Lake View," 2, Cities—Chicago, Ill., folder 2, box 283, CSM Collection; Mayberry interview; Cox interview.

17. For an example of the stereotypes, see Campbell and Pooler, "Hallelujah in Boom Town," 18–19; and Votaw, "Hillbillies Invade Chicago," 65–66.

18. Kaufman, *Religious Organization in Kentucky;* Weatherford interview; Tune interview. Alan Clive notes that "the local bar was one of the few urban retreats where rural migrants could sit at their leisure, drinking and listening to the commercialized rhythms of country music on the jukebox or over the radio, especially to Saturday night's 'Grand Old Op'ry' from a Nashville now more than geographically distant." See Clive, *State of War,* 175. See also Kirby, *Rural Worlds Lost,* 300–301; and Votaw, "Hillbillies Invade Chicago," 64–67.

19. See William Collins, "It's Not So Easy!" clipping (from *Cincinnati Enquirer*), Migrants II Folder, CSM Collection; Donald L. Benedict, "The Integration of Southern Appalachian Migrants into Northern Urban Centers," 10, Urban Migrant Project, folder 3, box 278, CSM Collection; Philliber, "Wife's Absence from the Labor Force and Low Income among Appalachian Migrants," 705–10; Evelyn S. Stewart, "It's a Hard Life for Women," *Detroit Free Press,* July 29, 1959; and Roscoe Giffin, "Newcomers from the Southern Mountains," 3, Southern Appalachia—General, folder 8, box 3, Roscoe Giffin Collection, Southern Appalachian Archives. Clara and Bill Belcher moved from eastern Kentucky to Chicago's Uptown, and Clara liked her new life in Chicago. But her husband always longed for home, especially in the spring; his foreman would ask him "When you taking off?" after the first warm spring day. Quoted in *Long Journey Home.* Even the male characters in James Still's novel, *River of Earth,* are much more romantic about "home."

20. Hensley interview, 9.

21. Lawson interview; Tune interview.

22. Cunningham, "Religious Concerns of Southern Appalachian Migrants in a North Central City," 348; McBeth, "Expansion of the Southern Baptist Convention to 1951," 40 (quote). On the rural nature of Southern Baptist congregations, see Flynt, "Southern Baptists," 24–34; and "Religion," Urban Migrant Project, folder 2, box 278, CSM Collection. An article in an Uptown (Chicago) newspaper in the 1960s noted that churches shunned southern migrants. See "Citizens' Tips Lead to 85% of Arrests, Capt. Fahey Says: Town Hall Chief Defends Migrants," *Edgewater Uptown (Chicago) News,* Feb. 13, 1962. Another source argues that ministerial associations in nearby Ravenswood, Edgewater, and Lake View deliberately excluded the twelve churches in Uptown. See Council of the Southern Mountains, Inc., *Report on a Meeting Held in Connection with the Opening of the Chicago Office of the Council of the Southern Mountains,* 6.

23. Livingston, "Southern Baptists in Michigan," 49–50, 55–56; McBeth, "Expansion of the Southern Baptist Convention to 1951," 33–34; Nettles, "Southern Baptists," 13, 19; Al Pikora, "Baptists Assist Kentucky Needy," *Dayton Daily News* [1965], folder 1, box 294, CSM Collection; Baker, *Southern Baptist Convention and Its People, 1607–1972.* For an earlier discussion of Baptists, see McCauley, *Appalachian Mountain Religion,* 201–37.

24. Jesse and Emma Martin interview. Jess's story is also interesting because he implies that "something" made him turn back to 1133 Gilbert.

25. Ibid.

26. Kimbrough, *Taking Up Serpents,* 171–86.

27. Lacy interview. For a history of the Michiana General Baptists, see *History of Michiana Association,* 34.

28. Baldridge interview, 2–3.

29. Livingston, "Southern Baptists in Michigan," 56; Lake View Citizens' Council, "Southern White Migrant to Lake View," 1–2. See also Elfers, Ashworth, and Reed, *Impact,* 40.

30. Ford, "Status, Residence, and Fundamentalist Religious Beliefs in the Southern Appalachians," 247–61. Moreover, small conservative churches without a strong national bureaucracy were often ephemeral, often reliant on dynamic (or ineffectual) clergy, congregants from the neighborhood, leases, and economic downturns. National surveys therefore do not capture these smaller churches that were doubtless important to some southern migrants. For more statistical information, see Berry, "Great *White* Migration," 293–96.

31. Cunningham, "Religious Concerns of Southern Appalachian Migrants in a North Central City," 374; Livingston, "Southern Baptists in Michigan," 55; Montell, *Singing the Glory Down.* One scholar argues that the national expansion of the SBC pushed the convention slowly toward cultural pluralism through increased contact with African Americans and other ethnic groups. See Halbrooks, "Growing Pains," 44–54.

32. Ledford and Bonnie Nell Stults interview.

33. Shelby interview; Lacy interview; McBeth, "Expansion of the Southern Baptist Convention to 1951," 40. See also Gregory, *American Exodus,* 193; and Neville, *Kinship and Pilgrimage,* 21.

34. Philliber and McCoy, eds., *Invisible Minority.* Perhaps not surprisingly, as

the migration leveled off in the 1970s, some SBC churches in the Midwest lost their southernness, having to rely on northern natives to fill pews vacated by migrants who retired and moved back South. As William Richard Livingston writes, these congregations "remain Baptist in doctrine and polity, and Southern Baptist in nature—they are just beginning to forget why." See Livingston, "Southern Baptists in Michigan," 132.

35. Wilgus, "Country-Western Music and the Urban Hillbilly," 160, 158–59, 161. See also Green, "Hillbilly Music," 204–28. Wilgus has defined hillbilly music as "of or pertaining to commercialized folk or folkish song . . . largely derived from or aimed at white folk culture of the southern United States, beginning in 1923." See Wilgus, *Anglo-American Folksong Scholarship since 1898,* 433.

36. Tribe, "Cultural Preservation among Appalachian Migrants," 263–70.

37. Wilgus, "Country-Western Music and the Urban Hillbilly," 162.

38. Asbel, "National Barn Dance," 20; Biggar, "Early Days of WLS and the National Barn Dance," 11–13; Biggar, "WLS National Barn Dance Story," 105–12; W. W. Daniel, "National Barn Dance on Network Radio," 47–62; Patterson, "Hillbilly Music among the Flatlanders," 12–18. Before long, barn dances were springing up throughout the new migrant borderland. WSM's fifty-thousand-watt *Grand Ole Opry,* which began in 1925 in Nashville, would soon become the most popular. In 1939, it achieved network status at NBC, and a thirty-minute abridged version of the four-and-a-half-hour show was beamed to millions each Saturday night. Others followed, including the *Midwestern Hayride* from WLW in Cincinnati in 1937 and the *Boone County Jamboree* from Renfro Valley, Kentucky, which was also supported by WLW, presumably to the delight of the thousands of southerners living in Ohio's Miami Valley. The *World's Original Jamboree* from WWVA in Wheeling, West Virginia, also was a far-reaching program. See Carney, "Spatial Diffusion of the All-Country Music Radio Stations in the United States, 1971–74," 59–60; Malone, *Country Music,* 195; and Grundy, "'We Always Tried to Be Good People,'" 1591–1620.

39. Patterson, "Hillbilly Music among the Flatlanders," 12–16.

40. *High Lonesome,* dir. Liebling.

41. Quoted in Asbel, "National Barn Dance," 22.

42. Wilgus, "Country-Western Music and the Urban Hillbilly," 169–70. See also Kirby, *Countercultural South,* esp. chap. 3.

43. In 1960, the Cleveland Committee on the Southern In-Migrants wanted to form a newsletter and play "mountain music" for the estimated 100,000 migrants in Cleveland, Akron, and Youngstown. See "City May Beam Mountain Music to Newcomers," *Petersburg (Va.) Progress-Index,* Mar. 28, 1960; "Mountain Music Planned for Immigrants to Cleveland," *Radford (Va.) News Journal,* Apr. 14, 1960; and "Back Home for South," *Santa Ana (Calif.) Daily Register,* Mar. 31, 1960.

44. Wilgus, "Country-Western Music and the Urban Hillbilly," 163, 165–66. See also Tichi, *High Lonesome,* 19–50; and Malone, "Writing the History of Southern Music," 385–404, esp. 394. An excellent article on anti-urban themes is Tribe, "Hillbilly versus the City," 41–51. See also Averill, "Can the Circle Be Unbroken"; Cobb, "From Rocky Top to Detroit City," 71–73; Peterson, "Class Unconsciousness in Country Music," 35–62; and Landy, "Country Music," 67–69.

45. Quoted in Horstman, *Sing Your Hear Out, Country Boy,* 20.

46. Lyrics in ibid., 23, 8.

47. For complete lyrics, see ibid., 13–14, 12, 7.

48. Quoted in ibid., 10–11.

49. Complete lyrics in ibid., 11.

50. Marglean C. Sutherland, liner notes to *South on 23*, Old Homestead 90018. See also Tribe, "Cultural Preservation among Appalachian Migrants," 263–70; Zill, "John Morris Talks about Old Homestead Records," 22–24; and Zorn, "Homestead for Unsung Talent," 24–26. A catalog may be ordered from Old Homestead Records, Box 100, Brighton, MI 48116.

51. *South on 23*. Lyrics appear under the copyright of Jaymore Music; all lyrics from *South on 23* are used with permission.

52. Ibid.

53. Ibid.

54. Ibid.

55. Clarkson and Montell, "Letters to a Bluegrass DJ," 219, 225, 221.

56. Ibid., 223, 225, 226–27 (ellipses in original).

7 *The 1960s and Beyond: Battling and Disproving Stereotypes*

> It is important to note that mountain people in the cities cause problems more because they are of lower social class origin than because of some peculiar features of mountain culture itself. So many people never fully understand or appreciate this.
>
> —Thomas R. Ford to Roscoe Giffin, May 31, 1960

> If they called me a Hillbilly, I'd say, "There's two kinds of people in the world: one of them's a Hillbilly and the other one's a sonofabitch. You know what I am."
>
> —Buddy Lee Ford, 1993, Kuttawa, Ky.

ON APRIL 19, 1959, an employee at Cleveland's City Water Department wrote a letter to J. A. Norton, the executive director of the Cleveland Metro Services Commission, regarding an invitation to attend a meeting about southern white migrants in the city. Having read Roscoe Giffin's "The Southern Mountaineer in Cincinnati," the writer maintained that he "could add a lot to that myself, from personal observation and experience with these 'mountaineers' and other in-migrants that are mentioned." He continued:

> Your organization has bitten off quite a chunk of social and economic problems when it attempts to deal with the in-migrant. Too many of

> these people are hard-headed and difficult to reach. They recognize no authority. They respect no authority. They disregard the rights of others in the community, and don't try to tell them what to do, just leave them alone to do what they please.
>
> Most of them are unschooled and unskilled. How can we give these people employment? Industry today demands highly trained technicians, and even the semi-skilled have a rough time getting a job. I know. I worked at Cleveland Welding Company on production work for almost 21 years.
>
> The simplest solution to the economic problem would be to encourage these people to go back home, and let their home states handle the problem. Why do they unload their problem children on us? It does not seem fair. With so many of our own local natives of 40 years and over unable to get jobs, it galls us to see these in-migrants get jobs while local residents walk the streets. That has engendered quite a bit of resentment here, and you also have probably heard people cussing at the "damn hillbillies." When I was out of work for 9 months, from October 1957 to July of 1958, I tried to get a factory job out at Chevrolet in Brookpark. They hired nine hill billies just arrived from Tennessee, and when the personnel man saw my application, and noted my age, 52, he told me he had nothing for me. Can you imagine how I felt?[1]

The letter to Norton was typical of the discovery of southern white migrants that took place once again in the 1960s. The recession in 1957–58 was an early shock to migrants who since World War II had been gaining fairly easy and welcome access into northern industry (the letter above shows how even during recession southern newcomers were preferred over natives). As the postwar economic boom tightened even further in the 1960s, hordes of eager but desperate migrants continued to be pushed out of the South. Conditions in the coalfields grew even more dire as mechanization made strides into even the smallest mines and a strike in the early 1960s dragged on. Small but evidently growing numbers of migrants never seemed to move up and out of such ports-of-entry as Uptown in Chicago and the Cass Corridor in Detroit as their southern white predecessors had for at least four decades.

The media were the first to notice. In 1959, a journalist in the *Louisville Courier-Journal* wrote, "The unskilled and semiskilled from Southern Appalachia exist precariously on the fringe of the labor pool, working some, idling much. They tend to huddle together in miserable housing, clannish, proud and difficult to get along with. Suspicious of city ways, they seek only the comfort of clinging to those of their own highland culture and folkways." Another article, describing a southern migrant, speculated that he "might make it. The statistical chances are he won't. Only a few of his clan have."[2]

This era in the history of twentieth-century southern white migration, which began in the 1960s, has become the most publicized, as journalists and social scientists for over three decades have focused on the relatively small number of migrants who for one reason or another were not improving their lot as the hundreds of thousands before them had. The literature produced during this era—what I would call the "pathology school"—was supplemented by stories told about people living throughout the southern Appalachians who lacked the motivation even to migrate northward to try to improve their lives.

In spite of the attention given to those migrants who were not succeeding economically, the vast majority of southern white migrants in the Midwest after 1960 were satisfying their own economic expectations. Migrants from the South who transplanted themselves in the Midwest had jobs—for the most part well-paying ones—mortgages, enough land for a garden, perhaps a fishing boat or a camper, and, most important, a good late-model car to carry them back to the South. Although the majority of migrants were not divided in their economic assessment of the Midwest, most continued to be divided in their emotional assessment of leaving what had always been home for a different culture.

This chapter details some of the stereotypical views of migrants in the Midwest, including the befuddlement some had over how such a "pure" race of people could go so wrong. Most of the differences nonmigrants were noticing, of course, stemmed from rural-urban and class differences, as the epigraph by Thomas Ford notes. Previous scholarship on (mainly Appalachian) migration has led to the notion that the majority of migrants spent their lives in maladjusted squalor in the urban Midwest. A better view of migration entails more diversity of experience, and three vignettes of such experience later in the chapter show how migrants themselves often battled, and sometimes disproved, these nefarious stereotypes. The chapter casts severe doubt on a pathological view of upland southern white migration.

Battling the Stereotypes

Newcomers to areas are often stereotyped by host populations, and southerners who moved out of their region and into northern urban areas had always had their fair share of labeling. Indeed, migrants had begun to be labeled while the great white migration was only a trickle. In the 1930s, an article in *Social Forces* cast a grim shadow on the "adjustment" potential of southern mountaineers who were moving intraregionally to Lexington, Kentucky. "As far as this study is concerned," the author

Morris G. Caldwell wrote, "these mountain families appear to be unable to make satisfactory social adjustments in an urban environment." Articles in popular magazines sensationalized and stereotyped those who were on the move because of destitution. Some even cast the migrants as subhuman. Advertisements for vacant homes in Detroit during the war carried the clarification NO SOUTHERNERS. In Chicago, one landlord explained, "We'd rather rent to a Negro, a Mexican, or a Filipino than to a white person from the South. A good clean colored person is a better tenant than a southern white anytime." Raymond Paul Hutchens, who studied attitudes in Hamilton, Ohio, toward the "Briar"—the term used in southwestern Ohio to describe Kentuckians—offered a summary of antisouthern sentiment:

> Thus, in a review of the attitudes of the Hamiltonian toward the Briar, we find the ideal-type Briar is one who is indolent in the use of his time; proliferous with respect to the number of his children; dishonest, particularly in the matter of petty thefts; physically aggressive in his solution of personal grievances; unclean in his person; shoddy in his dress; slouchy in his bearing; ungrammatical and provincial in his speech; illiterate; employed in the stead of native Hamiltonians during the Depression; and too often found enjoying the benefits of relief. The ideal-type Briar is not a golden mean of any sort; he is a caricature, a purposeful accentuation. He lives in the minds of native Hamiltonians and provides the rationale for certain categoric responses.[3]

By the 1950s and 1960s, the stereotypes of southern white migrants in general and southern Appalachian migrants in particular were becoming entrenched. In 1958, one of the most nefarious descriptions of "hillbillies" was penned in staid *Harper's* by Albert N. Votaw:

> These farmers, miners, and mechanics from the mountains and meadows of the mid-South—with their fecund wives and numerous children—are, in a sense, the prototype of what the "superior" American should be, white Protestants of early American, Anglo-Saxon stock; but on the streets of Chicago they seem to be the American dream gone berserk. This may be the reason why their neighbors often find them more obnoxious than the Negroes or the earlier foreign immigrants whose obvious differences from the American stereotype made them easy to despise. Clannish, proud, disorderly, untamed to urban ways, these country cousins confound all notions of racial, religious, and cultural purity.

Southern migrants, he summed, were "a disgrace to their race." Plenty of others would have agreed. An Indianapolis "native" quoted in the *Reporter* explained to the journalist James A. Maxwell that southerners "are creating a terrible problem in our city. They can't or won't hold a job, they flout the law constantly and neglect their children, they drink too much and their moral standards would shame an alley cat. For some reason or other, they absolutely refuse to accommodate themselves to any kind of decent, civilized life." Later in the article, Maxwell echoed Raymond Hutchens's description of southerners almost two decades later:

> In most Midwestern cities, these neighborhoods of Southern mountaineers are as easily recognizable as those made up of Italians or Jews or Negroes. The people from the mountains usually are tall, loose-limbed, and angular, with the blond hair and ruddiness traditionally associated with the English race. On the whole, both men and women are shabbily dressed—the men in sloppy, ill-fitting suits and colored shirts with garish ties, while the women seem to prefer nondescript dresses hanging loose from the shoulders. The hill folk speak with a twang of their own that sounds somewhat rustic and archaic and frequently use terms that were familiar at the time of the first Queen Elizabeth.

Just a few years before Votaw's piece appeared, Detroit residents were asked to identify the "undesirable people" who were "not good to have in the city." Criminals and gangsters came in at 26 percent, but "poor southern whites and hillbillies" provoked the disdain of 21 percent of respondents, significantly higher than "transients, drifters, dole types" (18 percent), African Americans (13 percent), and immigrants (6 percent).[4]

Underlying many of these accounts of southerners, particularly in the articles by Votaw and Maxwell, were both a perplexity and befuddlement about how such a "pure," "Anglo-Saxon" (and fecund) race could have gone so terribly wrong, a wonder particularly interesting considering the clamor many Americans had raised earlier in the twentieth century over the fecundity of many immigrant groups. Southern procreation was scorned not only because of the competition to elites but precisely because an Anglo-Saxon race was producing foul offspring. When the Russell Sage Foundation sent John C. Campbell on a fact-finding trip through the southern mountains early in the century, he celebrated and romantically tried, as David E. Whisnant has shown, to preserve a culture that was changing. Countless people have since been romantically obsessed with the historical depth and rustic purity of southern—especially mountain—culture. By the late 1950s, however, observers—most of whom were WASPs—were distressed at how far Anglo-Saxonism had "degenerated."[5]

By the 1960s and 1970s, southern migrants were assumed by many urban elites to be shiftless, lazy workers incapable of keeping a job. Superintendents of many northern school districts monitored the progress of migrant children, often expecting them to fail. Landlords continued to discriminate against migrant newcomers in housing because of their allegedly poor housekeeping, while health care officials bemoaned their distrust of modern medicine, especially their faith in "old-timey" cures. Police officers dreaded southern migrant populations because they believed the men were all-too quick with a knife or even a gun. Collection agencies assumed that southerners were too easily swayed by credit in the North and that southerners had never had experience with credit before migrating. Native northerners developed a repertoire of jokes based on stereotypes that were often not unlike jokes about immigrants or African Americans (for example, What is the best thing to come out of Kentucky? An empty Greyhound bus. The best thing to leave Ohio? A full bus.).[6]

What the creators and nurturers of stereotypes often did not realize, or cared not to realize, were both the peculiarities of southern *rural* culture that were discordant with northern *urban* culture and the differences associated with socioeconomic class. Southern workers, near the bottom of the employment pyramid, often tried simply to improve working conditions or wages in their frequent job moves because a labor shortage allowed them flexibility. Southern children who were transplanted in the North suffered not because of a lack of intelligence but because a child in the second grade in Kentucky was placed in the similar grade in the North, even though northern schools were often much more advanced in curriculum than southern schools, so that southern children began with a disadvantage. In the South, one gave food scraps to hogs and threw trash in a gully; trash cans were unnecessary and unavailable. Northern M.D.s and nurses singled out what was only one of several folk remedies for thrush: rinsing a child's mouth with urine. Other folk remedies were often successful, particularly since prescription drugs were unavailable or too costly. Police officers, too, were skewed in ascribing crime to southerners: a report in Lake View, in Chicago, for example, found that southerners there committed only a slight number of offenses, usually involving intoxication. Credit agencies also did not realize that buying on credit—whether in coal camps in the mountains or on lowland farms—was a hallmark of southern consumerism; the only big difference was that credit extension in the South was based on an intimate—if exploitative—relationship between buyer and seller. Credit was granted more on character than on financial ability to repay.[7]

Any problems that southerners were having making adjustments to urban life thus stemmed more from class and from migrating from a rural area than from ethnicity. Those newcomers who were displaying many of the stereotypes alleged of southerners in Chicago were frequently discovered to be not southerners but merely rural migrants from downstate

Indiana or Illinois or from western states. The labeling of nearly any rural migrant as a southerner or "hillbilly" in midwestern cities had several unfortunate consequences. Problems associated with southerners, especially with mountaineers, were often exaggerated. Moreover, by the 1960s, attention began to focus on understanding southerners, which would eventually lead to some sort of discovery whereby the urban adjustment of southerners could be guaranteed. Researchers, in short, were trying to find the adjustment "cure."[8]

There were two other unfortunate but related consequences. As social scientists flocked to areas of migrant concentration to understand white migrants from the South and to serve as their advocates, sometimes they ironically—and, I want to stress, completely unintentionally—seemed to strengthen and legitimize the stereotypes that had emanated from the media since the Great Depression. The other result is that their intense concern for and scrutiny of southern Appalachian migrants left flatland migrants whose origin lay outside of the mountain South without an interested party, which may have been as much a blessing as a curse.

Of all the migrant destinations in the Midwest, Cincinnati and southwestern Ohio have been studied in the greatest detail, and the scholarship produced reflects the unintended consequence of sometimes validating stereotypes. This occurred in a two-step process. First, the researchers who contributed to this scholarship—as products of a time when youthful idealism, perhaps, joined forces with intense optimism that poverty could be ended—seemed to focus not so much on the total group of migrants who had left the South for Cincinnati as on the city's southern white ports of entry, such as Over-the-Rhine and Lower Price Hill. The frequently grim and depressing portraits that emerged after many years of sound social scientific research seemed to consolidate the image of the southern Appalachian migrant (the overwhelming majority of southern white migrants to Cincinnati were probably from mountain areas) that many in the country had long accepted: poor, usually on welfare; handicapped in the North by a residual mountain culture; poorly educated and showing little or no interest in educating children; tightly clustered in urban ghettos characterized by dismal apartment houses and seedy taverns. In and of itself, this would not have been so validating. But second, when future scholars—particularly historians—even bothered to mention the southern white exile in their twentieth-century histories, they naturally cited scholarship already produced on Cincinnati and southwestern Ohio migrants who seemed unable to adjust or succeed. It became rather easy to assume, then, that most urban migrants from the South typified this portrait.[9]

Revisionist scholarship notwithstanding, it is difficult to be critical of a generation of scholars who donated immense time and energy to understanding and bettering the plights of hundreds of destitute people. My lament is not that scholarship about migrant tragedies (all done, after all, to help present and future migrants) was produced but that there was so very little about migrant successes to complement the overall understanding of the southern white hegira. I seek to balance the story of white upland southern migration to the Midwest by suggesting that the majority of those who left the South and toughed it out in the North seemed to find the economic rewards for which they were searching. In no way do I seek to sweep under the rug those who for whatever reason had difficulty adjusting to midwestern urban life. Again, emotionally, many remained unfulfilled in the North, but economically, according to oral testimony and census data, most migrants prospered, by both internal and external definitions.

Even by 1981, Phillip J. Obermiller, one of the tireless deans of Appalachian migration, was advocating a change in direction:

> We must begin to look at Appalachian success patterns and social competence, and not just the social disorganization that is present within some segments of the Appalachian community. . . . To spend all of our energy in pursuit of pathology can be a disservice to Appalachian people. There are two sides of victim blaming: one is to discover social dysfunction and to blame it on the individual or individuals involved; the other is to note success and attribute it solely to the individual or individuals achieving it. The successful Appalachian has manipulated the "system" for his or her own benefit, implying that to a certain extent the system does work. . . . We need to add the Appalachian middle class to our studies so that the opportunity structures they have either built or discovered can be made available to all.

More than ten years later, Obermiller reflected on what he called the "social problem approach to internal migration" and wrote that "defining urban Appalachians as only, or even primarily, uneducated residents of poor neighborhoods is simply inaccurate." "It is more accurate," he argued, "to balance the reality of grinding inner-city poverty with the reality of stable Appalachian families living in working-class neighborhoods scattered across the metropolitan area."[10]

As the literature proliferated, southerners began speaking out. One Hazard, Kentucky, native living in Detroit wrote a letter to the editor of the *Detroit News* complaining about the skewed portrait of southern Appalachia. "Some writers and speakers," he wrote, "go into the remote sections of our Kentucky mountains and pick out the very worst schools and homes they can find, then go back to the large cities and tell that our hills are full of ignorant, bloodthirsty and vicious people." He continued:

> These people are true, patriotic citizens of this nation. They have always been loyal to their country and flag and always will be. In the last war thousands of them laid down their lives on foreign soil as they [f]ought to make the world safe for democracy.
>
> These mountain children are starving not so much for food as for an education. The time for Christian leaders to give these children an education is now. Let's give it to them so they can carry on the great industrial work that is waiting and calling at the doors of the Kentucky mountains.

Similarly, a Lexington native living in Dayton railed against the *Dayton Journal Herald*'s 1961 reports on the mountain migrants: "If you can't find anything else for your staff writer Mary Ellen Wolfe, other than the mountain migrants she is now writing about, she should have another assignment—if it is only sweeping up the office." "I thought this was a free country and we could move as we please," the writer continued, suggesting that "it would help people more if Miss Wolfe would say a good word once in a while instead of trying to run mountain migrants down." Jokes of southerners proliferated, according to Benny Bailey: "The punch line in the mountain jokes is always that the hillbilly is dumb. I mean in the major industrial cities of the north, the hillbilly jokes are just as prevalent as the Polish jokes, especially wherever hillbillies congregate."[11]

The cumulative effect of the widespread belief that all southern migrants were ill-fated victims mired in urban poverty made them the targets of reformers who emerged by the 1960s to help them adjust to an urban life-style to which reformers believed migrants were incapable of adjusting on their own and in ways the reformers assumed migrants wanted. Two programs represent the range of concern expressed for migrants: the efforts of the Council of the Southern Mountains (CSM) and the JOIN (Jobs or Income Now) Project, sponsored by Students for a Democratic Society (SDS).

The Council of the Southern Mountains

The Council of the Southern Mountains, founded in 1913, had long been a conservative clearinghouse for southern Appalachia, but it took the CSM many years to acknowledge the exile that was draining the region of people. After World War II, the council only infrequently noted the vast number of Appalachian migrants in northern cities in the pages of its publication, *Mountain Life and Work.* David Whisnant has argued that while "officially the Council had no position on migrants," the "point of view most often represented . . . was that Appalachian people who *chose* to migrate must be helped."[12]

In the late 1950s, the CSM could no longer afford to give Appalachian out-migration superficial attention. In the summer of 1959, the organization, with twenty thousand dollars in Ford Foundation support, hosted a two-part workshop entitled "A Unique Social Exploration: A Workshop on Urban Adjustment of Southern Appalachian Migrants." In the first part, spanning twelve days in July, the CSM invited representatives from religion, welfare, education, law enforcement, housing, health, industry, and labor from New York, Cleveland, Chicago, Detroit, Dayton, Akron, Columbus, and Cincinnati to learn more about southern Appalachian culture and, in director P. F. Ayer's words, "to give urban leaders a close and intimate look at the conditions of life in the mountain counties which force people to migrate and to 'sensitize' these urban leaders to the attitudes and values with which the migrants come" through reading, lectures, discussion, skill training, and field trips. The second part consisted of a week-long bus tour between Berea, Kentucky, and Knoxville, Tennessee.[13]

A report by participants after the workshop recanted some stereotypes but perpetuated others. It noted that "all of us had come to Berea with preconceived notions about SAM [Southern Appalachian Migrants]. To the educator, he was that parent who permitted unexplained absences, tardiness, and school drop-outs. We had heard him labeled shiftless, troublemaking, suspicious, demanding, secretive and non-conforming. We knew his urban neighbor often pressured 'go home hillbilly.'" But much of the report lends credence to Whisnant's criticism that one of the council's biggest problems was its adherence to what he calls the Anglo-Saxon thesis—another stereotype of mountain people that predated the pathology thesis—which became a basis for the council's conservatism and occasionally racist and jingoist policies. At a 1927 annual meeting of the CSM, for example, a speaker trumpeted, "We have reached the point where we can . . . tell the whole country about these Anglo-Saxon, mountain-locked, one-hundred percent Americans." The 1959 workshop report continued this legacy, reminding the reader of the "Americanness" of migrants. "We concluded that SAM is probably the closest we get to an unadulterated, white, Protestant ancestry. We cannot . . . label him as a newcomer. His heritage began in America as early as 1639. A high birthrate, depletion of natural resources, and ambition are decreasing his chance of survival as he is. He must learn and adjust to change. City folk and city ways are diluting his culture."[14]

One of the biggest problems with the workshop, of course,was that the organizers—like the media and later many scholars of migration—seemed to assume that all white southern migrants were from the southern Appalachians.[15] Nevertheless, the workshops, which continued each summer until 1968, were probably important in publicizing the circumstances associated with southern Appalachian migration. The broad array of participants each summer was a credit to the organizers. Eventually, the Berea workshops resulted in a few local workshops in northern cities that focused on local factors; Dayton, Cincinnati, Detroit, and Cleveland all organized conferences on "SAMs."[16]

These midwestern cities also formed standing committees that addressed the needs of southern Appalachian migrants. Dayton formed the Committee on the Southern Appalachian Newcomer in 1960, and eventually committees were established in other cities as community activists and social workers discovered pockets of migrant poverty in their urban areas: Cincinnati's Urban Appalachian Council, founded by Ernie Mynatt; Dayton's Our Common Heritage; Columbus's Central Ohio Appalachian Council; and Hamilton's Appalachian People's Service Organization.[17] The committees served as task forces on migration, helped instill pride among migrants from Appalachia (often through crafts and music), and published a wide array of pamphlets on urban migrants for distribution to area agencies. Some were more successful than others, but they all constituted a notable effort in the history of southern out-migration.

One of the earliest pamphlets was *When Cultures Meet: Mountain and Urban,* published in 1962 by the Mayor's Friendly Relations Committee of Cincinnati. The pamphlet highlighted generalizations about southern Appalachian society and culture, noting the poor education of most migrants as well as speech patterns and their reputed distrust of modern medicine. It also advised agencies on how to deal more effectively with the "10% to 15% that come to the attention of the authorities—i.e. police, health department, welfare department or others." More significantly, the pamphlet stressed "one fact" that "should be made clear. *Most of the Southern Appalachian Migrants do find work, do eventually adjust to city living, do keep their children in school, do not get into trouble with the city officials, do become useful, producing citizens of their newly adopted home,*" a point sometimes forgotten as the decade of awareness wore on.[18]

Detroit also had a fair amount of organized activity for white migrants from southern Appalachia. On December 15, 1962, the inaugural meeting of the Southern Appalachian Center took place at the Cass Community Center. The poster announcing the meeting explained that "MANY

OF THE SOUTHERN WHITES FROM THE SOUTHERN APPALACHIA AREA HAVE MADE REPEATED REQUESTS FOR A PLACE TO MEET AND RENEW OLD FRIENDSHIPS AS WELL AS MAKE NEW FRIENDS. THIS IS YOUR GREAT OPPORTUNITY." Sixty-two people attended the meeting, which was followed by a potluck supper and southern music.[19]

About the same time, Kentuckians of Michigan, Inc., was organized, embracing Kentuckians from western as well as eastern counties. By 1974, the yearbook from the annual picnic listed over 350 members and a treasury of more than eight thousand dollars. The event included bluegrass and country music, raffles, and awards for Kentucky Queen Mother and King Father, the largest Kentucky family with all children present, and the longest married Kentucky couple. Information on elected officers listed their Kentucky county of origin, their employer, and the year they came to Detroit. The advertisements for the yearbook included many small businesses owned by southern migrants, including Ralph E. Whitfield Transmission (from Hopkins County), Bummie's Cafe (Hopkins County), Anderson's Market (Pike County), Dependable Sewer Cleaners (Hopkins County), and the Plymouth Burt Service Station (Clay County). Overall, the organization is a significant example of migrant associational activity transplanted in the North.[20]

The Council of the Southern Mountains continued looking northward during the 1960s. By January 1965, the council had produced a pamphlet titled *Are You Thinking of Moving to the City?* The pamphlet advised prospective migrants to take a birth certificate, social security card, employment records, school and vaccination records, and even divorce papers. Near the end, it also warned what not to take: "The law in most states says you cannot carry deadly weapons any time, anywhere without a permit from the police," including "shot guns, rifled guns, revolvers, pistols, daggers, straight-edged razors, knucks, black jacks or switch blade knives. In some states you cannot have guns in your house without a license from the police."[21]

After many years of ignoring northern mountaineers, the CSM moved into Chicago. Along Uptown's most eastern fringe was Lake Shore Drive's high-rise apartments, but farther west were the flats that had been divided into smaller apartments during World War II to make more housing; it was the beginning of Uptown's notorious slide into a ghetto. By the 1960s, at least 50,000 southern migrants (about half of whom were thought to be mountaineers—the rest were flatlanders) were estimated to be living there, along with 25,000 people over age sixty-five (the largest concentration of any Chicago neighborhood) and 10,000 Native Americans (of all tribes); as a port-of-entry neighborhood, it also had an increasing number of Puerto Ricans. Chicago alumni from the Berea workshops, learning of agencies in Uptown designed to help Native Americans, began rallying the CSM to open a Chicago branch office that would target urban Appalachians, particularly since Hull-House was said to have largely ignored the plights of migrants. In November 1963, the CSM responded but in a conservative way, in keeping with its long history. The major portion (twenty-five thousand dollars) of the funding for the Chicago Center came from none other than W. Clement Stone, the millionaire founder of the Combined Insurance Company of America, a company built at least in part on selling life insurance to the working poor. On the surface, Stone seemed an odd benefactor for southern migrant causes. He was author of the self-help classic *Success System That Never Fails* and encouraged CSM members to repeat Norman Vincent Peale–like phrases at board and annual meetings; he was also a heavy contributor to Richard M. Nixon. The political neutrality that the council was intent on maintaining made it easy to gratefully accept Stone's money, though. In 1962, Stone had given $7,500 to the CSM, 10 percent of its annual budget. A 1963 issue of *Mountain Life and Work* included a full-page acknowledgment from Ayer, concluding that the CSM "salutes Mr. W. Clement Stone and his philosophy." The first office was housed in a small storefront at 4606 North Kenmore Avenue, but later it moved to over twelve thousand square feet of space at 1028 West Wilson Avenue in the heart of Uptown, known popularly as Hillbilly Heaven. Eventually, the center received funding from the Kemper Insurance Company; the Robert R. McCormick Charitable Trust; Local 1540, Retail Clerks Union (AFL-CIO); and Berea College alumni.[22]

One of the center's most important policies was to encourage fellow southerners to help those migrants who needed it. Raleigh Campbell, a Berea graduate who was director of the center from June 1964 to August 1966, said other organizations in Chicago were simply not interested in southern migrants. Hull-House, for example, was always "snobbish," he said, toward those who lacked professional credentials and migrants themselves. The huge Urban Progress Center, funded by the Office of Economic Opportunity, was having little success reaching needy southern whites. The Chicago Southern Center saw itself as southerners helping southerners, and those in need were invited to take an active role; some were even eventually invited to serve on the board, but only after considerable lobbying by some board members.[23]

Although the center was eager to help all southerners, not just southern Appalachian people, its programs frequently concentrated on bread-and-butter goals that were in keeping with the council's history. For women, there were quilting and cookbook projects. Christmas baskets and used clothing were distributed. Men's clubs were organized. There were programs that taught children and adults how to get around Chicago—even how to negotiate through a turnstile for mass transit (the CSM reminded those migrants from the farm that most Chicagoans would not know how to get through a farm's drawbar gate). Other programs were designed to administer inoculations and to provide a quiet place for children to study. A very active Alcoholics Anonymous program helped those with drinking problems, and an emergency food pantry and rotating fund kept migrants from going hungry and running out of money. The center also served as their public relations center, trying to improve the image of southern migrants among Chicagoans, particularly employers.[24]

The center eventually was perceived as conservative by activists in Uptown and some migrants themselves. In spite of the conservatism of the council and its urban office, the Chicago Southern Center, like the CSM's workshops, was an important factor in easing the adjustment of southern white migrants. From the records that survive, there is some indication that there were at least glimmers of popularity among migrants. In 1966, for example, the center was hosting a square dance with migrant music talent. The organizers hoped that perhaps eight sets—32 people—would attend. When the doors opened, more than 350 people were outside in line.

As time passed, however, Uptown became the home of more groups, each with different goals—from easing adjustment of migrants to converting them to Christianity to overthrowing the local political structure. Similar factions were also plotting for control of the Council of the Southern Mountains, and as the political neutrality of the CSM was challenged, corporate and foundation supporters changed their rating of the CSM from *safe* to *risky.* As council moneys dried up, so, too, did the Chicago Southern Center. In spite of its separation from the CSM on January 1, 1968, designed to make it more attractive to Chicago support, particularly the United Way, the center seemed to peter out by the late 1960s. Stone, in particular, withdrew his grant of ninety thousand dollars after attending the fiery 1969 annual meeting of the CSM in Fontana, North Carolina, because he was frightened that "communist radicals" were overthrowing the rightist direction of the council. It was always difficult, after all, to balance the needs of needy migrants with the positive mental attitude and faith in American capitalism that such conservative benefactors as Stone considered sacred. Moreover, according to Raleigh Campbell, an arrogance among leaders of President Johnson's War on Poverty emerged that patronizingly maintained that government programs negated the need for such smaller organizations as the Chicago Southern Center. As many people during the War on Poverty would discover, people associated with the center, such as Campbell, soon learned that "change was really dangerous at that time. You had to be careful not to step on Mayor [Richard J.] Daley's toes." In short, the dynamics of interest, funding, and energy that formed the Chicago Southern Center in the early 1960s vanished by the end of the decade.[25]

JOIN in to Help

After white activists were told "thanks, but no thanks" by black leaders in the civil rights movement, much of the energy of white activism had to find another outlet. In Chicago, a great deal of this energy was centered in Uptown, where by 1968 there were over twenty-six public and private agencies that focused more or less on southern white migrants. The *Chicago Tribune* noted glibly that these agencies' "representatives stumble into one another on the street and compete, often with shockingly bad tempers, for a share of the humanitarian good works." Raleigh Campbell, for example, recalled members of Students for a Democratic Society working in Uptown while he was there. The SDS Chicago project was called JOIN (Jobs or Income Now), which was designed to be an organization of the "unemployed scattered over the white North Side of Chicago," write organizers Todd Gitlin and Nanci Hollander. SDS soon found this goal to be unattainable, so instead it tried "to bring poor whites together to fight for seemingly more accessible rights—changes in welfare policy, recreation, schools, decent housing, *whatever needs were felt* by a definite community of hitherto powerless people." In January 1965, organizers moved JOIN to Uptown and added "Community Union" to its name. The biggest difference between the efforts of JOIN and the Council of the Southern Mountains was political: JOIN was organizing rent strikes, fighting welfare bureaucrats and unscrupulous landlords, challenging class-biased urban renewal that was leaving scars on an already pocked landscape, and renouncing police brutality, while the Chicago Southern Center seemed more intent on instilling pride in southern Appalachian handicrafts and changing commonly held stereotypes of southern migrants.[26]

Todd Gitlin and Nanci Hollander saw in Uptown what most others, including the media, saw when they stopped long enough to look around. By the 1960s, over 50 percent of the housing units were one or two rooms, 38 percent were in some state of deterioration, and over 25 percent lacked adequate plumbing. As Gitlin and Hollander note, Uptown was Chicago's white ghetto; it had the second highest population density in the city (first was Lawndale, the black ghetto) despite its 13 percent vacancy rate. The organizers also point out that in 1966 there were more than a hundred cases of tuberculosis, almost as many as Skid Row on West Madison. In 1961, 11 percent of the stores were vacant; 21 percent were used "marginally" for such businesses as pawn shops; and 17 percent were taverns. In contrast to this were the headquarters of insurance giants Kemper and Combined. Gitlin and Hollander believed JOIN could change Uptown.[27]

Gitlin and Hollander began interviewing residents of Uptown in August 1965 for the book they would publish five years later. They admit those they tape recorded are "probably . . . not typical of Uptown as a whole, even of the migrants. They are less settled, less centered on family and work than is the norm." They also note that their two years in Chicago were times of low unemployment and a booming war, factors they recognize as not unrelated. They also observe that "white skin and an able body were rather good guarantees of a job," though the job's permanence and its wages were likely to be short and low, as the many signs in Uptown for "Manpower" and other day-labor agencies suggested. But the question of representative sampling for Gitlin and Hollander was moot, as they explain:

> The residents of Uptown had been subjected to so many questionnaires, so many earnest surveys from Ph.D. candidates and anthropologists, Labor Department and war-on-poverty agents, we could not bear to inflict still another battery of tests for what would be, with the best of intentions, another round of exploitation, another display of people boiled down into a statistical population to be digested as tasty or fashionable objects. A deep and passionate engagement with one life matters more, teaches more than a nodding acquaintance with ten or a door-to-door survey of a thousand, if the passion does not obscure one's faithfulness to what one sees. Better to let some people stick in your [the reader's] throat.[28]

An accurate picture of southern migration would be incomplete if some of the people that stuck in people's throats—even if they were not necessarily "typical"—were ignored. Much of what we think we know about southern white migrants was conditioned by the scholarship that began to be produced about the time the War on Poverty began in which those who came to study or improve or change the Uptowns of the Midwest often saw not the dynamics of a port-of-entry community but the stasis, and they seemed to believe that those who entered never left, instead continuing to lead lives of victimization. Those migrants who came to live in Uptown because kith or kin preceded them often found a job, saved money, and moved out into a working-class suburb, but those who *made it* are too frequently left out of the historical record of migrants. What comes to mind, then, when one thinks of a southern migrant is a poor, dumb, welfare grabbing, honky-tonk drinking, knife-fighting individual who does not "care" to improve his or her situation. What follows is a story of family members in Uptown who were leading a difficult and heart-wrenching life at the time they were interviewed (and who also likely continued to lead difficult lives long after their interviews), but I also include the story of a young man who entered Uptown, met his measure of success, and moved out—one who *used* Uptown, not one who was used by it.

I begin with Virgie.[29] At the time of one of her interviews, Virgie, aged thirty-two, had been in Uptown for about ten years, but she and her husband, Tom, from whom she was separated (leaving her to care for their ten children), had made countless trips between Logan County, West Virginia, their home, and Chicago. "About all my life," she said, "I lived in Logan, and we come out here cause there wasn't no work out there," particularly after her husband, who had worked "practically about all his life" in the coal mines, lost his job when the mine shut down. "I never did work out here but Tom did; he was always able to find a job when he wanted to work," she added, proving that Virgie's troubles had more to do with her husband than with anything else. Tom and Virgie had sojourned because, like many migrants, their hearts were divided between attachment to the South and opportunities in the North:

> When you grow up in a place, you're born and raised there, it always seems like home to you. No matter where you go you always think about that, I guess, it's one thing that you think of your whole life. I guess you'll just go through it thinking about, you know, things that you done when you were back home. Times were hard and everything, but still it still seems like home to you. And you would rather be there. The way I feel, I don't know if everbody feels the way I do. But anyway I would rather live out there than live out here. One thing, I have such a big family I think if it was just me, you know, if I was just by myself, me and Tom, if we was together and just us, you know, and we didn't have kids, I guess I would choose Chicago because I think there's more work out here and everything and we could really live better out here cause I do know that.
>
> But the coal mines really pays good money but most of the mines are shut down out there, and he wasn't able to ever find another job out there.

With her husband gone, Virgie and her ten children were on welfare, receiving, she thought, $390 per month (of that money, $125 went for rent) and plenty of indifference, humiliation, and even cruelty from welfare caseworkers. "I think they should pay your people more to live on," she said, "because [the] amount of money they've given me we sure can't make it on. I've got a hundred and twenty-five dollar check and I owe my back rent and I owe another month's rent. I don't see how in the world I'm gonna make it"; in the past, she had gone to the Chicago Southern Center for food and clothing, demonstrating the small world of Uptown. "All at once your bills all piles up on you." Virgie was again having trouble clothing her children; on snowy days, she would keep one of her daughters home because she had only sneakers to wear, which got her into trouble with truant officers. Virgie had been on welfare for about a month when Nanci Hollander interviewed her the first time.

Virgie first met her husband when she was fourteen. "I were real young," she said, "and I hadn't ever really went with no boys, and I didn't know if it was okay by my mother or not, so I asked her. And she said she didn't see why not, that he was a good boy, that she knew the family, you know, and they were good people, and I just started going with him then from that. And I dated him three year before I married him," on October 26, 1950. At that time, she said, "He was real good to work. He worked in the coal mines and he made good money, and we both were just young": she was seventeen, he was twenty-five.

After the coal mines declined in West Virginia, a problem emerged that would characterize Tom for the rest of their marriage and cause much hardship for the family: he could not, or would not, keep a job. Perhaps he was distressed over the decline of coal mining, or perhaps he simply wanted to return to the farm. Whatever the reason, it became a thorn in Virgie's side.[30] "Well, he worked until after we had two kids, and then after I'd had the two children we just broke up housekeeping and he wanted to go to his mother's," which was two hundred miles from Logan, West Virginia. After trying to make it as farmers, "I just got where that I just didn't want to stay over there," she said, "and we came back to Logan by me nearly forcing him to bring me back to my mother's. And I stayed there for a while and finally we just broke up. Right then I was expecting another kid and we were separated then for seven months; Tom came to Chicago and he stayed out here without us and never sent me no support of no kind." Virgie applied for welfare in West Virginia, had her third child—a girl—alone at home because the caseworker told her she was not qualified to go to a hospital. "I think," Virgie recalled, "she was about three months old when Tom come back then":

> It was during Christmas and the children didn't have anything for Christmas. I never will forget—they didn't have a toy or I didn't have anything.

> And he asked me to take him back, and things was getting really rough on me then. I had three children and it was just so hard. They cut my check down to forty-seven dollars a month, which I hadn't never signed the baby on it, but that was all I was getting and they said that she would have to be six months old before they would sign her up down there.
>
> Well when he came back from Chicago, I took him back, but I didn't go right with him right away; I waited for a while to make my mind up whether I would take him back because I had went through so much—it wasn't just something that I could just say I would go on and take him back, you know. I had to have time to think about it, so I did, and at that time my sister, one of my sisters had three children and she had come to my house and started staying with me too, and I just couldn't keep them all, so I made my mind up by that that I just couldn't go on with the kids trying to raise them, and they needed clothing and things I couldn't give them. And I just came to Chicago then on a bus.
>
> It [Chicago] was really scary more than anything else—I could just look out and see these big buildings and I never saw anything like that before and it—it just really seemed frightening. But I got to like Chicago. We stayed here for a while and then finally my mother took real bad sick, and I had to go back and they were looking for her to die, but she didn't die right then. She got over it and we stayed out there I guess about five or six months again and we came back and I started running a apartment building over on Winthrop, and I stayed there, I guess, four or five years. Tom was still with me.

During these four or five years, life improved greatly for Virgie and Tom and their four children, particularly since their rent was paid by Virgie's job in the apartment building. But shortly after their fifth child was born, Tom "took a notion to go home." He quit his job (he was earning $3.10 an hour), and they packed up and returned to his mother's place, where problems had first surfaced. "So I tried to live with him every way I know how," Virgie said. "It seems like it's getting harder and harder." Virgie and her mother-in-law were fighting, perhaps because Virgie said she was taking out her frustration with Tom on his mother. So after a year or so they moved back to Logan. "My mother and father both was dead by that time," she said, "and we went back again to try to make it, and he worked around there a little bit and he really couldn't find a job in Logan or nowhere out in there—works were real bad then and finally we sold out everything we had again and we come back to Chicago." They moved around to several addresses on Kenmore and Winthrop—in the heart of Uptown—while Virgie was pregnant again. Once she had her sixth baby, they moved back to Logan. "He just wanted to go back again. Then it were getting really tough on the kids. We didn't have them all in school at that time, cause they all were school age, and he thought it would be better if we take them back there and put them in school. And so we went back again to try to make it and we stayed, I guess, about three months that time and come back again." So many mines had closed in Logan County during this time that one of the only jobs to be found was in the scrap metal business. Tom found such a job working for Virgie's uncle. "These old mines that had been worked out—they go in there and take this steel all out and sell it for scrap iron and he had several men working for him," Virgie explained. Two more trips between Logan and Chicago brought four more children for Virgie, who, only in her thirties, was growing weary of childbirth, sojourns, and marriage.

Tom, however, threatened to kill Virgie unless she returned to West Virginia with him. Once they went back, Tom found a job in a coal mine, making it possible to buy a house for $2,700. But what ensued were more difficult periods, marked by garnished wages for outstanding bills, Tom's threats, and intermittent welfare. The garnished wages, in particular, were resulting in paychecks being cut in half; with $1,200 left to pay on their home, they lost it (it was the fourth consecutive time that the house was put up for public auction). Virgie wanted to return to Chicago. "I just finally made my mind up that I were coming back and he could stay out there if he wanted to and he knew that I was coming. And I guess that he just thought well, there ain't no other way and then him and his boss got into it so he quit. He just quit his job."

In 1965, the thing Virgie wanted most was a stable life in a home: "Well, I think the most thing I want for my kids is a home, which I don't know if I'll ever have. 'Cause I've been drug from here to there with them so much that I would really like to settle down and have a home where I would have to go no more." Once they returned to Chicago, they were living in a decrepit building at 4436 Magnolia with nine of the children (the oldest daughter had married at age fourteen and had moved to Ohio); Tom had also come back to live with her. They lived in what was supposed to be a furnished three-room apartment for four weeks until the landlord gave them a couch, which was their only piece of furniture in the living room. "I don't think anybody with their right sense would want to move in[to] this building," Virgie said, "cause they's rats and roaches and they don't do anything to the building, they don't do *anything*. I do believe this is the worst one I've lived in since I been in Chicago."

According to the last interview with Virgie, Tom had gone off to Dayton (where their oldest daughter had moved) and had found a job, but Virgie did not expect him to keep it for long. "It's hard to say in a way," she said. "You might consider that we've lost everything we had, and he might keep it for a while, but not always, he won't." Virgie intended to return to West Virginia and enroll her children in school there. "Then after school's out, it's hard to say. I might go out there" to Dayton "and stay till after" the birth of her first grandchild. "But I don't want to go to Ohio to live," she said, "I never did like Ohio."

For plenty of other West Virginians, however, Ohio and other midwestern states were the Promised Land. Ozzie Stroud's migration began as soon as he finished high school. "It was a trend there that once you graduated from high school," he explained, "you went off to Chicago, Cleveland, Columbus, Baltimore, Detroit. I graduated at two o'clock on Sunday, June the fourth, 1967. Two o'clock Monday afternoon I was sitting in Columbus. And I looked for a job for about two weeks here and couldn't find one." "I had a sister living in Chicago at the time," he continued, "and I called her and told her I was coming up. I left home with twenty dollars in my pocket. Haven't looked back since."[31]

Stroud grew up in Mingo County, West Virginia, amid the heartland of southern Appalachia's coal country. His father worked in a coal mine, and his mother stayed at home rearing the seven children. His father had managed to survive the mechanization programs that began in the late 1940s, and life was generally good (his family had the first television in the community) until in 1959, when Stroud was eleven, his father slipped on ice outside a mine and fell on a rail of track, suffering a cracked spine. Because the mining company disputed his injury, the family had no income for three years. "You couldn't buy a job," he recalled. "You know like teenagers today, they can go out to Kroger's or any of the shopping centers and get a job in the shoe store. There was no jobs like that when I was a teenager." "As I remember most," he explained poignantly, "you either worked in the coal mines, or you was a schoolteacher, school bus driver, or you was on welfare."[32]

Stroud spent his adolescent years counting the days until he would have to leave, because people were leaving all around him. "It was kindly disappointing," he said:

> Because you knew when you got out of high school if you didn't go off to college you had to go off to work someplace. You were leaving home. It's hard to break the tradition or the culture of knowing that, okay, when I graduate from high school I'm going to be out on my own. Because I've got to leave home. I can't stay at home. And I was one of those individuals—like I knew from '59 to '62 we had no income, from '62 to '66 we were on welfare. My mom got $165 a month. And that's all we had from '62 to '66. And there were still seven of us. My sister left home in '64. She got married at the age of sixteen, and they went to Chicago. They both started working. But all of us graduated from high school. I don't see how she did it.[33]

While Stroud was in high school, the War on Poverty's job corps program was active in West Virginia. During one summer, he got a job through the program as a timekeeper for the other workers who cleaned high schools. He was making $22.50 a week and gave his check to his parents so that the family could survive. "I remember one Friday I came home," he explained, "and I just got my check the day before or something. And I put it up on what we called the shadow box on the wall. I just stuck it up there like you would in a picture frame. And I came home and it was on a Friday night and I said, 'Dad, you think I could have two bucks tonight to go down to the restaurant and stuff?' And he said, 'Well, you can have your whole check.' That day he got his back pay from his social security. He got seven years back pay." That, he said, "was a good memory."[34]

Stroud also spent another summer working in Uptown after his oldest sister married and moved to Lake View, an adjacent neighborhood. The family was in such a desperate condition that his mother came along to work as well. "It was a unique feeling," he said, "especially if you get on your own. The first summer I went up there it was a common thing that if you wanted a job you could go to Chicago, and you could go to this one certain factory and get a job. It was a candy factory. It was the Williamson Candy Company, on the corner of Armitage and Cicero. They made O'Henry candy bars." Like the chocolate factory that Buddy Lee Ford went to in Milwaukee, Williamson was filled with southerners and Mexicans. "I went out," he recounted, "and got a job there—they hired me. This was the summer before my senior year—summer of '66." Along with his mother, he said, "I went and got a job there." His job was to take the centers of the candy bar and dump them on a conveyor belt. "I never will forget it," he said, "$1.53 an hour. And that was pretty good money when you figured that a tool and die maker back then, I think the top pay was $4.00 an hour." He was making about sixty dollars a week, three times what the West Virginia Job Corps paid. After he was on the job two days, his boss wanted to make him an order-filler in the shipping department for a nickel an hour more. He agreed, and on the dock he soon learned why personnel wanted to move him there: he was the only one who could read. The dock loaded about twenty semitrailers each day. "That was an experience," he said. "Because you know you don't tell them you're going to quit and go back, you know. When you hire in you don't tell them you're just going to be there for three months. So, when it got late August, I went in and I told them that I was going to quit and go back to school and stuff, and the personnel manager there at the time said, We'll give you a raise to stay and everything." After he refused, the manager told him he would have a position waiting for him the following June. Stroud and his mother returned to Mingo County, and he spent a portion of his wages buying school clothes for his siblings.[35]

After graduation, Stroud and his younger brother left for Columbus, Ohio, to find work. Fortunately, his grandparents and uncles were living there, so they had a place to stay. His brother's plans were to work over the summer and return in the fall for high school, and he found a job bagging groceries at a local store. Stroud, however, was intent on a factory job, and for two weeks he searched to no avail. Not wanting to return to West Virginia because it would have been another mouth for the struggling family to feed, Stroud had his father come to Columbus and drive him to Uptown. In Chicago, unlike Columbus, there were jobs for the taking, and Stroud readily exercised his ability to choose; the first week he was there, he worked at five different places. He would hire in, work a shift, and leave, not because of a peculiar cultural trait but because it was a miserable job. Eventually, his brother-in-law managed to get him a position at the machine shop where he worked; he began at $2.10 an hour. Stroud was still homesick, even though he was staying with his sister and brother-in-law in Lake View. "It still wasn't like home, you know. You felt like the third wheel."[36]

Moving from Mingo County to Chicago's Near North Side entailed many adjustments, but Stroud seems to have made them well and rather quickly. About the time he moved, he said Uptown was discovered as an Appalachian mecca, but he refused to live there. He did not want to live in one of the three-room apartments in which you shared a bathroom. He also said there were too many prostitutes. Instead, he found an apartment for himself in Lake View and then in Logan Square. But he enjoyed going to Uptown for shopping, movies (which he said was his major entertainment), and the bars, although he never drank in them. He said two pickpockets made him quickly realize the way of the city. After several months of work, he saved eight hundred dollars to make a down payment on the one thing, it seems, that was first on many male migrants' wish list: a new car. In January, he returned to West Virginia for a funeral in his new Ford Fairlane. At a high school basketball game, he learned that he was making five hundred dollars more per year than his old basketball coach, and at that time he realized that even the one occupation he thought would allow him to remain in West Virginia—teaching—was not feasible. "You know," he said, "the world seemed to open up after you got out of the state of West Virginia."[37]

In 1973, two events occurred that would coax Stroud into leaving Chicago. His older sister, who had been the primary reason why he had come to Chicago, divorced her husband, and both moved away. Stroud suddenly had no family nearby. In September, his grandmother, who was living in Columbus, died. When he went home for the funeral, his family told him they wanted him closer, so he returned to Chicago, quit his job, and moved to Columbus on October 10. After a few days, he found a job, ironically, at Jeffrey Mining Equipment, one of the industries that was helping mechanize West Virginia's coal mines.[38]

While Virgie and Ozzie Stroud were making the adjustments to urban life as first-generation migrants, there were, of course, second-generation southerners trying to reconcile the vestiges of an old life with the realities of a new life. Some were successful, drawing on the improvements their parents made as migrants. A few, however, were struggling in 1960s—battling poverty, declining opportunity, lack of (especially male) role models, and welfare caseworkers. Some second-generation southerners, most of whom were young, were betwixt and between.

Take the case of Larry Redden, born in 1947 into the ugliness of Cincinnati's migrant cluster. His parents, who were from eastern Kentucky but had met in Cincinnati, were having difficulty surviving economically, let alone moving up and out of poverty, as many other migrants had. Thirteen children only made matters worse. Many times, his mother told Redden, the family slept where it could—on the streets, in the bus station. Redden said his father had absolutely no pride left because all the unskilled jobs for which he was applying were filled. Because welfare regulations were predicated on the assumption that there was no reason for an able-bodied male to be unemployed, benefits were difficult to get. Consequently, Redden's father left the household periodically. "When I was born, my mother was on welfare, which caused a problem," he said. "She had my older sister with her, but at that point in time, being on welfare, you weren't supposed to have a man in your life." "No kind of man was supposed to be even around, or else you could get kicked off welfare." "That," he continued, "created a problem for my mother when she was pregnant because once she went to the hospital, she would have been cut off welfare because of being with a man," the pregnancy certainly "proof that she had been with a man within the last nine months." Even by the late 1940s, southerners had come to display a shrewd resourcefulness against a system that was designed to make life as miserable as possible. "When she went to the hospital," he said, "she used a fictitious name. She took her middle name, took my father's name, and cut off the last letters and added others, which made her be Louise Redding. My father did the same, so when I was born, I was born as Larry James Redding instead of Redden. My mother said other people did that, and that she got the idea from a friend of hers."[39]

Redden recalled the horrific memory of a caseworker barging into his family's apartment and finding his father at home in bed. The caseworker cut off their relief for three months, and they were forced out into the streets. Unannounced visits were something a welfare family had to endure:

> From the bottoms, we moved to Riverside, which was in a house that was really close to the River, and every year we used to be flooded out. My mother was still living on welfare. Then we moved into Laurel Homes because in a sense it was like subsidized housing back in the early fifties. I went to Washburn School. We moved to Vine Street, which was basically Over-the-Rhine, and from about age 6 that was where I grew up. That's the beginning, my kind of life living on welfare. Between the ages of 6 and 7, I went to five different schools. The remarkable thing is that I did very well. I was a straight-A student and very rarely ever got a B. When I transferred to junior high, I started failing. That was at the same time when I started living on my own. I was almost 12, and I was out on the streets on my own. The reason for that was that we were sitting in the house on Vine Street and a welfare worker came in without knocking. She just opened the door, and we had a television, a little Philco TV that my uncle had given us because we didn't have a radio or TV or anything in the house. At that point in time, you weren't allowed to have what they called "luxuries" in the house, or you would be thrown off welfare.

With little recourse, and still no job, Redden's father was forced to leave his family in order to feed it. He went to California and found a job as a janitor, and his absence made it easier for Redden's mother to reapply for welfare. Redden attributed the breakup of his family (and, he said, many other southern Appalachian families in Cincinnati and other northern cities) to a welfare system that maintained "if you couldn't find a job, it was your own fault."[40]

When his father left, suddenly, Redden said, he realized he was on his own. His mother was getting $120 each month; after rent and utilities were paid, the family—at that time six children—had $20 to buy food for the month. In 1958, shortly after his father left, Redden also left the apartment so that the money could be stretched further. He began sleeping anywhere he could find, including attics, people's homes, abandoned buildings. Although he was still in school (because his mother's welfare check would have been reduced had he quit), he was finding it increasingly difficult because he was working at three different jobs. Redden was only the most recent in a long tradition of southern males going to work as soon as possible.[41]

In 1963, Redden dropped out of school. The following year he went into the service. At the age of twenty-one, after his military stint, he went back to Cincinnati and discovered his own identity by working at the Appalachian Identity Center, now a part of Cincinnati's Urban Appalachian Council (UAC). He said he was surprised to think of himself as either an "Appalachian" or a "hillbilly" because he was "urbanized" as a second-generation migrant. Seeing the lack of role models for the children of Cincinnati's Lower Price Hill and other migrant neighborhoods, Redden realized that he had to go back to school to gain the integrity needed to persuade children to stay in school. Eventually, he graduated from the University of Cincinnati and has been a part of the UAC staff since then.[42]

Disproving the Stereotypes

Certainly not all scholars who studied migrants have focused on pathology. Some were designing hypotheses in their research that would test the validity of common assumptions about southern migrants. Earl Harold Cunningham, for example, studied Cleveland migrants and discovered most of his assumptions were false. Migrants there were not dissatisfied or disappointed in Cleveland; migrants did not possess "sect-like" attitudes; and associational activity, particularly with churches, did not decline upon migration. More important, Cunningham did not find serious economic or emotional distress. Many migrants he interviewed had experienced unemployment, but the overwhelming majority were not dependent on public assistance. Most believed it better to be in the North during unemployment than in the South (a change from the beliefs of many depression-era migrants), primarily because they had friends and kin to whom they could turn. John D. Photiadis also studied migrants (mostly West Virginian) to Cleveland and found the typical pattern was that migrants first moved to inner-city areas and then on to better neighborhoods as soon as they could. Those who left West Virginia and stayed in Cleveland attained more than those migrants who returned to West Virginia or those who never left.[43]

In the late 1960s, the sociologists Harry K. Schwarzweller, James S. Brown, and J. J. Mangalam did a follow-up study of Brown's doctoral thesis on Beech Creek in Clay County, Kentucky. The most significant finding was the massive out-migration of as many as three-quarters of the community, many of whom went to southwestern Ohio. But in the host city, they found little of the misery and despair among Beech Creekers that those in Cincinnati experienced. The changes associated with moving from farm to factory were compensated by monetary rewards, kinship (through neighbors, friends, and family, many of whom hailed from

Beech Creek), and frequent visits back to Kentucky. Beech Creekers, the authors note, "looked toward the hills for renewal of their strength." In short, what the authors found economically was what one might expect: a few did very well, achieving professional careers or supervisory roles in industry, while the vast majority attained "a reasonably adequate, though relatively modest, level of living, and their incomes compare favorably with those of the American working class in general." A few, however, continued to struggle economically in urban areas, where "the inadequacies and injustices of the past linger as an ever present reality."[44]

Finally, the historian James N. Gregory has mined the Public Use Microdata samples (PUMS) from the 1970, 1980, and 1990 censuses to provide quantitative data that go far in refuting the belief that southern migrants lived in ghettos characterized by poverty, victimization, and hopelessness, data that complement evidence from chapter 5 dealing with 1960. By 1970, almost 40 percent of the 7.3 million white southerners who were living outside the South resided in the five midwestern states of Wisconsin, Illinois, Michigan, Indiana, and Ohio, and according to PUMS data, there is no evidence of exceptional poverty among migrants. For example, southern migrants had an average family income that was only $382 less than midwestern-born whites, and the percentage of southern whites below the poverty line was only slightly higher than their midwestern-born white counterparts. This evidence contradicts Jon C. Teaford's presentation of the entire migratory population as mired in poverty. Indeed, the figures for southern white migrants mirror approximately the figures for whites as a whole, indicating that migrants were not economically different from other white groups, again evidence congruent with data from 1960. When data on impoverished households are further analyzed, southern whites do not constitute anywhere near the bulk of those in poverty in the Midwest; of those living in poverty in 1969, 7 percent were southern white, 55 percent were midwestern-born white, 10 percent were other U.S.-born white, 8 percent were foreign-born white, 18 percent were African American, and 2 percent were Hispanic.[45]

The PUMS figures also indicate that by 1970 white southern migrants had become more suburbanized than most other population groups had, directly refuting the long-held assumption that migrants lived in central-city "hillbilly ghettoes" because they could not afford anything else. In the Midwest, 47 percent of southern white families lived in suburban communities outside major metropolitan areas, and another 23 percent chose to live in small cities and rural areas, a figure confirmed in oral histories with such people as Dewey and Marie Thompson in Osceola, Indiana; Jess and Emma Martin near Indianapolis, Indiana; Joe and Lucille Clardy in South Bend, Indiana; and Ozzie Stroud near Columbus, Ohio. Southerners seemed to have maintained their strong attraction to land and to rural life once their economic success allowed them to move out of urban neighborhoods.[46] Gregory notes that the salaries that made suburbanization possible among southern white families in the Midwest were based solidly on blue-collar jobs in 1970: 66 percent of southern white males employed in the civilian labor force held blue-collar positions, compared with 50 percent for other whites. Among southern white women, approximately 33 percent worked in blue-collar jobs, compared with 17 percent for other white women. Although African Americans and Hispanics were also blue collar, southern whites held a higher percentage of skilled, craft, and supervisory positions, 25 percent compared with 15 percent for African Americans and 17 percent for Hispanics. The data indicate that although southerners often came northward unskilled, by 1970 they had moved into skilled positions, many of which were in unionized, highly paid industries (southerners brought home the highest average blue-collar salaries of *any* other group, including whites), a trend that indicates that racism likely accounted for southerners' gain over minorities in these positions.[47]

Gregory's examination of census data for 1970 provides a clear and concise summary of one of the largest internal migrations in U.S. history. Frequently ignored except during economic crisis, southern whites realized the lack of economic opportunity around them and embarked on a journey to areas north of the Ohio River that looked far more promising. In contrast to the stereotypes associated with journalists who were looking for scapegoats or even unintentionally spread by scholars trying to uncover solutions to poverty and maladjustment, by the 1970s the vast majority of southerners were enjoying the benefits of several decades of a booming postwar economy. The model of southern white migration was clearly based on success, not on failure. Indeed, it is doubtful whether such a mammoth northward migration would have occurred were migrants not improving and remaking their lives in the North. In spite of the comparisons with African Americans, who had embarked on what for them was a true exodus about the same time as southern whites began their exile, southern whites had won out in a northern economy and society that was peppered with racism.

When the postwar economic boom began to founder as the 1970s progressed, southern migrants, who had constituted so much a part of the midwestern industrial belt, began to feel the effects of layoffs and plant closings associated with deindustrialization, but the distress associated with the movement of industry southward (even to Mexico) was felt by everyone whose life was bound up with a factory, not just southerners. To emphasize southern distress is to perpetuate the stereotype.[48]

Although the evidence proves that southerners did well economically by migrating, emotionally they were frequently still divided in their feelings about the South and the Midwest. The divided heart often was manifest in the 1980s and 1990s when migrants faced retirement and the prospect of staying in the Midwest or returning to the South to finish out their lives.

Notes

1. Letter to J. A. Norton, Apr. 19, 1959, Urban Migrant Project, folder 6, box 278, Records of the Council of the Southern Mountains (hereafter CSM Collection), Southern Appalachian Archives, Hutchins Library, Berea College, Berea, Ky. See also Giffin, "Appalachian Newcomers in Cincinnati," 79–84.

2. Allan M. Trout, "Why South's Mountaineers Migrate Is Workshop Topic," *Louisville Courier-Journal,* Aug. 2, 1959; John Fetterman, "'Man Can Make It Up Here If He Really Tries,'" Newspaper Clippings, folder 1, box 294, CSM Collection; American Friends Service Committee, "Preliminary Report on Conditions and Problems Observed in the Kentucky Mountain Counties," Southern Appalachia, folder 3, box 8, Roscoe Giffin Collection, Southern Appalachian Archives. See also Maxwell, "Down from the Hills and into the Slums," 27; Bruno, "Chicago's Hillbilly Ghetto," 28; Richard Martin, "City 'Hillbillies': Appalachian Migrants in Slums Fail to Benefit from Antipoverty Drive," *Wall Street Journal,* Sept. 30, 1965; and Dorothea Kahn Jaffe, "Hills Still Call Job Refugees," *Christian Science Monitor,* Aug. 4, 1964. Jon C. Teaford and Jacqueline Jones are the latest scholars who have emphasized those who did not seem to experience the mobility of past migrants over those who moved northward and vastly improved their lives. See Teaford, *Cities of the Heartland,* 232–33; and J. Jones, *Dispossessed,* esp. 249–65. Meanwhile, recall that in 1960, only 4 percent of southern white migrants were unemployed. See 1960 Integrated Public Use Microdata Samples: One Percent Sample. There were exceptions, however, to the growing body of newspaper reports stereotyping southerners in the Midwest. See Julian Krawcheck's six articles in Cleveland, "Smile When You Say 'Hillbilly,'" *Cleveland Press,* Jan. 29–Feb. 4, 1958. On population trends, see Pickard, *Population Change in the Appalachian Region,* sec. 3, 6; and Pickard, *Population and Net Migration Trends in the Appalachian Region,* 1–4.

3. Caldwell, "Adjustment of Mountain Families in an Urban Environment," 395; *Michigan Chronicle,* May 1, 1943; Killian, "Southern White Laborers in Chicago's West Side," 133 (landlord quote); Hutchens, "Kentuckians in Hamilton," 13. See also Murphy, "Orphans of Willow Run," 110.

4. Votaw, "Hillbillies Invade Chicago," 64, 67; Maxwell, "Down from the Hills and into the Slums," 27, 28; Dale Nouse, "Detroiters Like City Just Fine, Survey Reveals," *Detroit Free Press,* Nov. 18, 1952. Harry Woodward Jr., in an extensive study of migrants in Lake View (Chicago), explained that "although the metropolitan newspapers have labeled this group 'hillbillies,' indicating they come from

the Appalachian mountains of the southern part of the United States, there is little evidence to support this assumption; rather, the people seem to come from all parts of the rural and small town South with little regional distinction among them." See Woodward, *Southern White Migrant in Lake View,* 2A.

5. Whisnant, *All That Is Native and Fine.*

6. These stereotypes are uncritically analyzed in Teaford, *Cities of the Heartland,* 232.

7. Cabestro and Hill, *Appalachian Culture;* Woodward, *Southern White Migrant in Lake View,* 30A; Stekert, "Focus for Conflict," 95–127.

8. Woodward, *Southern White Migrant in Lake View,* 9A; Fisher, "Victim-Blaming in Appalachia," 185–94; Galloway, McBride, and Vedder, "Mobility of Appalachian Americans," 53–64.

9. Teaford does even worse by borrowing from media reports for much of his discussion of southern whites. See Teaford, *Cities of the Heartland,* 291. Jacqueline Jones borrows heavily from literature on Cincinnati. See J. Jones, *Dispossessed.* For early studies, see Roscoe Giffin and Mayor's Friendly Relations Committee, *Report of a Workshop on the Southern Mountaineer in Cincinnati.* See also *Peoples Appalachia,* 1–40. For background on the Urban Appalachian Council, see Michael E. Maloney, "The Urban Appalachian Ethnic Movement," paper presented at the annual meeting of the American Anthropological Association, Cincinnati, Nov. 30, 1979, copy in Frank Foster Library, Urban Appalachian Council, Cincinnati. See also *Cincinnati Enquirer* Staff, *Urban Appalachians.* The literature is prodigious, and although many of the following items are part of this school, I in no way mean to indict all the titles or to discount the contributions that these authors made: Philliber, *Appalachian Migrants in Urban America;* Hanrahan, "Public Budget Effects of Eastern Kentucky Migration to Cincinnati, Ohio"; Henderson, "Poor Urban Whites," 111–14; Borman, *Urban Appalachian Children and Youth at Risk;* Fowler and Davies, "Urban Settlement Patterns of Disadvantaged Migrants," 275–84; Maloney, "Prospects for Urban Appalachians," 163–73; McCoy and Watkins, "Drug Use among Urban Ethnic Youth," 83–106; Obermiller and Philliber, eds., *Too Few Tomorrows;* Weiland, Wagner, and Obermiller, eds., *Perspectives on Urban Appalachians.* The following are available at the Foster Library: Michael E. Maloney, "School Dropouts: Cincinnati's Challenge in the Eighties," Working Paper 15, Apr. 25, 1985, Urban Appalachian Council (UAC); David P. Varady, "Elderly Appalachians in Cities: A Case Study of Cincinnati," Working Paper 13, Dec. 1980, UAC; Dan M. McKee, "A Comparison of Appalachian Black and White Neighborhoods of Cincinnati," Working Paper 9, Nov. 1977, UAC; Marvin J. Berlowitz and Henry Durand, "School Dropout or Student Pushout? A Case Study of the Possible Violation of Property Rights and Liberties by the De Facto Exclusion of Students from Public Schools," Working Paper 8, Spring 1977, UAC; David Bruning, "Socioeconomic and Ethnic Composition of Catholic Parishes in Cincinnati and Norwood, Ohio," Working Paper 7, Mar. 1975, UAC; Thomas E. Wagner, "Urban Appalachian School Children: The Least Understood of All," Working Paper 6, UAC; Thomas E. Wagner, "Report of the Appalachian School Study Project," Working Paper 4, June 1974, UAC; Phillip J. Obermiller, "Essay on Minority Populations," typescript, Apr. 1983; Aloys Schweitzer, "Who is SAM? A Friendly Study of the Southern Appalachian Migrant," typescript, 1964. In the 1970s and 1980s, *Mountain Life and Work* also

kept a close watch on conditions in Cincinnati. See *Mountain Life and Work* 52 (Aug. 1976): 3–29; 52 (Sept. 1976): 35–39; 52 (Nov. 1976): 38; 53 (Jan. 1977): 28–30; 53 (Feb.–Mar. 1977): 35–37; 53 (June 1977): 35–36; 53 (July 1977): 24–26; 54 (May 1978): 35–36; 54 (June 1978): 22–26; 54 (Oct. 1978): 16–19; 54 (Jan. 1978): 29–31; 55 (May 1979): 30–31; 56 (Sept. 1980): 23; 56 (Oct. 1980): 29; 59 (Sept. 1982): 14–20; 60 (Sept. 1983): 3–23; and 64 (Oct.–Dec. 1988): 3–41.

10. Obermiller, "Question of Appalachian Ethnicity," 18; Borman and Obermiller, eds., *From Mountain to Metropolis,* xix. For another critique of the emphasis on pathology, see Bailey, "'I Never Thought of My Life as History,'" esp. 238–39; and Feather, *Mountain People in a Flat Land.*

11. Robert Oliver, "Ex-Kentuckian Pleads for Mountain Children," (from *Detroit News*), Newspaper Clippings, folder 1, box 294, CSM Collection; M. Martin, "Mountain Migrants," (from *Dayton Journal Herald,* July 26, 1961), Newspaper Clippings, folder 16, box 293, CSM Collection; Bailey interview, 28. For an example of one of Mary Ellen Wolfe's articles, see "Integration Puzzle Confronts Dayton," *Dayton Journal Herald,* Feb. 24, 1960. One of the most notorious series on mountain pathology began in May 1957 in the *Chicago Tribune.* See, for example, Norma Lee Browning, "A Trip to Appalachia: Visit to Middle Ages," *Chicago Tribune,* May 5, 1957. The article series, "Otter Holler, Appalachia, U.S.A.," was picked up nationally by newspapers. See, for example, Norma Lee Browning, "Backward, Even for Hill Folk," *Kansas City Star,* May 8, 1957.

12. Whisnant, *Modernizing the Mountaineer,* 37n70. For examples of mention of the out-migration, see *Mountain Life and Work* 30 (Summer 1954): 23–25; 34 (Fall 1958): 42–44; and 36 (Fall 1960): 52–53. For an overview of the council, see Whisnant, *Modernizing the Mountaineer,* 3–39.

13. "Participants, Workshop on Urban Adjustment of Southern Appalachian Migrants, 1959–1966," Workshops—Urban Migrant, folder 1, box 280, CSM Collection; "Unique Social Exploration," ibid.; P. F. Ayer to Lena Brown Ainsworth, June 1, 1959, Urban Migrant Project, folder 5, box 278, CSM Collection. For more on the Berea Workshop, see Chicago Commission on Human Relations, Mayor's Committee on New Residents, "Southern Appalachian Tour Workshop," Urban Migrant Project, folder 1, box 278, CSM Collection; Gissen, "The Mountain Migrant," 67–73; Evelyn S. Stewart, "Hill People—Proud and God-Fearing," *Detroit Free Press,* July 31, 1959; John Fetterman, "Mission to Appalachia," *Louisville Courier-Journal,* Aug. 2, 1964; and Trout, "Why South's Mountaineers Migrate Is Workshop Topic."

14. Participants quoted in [B. Farris], "The Southern Appalachian Mountain Migrant," 3 (first quote), 7 (third quote), Urban Migrant Project, folder 1, box 278, CSM Collection; Whisnant, *Modernizing the Mountaineer,* 9 (second quote). See also Fetterman, "Mission to Appalachia"; and "10 to See Where Hill Folk Came From," *Chicago Sun-Times,* July 7, 1959.

15. At the opening of the CSM's Chicago Center in 1963, William H. Meyers, a member of the board, regretted that there was no "Council of the Southern Flatlands." See Council of the Southern Mountains, Inc., *Report on a Meeting Held in Connection with the Opening of the Chicago Office of the Council of the Southern Mountains,* 1, Migrant Centers, folder 3, box 284, CSM Collection.

16. See Workshops—Urban Migrant, folders 6 and 7, box 281, CSM Collection;

and miscellaneous documents, Urban Migrant Project, folder 4, box 278, CSM Collection.

17. J. Jones, *Dispossessed,* 255; "Report of the Committee on the Southern Appalachian Newcomer," Urban Migrant Project, folder 6, box 283, CSM Collection.

18. Mayor's Friendly Relations Committee of Cincinnati, *When Cultures Meet,* 3.

19. See Southern Appalachia Center, Workshops—Urban Migrant, folder 3, box 281, CSM Collection.

20. Kentuckians of Michigan, Inc., *Annual Picnic, '74.* I thank Lynwood Montell for bringing this to my attention.

21. Council of the Southern Mountains, *Are You Thinking of Moving to the City?*

22. *Mountain Life and Work* 39 (Spring 1963): 9; Guy, "Diversity to Unity"; Stone, *The Success System That Never Fails.* On Hull-House, see Council of the Southern Mountains, Inc., *Report on a Meeting Held in Connection with the Opening of the Chicago Office of the Council of the Southern Mountains,* 7. See also William H. Meyers to Elinor Griest, Mar. 22, 1966, Migrant Centers, folder 9, box 283, CSM Collection; Donald Yabush, "Aid Migrant Whites in Finding Work," *Chicago Tribune,* May 30, 1965; "Southern Mountain Council to Expand," *Chicago Tribune,* May 6, 1965; and Peter Gorner, "Mountain Folks Learn Ways of Urban Life," *Chicago Tribune,* Nov. 28, 1965.

23. Meyers to Griest; Campbell interview.

24. Meyers to Griest. See also Guy, "Chicago Southern Center"; William H. Meyers to Hollie D. Sizemore, Sept. 2, 1965, Migrant Centers, folder 8, box 283, CSM Collection; and Campbell interview.

25. Meyers to Griest; "A Survey of Our Past," miscellaneous, folder 5, box 284, CSM Collection; Whisnant, *Modernizing the Mountaineer,* 26–28; Jones interview; Campbell interview. For more on community action programs in the 1960s, see B. Montgomery, "Uptown Story," 8–18; and Matusow, *Unraveling of America.* One very important agency for southern migrants is the Chicago Area Black Lung Association. See "Uptown Chicago Gains Community Clinic," 34–36.

26. Carson, *In Struggle;* Miller, *"Democracy Is in the Streets";* Whisnant, *Modernizing the Mountaineer,* 23; Clarus Backes, "Poor People's Power in Uptown," *Chicago Tribune Magazine,* Sept. 29, 1968, 46; Gitlin and Hollander, *Uptown,* xxi–xxii; Herman, "Uptowners Call Him 'Preacher,'" 11–14. Another major difference between the JOIN project and other programs was that activists did *not* try merely to change the southern migrant's outlook on life into one that resembled a middle-class view. One agency, for example, promoted a contest in which an award ("inedible, unwearable, and nonnegotiable") was given to the people with the neatest lawns. See Backes, "Poor People's Power in Uptown," 49.

27. Gitlin and Hollander, *Uptown,* xix. For more on Uptown, see Clarus Backes, "Uptown: The Promised Land," *Chicago Tribune Magazine,* Sept. 22, 1968; Backes, "Poor People's Power in Uptown," 46–56; Clarus Backes, "Appalachia: The Source," *Chicago Tribune Magazine,* Oct. 6, 1968, 30–33; and Harry Ernst, "Appalachians in a Hostile World," *Charleston (W.Va.) Gazette-Mail,* Oct. 9, 1966.

28. Gitlin and Hollander, *Uptown,* xxiv–xxv.

29. I am grateful to Todd Gitlin for sharing with me the large number of oral history transcripts produced from his time in Uptown. One of the requirements I agreed to was that I would not disclose the identity of the interviewees (for a number of reasons, all the names of interviewees in *Uptown* were changed). Nanci Hollander interviewed "Virgie" (a fictitious name) on three separate occasions in 1965; the transcripts from the tape-recorded interviews are in the author's possession.

30. An unidentified University of Chicago sociologist quoted in the *Chicago Tribune Magazine* came to the controversial conclusion that "hard-core poverty as a way of life is relatively rare among Chicago's southern migrants, that good jobs (averaging $2.50 an hour for men, $1.90 an hour for women) are there for the asking, and that migrants are earning and spending more money than they have ever before seen in their lives. This bit of blasphemy strikes directly at the foundation upon which most welfare agencies in Uptown were built, and many social workers—despite the sociologist's well-documented statistics—are still unable to accept it." Quoted in Backes, "Poor People's Power in Uptown," 47. Virgie's problems stem primarily from Tom's not keeping a steady job—for whatever reason, which meant frequent trips between Chicago and West Virginia, disrupted education for her children, intermittent welfare, and housing in some of the worst places Chicago had to offer. The other controversial notion is that some scholars studying migrants have implied that those who would have been "problem cases" in the South often became "problem cases" in the North, a view I do not necessarily accept. See, for example, Brown, "Social Organization of an Isolated Kentucky Mountain Neighborhood"; and Schwarzweller, Brown, and Mangalam, *Mountain Families in Transition.* Jacqueline Jones rightly notes that an individual's adjustment often reflected "indefinable qualities, such as a yearning (or lack thereof) for a Southern home place," which certainly seems to be the case with Tom. See J. Jones, *Dispossessed,* 245.

31. Stroud interview. I am grateful to Lea Ann Sterling for introducing me to Ozzie Stroud.

32. Ibid.

33. Ibid.

34. Ibid.

35. Ibid.

36. Ibid.

37. Ibid.

38. Ibid.

39. Redden quoted in Borman and Stegelin, "Social Change and Urban Appalachian School Children," 178; Redden interview.

40. Quoted in Borman and Stegelin, "Social Change and Urban Appalachian School Children," 178. Redden's parents never officially divorced; more than a decade later, his mother was able to rejoin her husband in California and spent time with him before his death. Redden interview.

41. Redden interview. See also Stroud interview.

42. Redden interview.

43. Cunningham, "Religious Concerns of Southern Appalachian Migrants in a North Central City," 372–75; Photiadis, *Social and Sociopsychological Characteristics of West Virginians in Their Own State and in Cleveland, Ohio.* See also

Petersen, Sharp, and Drury, *Southern Newcomers to Northern Cities;* Nelson and Whitt, "Religion and the Migrant in the City," 379–84; Crissman, "Analysis of the Family Structure and Family Values of Central Appalachian Migrants in Akron, Ohio"; Kukin and Byrne, *Appalachians in Cleveland;* Crowe, "Occupational Adaptation of a Selected Group of Eastern Kentuckians in Central Ohio"; and Deaton, "Private Costs and Returns of Migration from Eastern Kentucky to Cincinnati."

44. Schwarzweller, Brown, and Mangalam, *Mountain Families in Transition,* 218–19.

45. 1970 Public Use Microdata Sample: Five Percent Sample, cited in Gregory, "Southern Diaspora and the Urban Dispossessed," 111–34; Teaford, *Cities of the Heartland,* 232–33.

46. Gregory, "Southern Diaspora and the Urban Dispossessed," 123–24.

47. Ibid., 124–28. That southerners received higher paychecks than other midwestern groups refutes those who maintain that southerners did better than those they left behind but not as well as other northern groups. For evidence of this assumption, see, for example, Philliber and McCoy, eds., *Invisible Minority,* 5. It also shows a bias and a lack of understanding about southern white migrant motive on the part of scholars who are critical of their "underachievement." Jon Teaford has written that "even the 'successful' southern migrants were employed chiefly in blue-collar jobs, which could lead at best to a house in Huber Heights [Ohio]," as if migrants should have aspired for much more. This criticism echoes those by employers and unionists in previous decades who were critical of southerners because some were willing to work for low wages in the most menial of jobs. See Teaford, *Cities of the Heartland,* 232–33, 194.

48. For those who emphasize southern migrant economic distress, see J. Jones, *Dispossessed,* 264–65; Hundley, "Mountain Man in Northern Industry," 37; and Mary Ellen Wolfe, "Migrants Loyal, Easily Adjust to Jobs," *Dayton Journal Herald,* Feb. 26, 1960.

Epilogue: Return from Exile?

> I was born in eastern Kentucky in 1912. At the time, it was very, very isolated. We didn't have too much to look forward to. I have seen many, many changes. I have left eastern Kentucky and lived for a while in the East and in the North, and I came back to eastern Kentucky because I couldn't find the people anywhere else in the world like they are in eastern Kentucky.
>
> —Woodrow Allen

> I been here since 1947 and I'd like to leave before daylight if I could. But I got seven more years to go at Chrysler, then it's 30-and-out, and I head for Kentucky. . . . I'm going back to Kentucky to sit on the front porch, chew tobacco, and pick guitar. I've never chewed tobacco, but I'll learn.
>
> —Elden Partin

ALTHOUGH THE GREAT white migration slowed after 1970, it never completely stopped; hundreds of high school students, like Ozzie Stroud, graduated one day and migrated the next. But the migration northward seems to have been checked after 1970 by a significant southward migration. Even during the 1960s the Tennessee Valley region reversed the population decline from the three previous decades; as a whole, the 201 counties grew by 9 percent (in spite of the 64 that lost population—a total of 120,000 out-migrants), posting significant gains around the region's seven largest cities. Between 1975 and 1980, for example, 280,000 white southerners migrated to Illinois, Indiana, Michigan, Ohio, and Wisconsin, but 340,400 left there; between 1985 and 1990, 294,609 came northward, and 262,759 left the Midwest. By 1970, the first wave of southern migrant retirees was emerging, and once retirement dawned, of course, these exiles (many of whom had come north and convinced themselves that they would stay for only a short time) had to face the question of where they would spend the last years of their lives.[1]

Because kinship dictated so much of the southern white migratory experience, it should not be surprising that attachment to kin continued to be a factor—most often it was the deciding factor—as migrants decided what to do after their job no longer existed, which, after all, was the main thing that kept southerners in the Midwest. There were three basic options, although they usually wrestled most with the first two: one could leave the Midwest and return to one's original southern homeplace or community; one could stay in the Midwest and be near the children; or one could move away from the Midwest to a retirement area, such as Florida or Arizona.[2]

Anthropologists, such as Gwen Kennedy Neville, have argued that much of southern white culture concerns a world in which "the person lives in a constant state of individual striving and self-actualization but in which the religious imperative calls for communal life and loyalty to one's family and kin," another version of the divided heart. Clearly, individual attainment and attachment to one's family in a depressed region were contradictory cultural demands, but southern families who did not have large extended families in the Midwest particularly grappled with these competing demands because they had a family of procreation in the North and a family of origin in the South.[3]

Those who decide to move northward, save their money, and return to their southern homeplace with a pension often do so, it seems, out of a connectedness to place but also to be near their families of origin, particularly to care for an ailing parent. When I interviewed Pauline Mayberry in East Detroit in 1992, she talked of going back to be near her relatives, and a year later, she had returned to Tennessee to be with her mother, who lived in a nursing home in Waynesboro. Earl Cox's mother became ill just as he was set to retire in Detroit, and instead of moving to Alaska as he had planned, he reluctantly moved back to north Georgia to care for her. "If it hadn't a been for her," he said, "I would never have come back here, because I had to leave this place in order to make a decent living, and I couldn't see no reason to bring my money back here." Ed and Opal Martin lived a number of years in northern Indiana, but after Ed retired, they returned to Cypress Inn, Tennessee, and lived the remaining years of their lives comfortably and happily in a mobile home. Officially, they returned because Opal's widowed mother did not want to stay alone. Dewey Stults (who first came to Mishawaka, Indiana, to be with his seventeen-year-old son who had migrated) and his wife, Jewell, also retired and moved back to Tennessee because of Jewell's ailing mother.[4]

Those who returned to be near family in the South, however, often had to reconcile their family of procreation. Daymon and Betty Morgan moved from Dayton, Ohio, to Daymon's birthplace in Leslie County, Kentucky, after he retired and their youngest son graduated from high school. "I always said I would come back here," Daymon explained. "I had a feeling towards the mountains. There's other mountains but it seems like these had a special place." The Morgans' decision was made easier not only because they were able to return and live comfortably but also because they did not have to leave their children behind, since all three moved back with them, two of them permanently. R. G. Hudson and his wife, Pat, never had children, so when R. G. retired from Youngstown Steel in northwest Indiana, their decision to return to Blue Ridge, Georgia, to be with R. G.'s widowed mother was relatively easy, though more difficult for Pat, who was born and reared in the Calumet region. Conversely, Charlie and Charis Crooks miss their children and grandchildren in Milwaukee, but the Crooks decided to return to western Kentucky because of Wisconsin's high tax rate.[5]

Jim and Sally Etter ultimately chose their family of origin, because Jim, at least, was certain that he did not want to continue living in Whiting, Indiana. "I never did plan," he said. "I just never planned to continue to live there after I retired." He continued:

> Now I had friends, the Kirks, he planned to stay there when he retired. It was just always their plans, they would stay there when they retired. I never intended to. I really never intended to come back to Kentucky here. We went to Raleigh in North Carolina, we looked around there. And it was too high. We looked in east Tennessee before we came here. And probably would have settled there, we liked the area and all. But certain things—my mother and dad and her mother was still living and that had some drawing, you know. I mean, over the years we had been away always when there was sickness or something, it fell to some of the children close by to take care of them or something. Well, when we came back here we have had our part of it since that [laughs]. And I'm sure deep down that that had something to do with us coming here. . . .

Of their three children, only Don lived in Whiting, so their decision to be with their family of origin was less difficult, although the transition was harder for Sally. "I'm a nest builder," she said, "and it took me a while to make my nest."[6]

Other southerners have lived longer in their northern nests than their southern ones, however, and many of them find it too painful to leave their children and grandchildren by retiring and moving south. "It makes a difference about your family," Adolph Lacy believed. "For the wife and I, this is home to us. Our children are here and our grandchildren are here. They may leave sometime (I doubt it), but until they do we'll stay with them because this is home," he said of northern Indiana. Reuben and Mary Tune never had children of their own, but they have grown particularly fond of their nephew and therefore refuse to return South.[7]

For migrants whose parents were dead by the time retirement came, the decision about moving back was conditioned only by children living in the North. For Frank Plemons, for example, the specter of retirement came suddenly, as the Gary Works of U.S. Steel began eliminating jobs in the early 1980s. Frank had only sixty days to consider early retirement, but he took his retirement package just after Joyce's mother died in Tennessee. With her parents gone, Joyce's feelings of Tennessee died, too. "After then," she said, "I never thought anything, I never even gave it another thought about moving back. Because if I didn't have my parents, I didn't want to go back, you know. And naturally, I wouldn't want to leave Gary," her only child. Asked if Gary were to get a job transfer to east Tennessee, however, she quickly answered, "then I'd probably pack up tomorrow and go. I wouldn't go off and leave Gary."[8]

Some migrants become shuttlers, perhaps attempting to reconcile divided hearts, even after retirement. James Shelby went back to Hardin County, Tennessee, after he retired from Uniroyal in Mishawaka but stayed there only a few months and then returned to Indiana. "I think a lot of them, you know," he said, "figured their whole family is there on both sides—a man's family and his wife's, too. You'll see that the majority of them that move back there, they're not satisfied. This is more home to them—they've lived here, their kids are all here or part of them, and they're just not satisfied." Many of his acquaintances that did move back, he added, did not have children nearby in the North anyway. "People like that didn't have nothing here to keep them here; all their family's down there. If you've got a family and you got children living here, and you go back down there, you're not happy with being down there and them up here. You don't see them that often. So that's the reason a lot of them don't stay who moves back."[9] John Weatherford's actions are proof of this attachment to children. He and his wife had sold their house and were ready to move back to Tennessee with their son (he was intending to get his son a job at the nearby Saturn plant), but when their son backed out, he canceled his retirement plans, and all three are still in Mishawaka. Pauline Mayberry, in 1999, was considering a move back to Detroit to be near her children and grandchildren.

Nevertheless, kinship and the attraction of things and even people past are still strong in migrants' lives, and hearts are still torn between North and South. Some migrants refused to rule out a return move, saying instead, "Well, someday we might go back." Nellie Austin realized that the desire to go back was nostalgic. "We had some really good times when we come here adjusting," she said, but "it was rough. I look back now, and I wouldn't want to live through it again, the adjusting part, leaving family. It was a way of life down there, cause I grew up on a farm. And I think that I have always wanted to move back to the country, where I could see the hills." But "the hard work part," she added, "see, I don't remember that, and if I had to work real hard on the farm I would not have wanted to go back." Adolph Lacy concurred: "I think why most people want to go back, see, they remember how it was when you left. Everybody was in a group, they really wasn't a lot of responsibility other than just, you know, you had to make a living, and it was comfortable. Leave the doors open." He continued, "That's what you want to go back to. Now I'd like to go back to that, but that's not there anymore, and I really think that's what draws back a lot of people—they've forgot that it's a new world." Clearly, some southerners have overcome the ambivalence associated with migration.[10]

The strongest indication of where one's home really is concerns burial places, and the responses were split between burial in the North and the South. For some southerners, the decision about where to be interred was bound up in the complexity of deciding where to retire. Dewey and Marie Thompson answered both questions by deciding to be close to their nine children. "This is home," Marie said. "Yeah, I said I couldn't see going back down there to be buried and having the kids all have to go way down there. And if they ever wanted to visit the cemetery, they'd have to go way down there. And I know that they'd all want to be buried up here because the families is up here, so we just bought our plots out there in the Osceola cemetery." Other southerners did not care to return to the South to live but were quite adamant about being interred in a particular place in the South, often the family cemetery. John Weatherford had a fondness for a church graveyard outside Lutts, Tennessee, set on a hill facing east. Other migrants, such as Alvin and Ruby Berry, tried to reconcile both worlds by buying lots in the South and in the North, though after a daughter died in the North, the couple decided to make their final resting place in the same northern mausoleum; family of procreation won out.[11]

Immigrants have also struggled with questions of family of procreation and family of origin when circumstances in life opened the possibility of returning to one's premigration home. But southerners, given the proximity of "home," were probably better able to consider seriously a return than other groups were. Distance mattered; returning to one's original community in Budapest or even Chihuahua entailed much more discord than returning to east Tennessee from Detroit. Distance had always allowed southern whites the possibility to sojourn, and retirement again allowed them to choose between kin.[12]

Packing up and moving is rarely easy, and for a people with a strong sense of place, it was among one of life's most difficult decisions. There was a host of experiences in the southern exile to the Midwest, but there are common patterns. A combination of pushes and pulls sparked one of this country's largest internal migrations, as people set out looking for sustenance, shelter, even dignity and autonomy. Many southerners found these in the fields and factories of the Midwest. Some found satisfying jobs and adjusted reasonably well; others had a more difficult time and returned to the South. Virtually all migrants sojourned between midwestern jobs and their southern homes because of the two very different worlds in which they lived.

Southerners in the Midwest were intimately involved in twentieth-century history that was being made all around them, but they also made their own history. Their sweat and muscle helped win world wars, build great products, and sustain a remarkable economic boom. They were alternately welcomed in the North and discouraged from coming; they were sometimes noticed, sometimes ignored. But as the words of southerners themselves indicate, they were their own agents. Both mountaineers and flatlanders acted on the problem of poverty by moving to where they believed they could find prosperity. They tried to keep kin relationships alive by encouraging friends and family to move with them or by traveling on divided highways to see relatives in the South. They attempted to make what was for some a very difficult adjustment easier by bringing elements of upland southern life with them, such as gardening or music or transplanting the southern evangelical church. They struggled to fight and disprove stereotypical notions of what it meant to be a newcomer from the South. For the overwhelming majority, this perseverance paid off. A previously poor group of people for the most part neared the end of their lives with a home, a pension, and a bountiful table, even if they had divided hearts that resented having to leave their southern home to attain such things.

Notes

1. Tennessee Valley Authority, *Tennessee Valley Region,* n.p.; 1980 and 1990 Public Use Microdata Samples, Sample B: One Percent, cited in Gregory, "Southern Diaspora and the Urban Dispossessed," 130–32. See also Irene Nolan, "Their Mountain Homes Bring City Dwellers Back," *Louisville Courier-Journal and Times,* July 14, 1974.

2. Some maintain that kinship ties and community attachments were reasons for not leaving. See, for example, Uhlenberg, "Noneconomic Determinants of Nonmigration," 296–311.

3. Neville, *Kinship and Pilgrimage,* 22.

4. Mayberry interview; Cox interview; Ed and Opal Martin interview; Dewey and Jewell Stults interview.

5. Morgan interview; Hudson interview; Crooks interview.

6. James and Sally Etter interview, 39–44. See also Kirk interview; and Donald Etter interview, May 15, 1991, Aug. 4, 1992.

7. Lacy interview; Tune interview.

8. Plemons and Collins interview, 37.

9. Shelby interview.

10. Austin interview; Lacy interview.

11. Thompson interview; Weatherford interview; Alvin and Ruby Berry interview. John Weatherford's cemetery that faces east is a common allusion in southern Protestantism, because the dead were to rise and face Christ in the East on judgment day.

12. On immigrants' returning, see Bodnar, *Transplanted,* 53–54.

Bibliography

Interviews

AOHP	Appalachian Oral History Project, Special Collections Library, Alice Lloyd College. Transcripts available on microfilm.
CB	Tapes and/or transcripts in author's possession.
IUOHRC	Transcripts available from the Indiana University Oral History Research Center, Bloomington, Indiana.
UAC	Available from the Urban Appalachian Council, Cincinnati, Ohio.

Adams, Frazier B. By Ron Allen. July 6, 1972. AOHP

Allen, Alice T. By Ron Allen. Quicksand, Ky. June 15, 1972. AOHP

Ashley, Polly. By Curtis Caudill. Dec. 31, 1971. AOHP

Austin, Harvey and Nellie. By Chad Berry. South Bend, Ind. Dec. 21, 1989. CB

Bailey, Benny. By Bill Weinberg. Dec. 11, 1975. AOHP

Baldridge, Olus. By Ron Daley. Nov. 5, 1975. AOHP

Barkley, Allen and Earlene. By Chad Berry. Iron City, Tenn. May 22, 1985. CB

Berry, Alvin and Ruby. By Chad Berry. Granger, Ind. Jan. 6, 1990. CB

Berry, Orbie and Irene. By Chad Berry. Collinwood, Tenn. May 22, 1985. CB

Bowen, Altie. By Chad Berry. Cypress Inn, Tenn. May 24, 1985. CB

Brown, Helen [pseudonym]. N.d. UAC

Brummett, Charles. By Chad Berry. Whiting, Ind. Apr. 9, 1992. IUOHRC

Butler, Matt and Reba. By Chad Berry. Mishawaka, Ind. Dec. 22, 1989. CB

Campbell, Riley. By Chad Berry. Roanoke, Va. Jan. 17, 1995. Notes based on telephone conversation. CB

Clardy, Joe and Lucille. By Chad Berry. South Bend, Ind. Dec. 22, 1989. CB

Combs, Ed. By Diane ?. N.d. AOHP
Cox, Earl. By Chad Berry. Blue Ridge, Ga. May 30, 1993. CB
Crabtree, Riley. By Joey Elswick. N.d. AOHP
Crooks, Charlie and Charis. By Chad Berry. Kuttawa, Ky. July 11, 1993. CB
Dixon, Clemeth and Thelma Mae. By Chad Berry. Iron City, Tenn. May 21, 1985. CB
Dodd, Leonard and Ora. By Chad Berry. Iron City, Tenn. May 23, 1985. CB
Etter, Donald. By Chad Berry. Whiting, Ind. May 15, 1991; Aug. 4, 1992. IUOHRC
Etter, James and Sally. By Chad Berry. Hartford, Ky. June 25, 1992. IUOHRC
Fields, Simeon. By Ron Daley. Dec. 8, 1975. AOHP
Ford, Buddy Lee and Anita. By Chad Berry. Kuttawa, Ky. July 11, 1993. CB
Fowler, Dick. By Chad Berry. Waynesboro, Tenn. May 17, 1985. CB
Frazier, John C. N.d. AOHP
Gabbard, Fred. By Phyliss Combs. Booneville, Ky. Apr. 11, 1974. AOHP
Giardina, Denise. By Chad Berry. Charleston, W.Va. May 21, 1993. CB
Green, Max. By Chad Berry. Blue Ridge, Ga. May 30, 1993. CB
Hammittee, Jim. By Mary Thompson. Nov. 23, 1974. Special Collections, Samford University Library, Birmingham, Ala.
Hensley, James L. By Greer Warren. Anderson, Ind. June 19, 1982. IUOHRC
Hudson, R. G. and Pat. By Chad Berry. Bloomington, Ind. Sept. 28, 1991. CB
Isenhour, Bernice. By James R. Martin. June 12, 1973. AOHP
Jackson, Clifford and Ethel. By Chad Berry. Cypress Inn, Tenn. May 22, 1985. CB
Jett, Zeke. By Sari Tudiver. Highland, Ky., Jan. 25, 1972. AOHP
Jones, Loyal. By Chad Berry. Berea, Ky. Jan. 17, 1995. Notes based on telephone conversation. CB
Kirk, Leonard and Lucille. By Elisabeth Orr. Whiting, Ind. July 20, 1991. IUOHRC
Lacy, Adolph and Jemae. By Chad Berry. Mishawaka, Ind. Dec. 21, 1989. CB
Lawson, Vera. By Chad Berry. Mishawaka, Ind. Aug. 26, 1989. CB
Little, McKinley. By Laurel Anderson. May 25, 1975. AOHP
Martin, Ed and Opal. By Chad Berry. Cypress Inn, Tenn. May 18, 1985. CB
Martin, Jesse and Emma. By Chad Berry. Indianapolis, Ind. December 7, 1993. CB
Mayberry, Pauline. By Chad Berry. East Detroit, Mich. Aug. 4, 1992. CB
Morgan, Daymon and Betty. By Chad Berry. Bad Creek, Ky. Dec. 13, 1993. CB
Pennington, Will. By Laurel Anderson. Cincinnati, Ohio. Sept. 25, 1975. Nov. 14, 1975. AOHP
Plemons, Frank and Joyce, and Carol Collins. Whiting, Ind. May 15, 1991. IUOHRC
Profitt, Melvin. By Laurel Anderson. Hazel Green, Ky. May 30, 1975. June 1, 1975; June 23, 1975. AOHP
———. By Bill Weinberg. Hazel Green, Ky. Aug. 11, 1975. AOHP
Redden, Larry. By Chad Berry. Cincinnati, Ohio. Oct. 29, 1993. CB

Reeves, Sterlin and Nadean. By Chad Berry. Iron City, Tenn. May 21, 1985. CB
Rich, Hardin. By Chad Berry. Iron City, Tenn. May 21, 1985. CB
Roberson, Grady. By Chad Berry. Mishawaka, Ind. Oct. 8, 1989. CB
Shelby, James. By Chad Berry. Granger, Ind. Jan. 6, 1990. CB
Smith, Hazel [pseudonym]. N.d. UAC
Stroud, Ozzie. By Chad Berry. Columbus, Ohio. Oct. 27, 1993. CB
Stults, Dewey and Jewell. By Chad Berry. Collinwood, Tenn. May 20, 1985. CB
Stults, Ledford and Bonnie Nell. By Chad Berry. Mishawaka, Ind. Aug. 26, 1989. CB
Thompson, Dewey and Marie. By Chad Berry. Osceola, Ind. June 18, 1992. CB
Tune, Reuben and Mary. By Chad Berry. Mishawaka, Ind. Dec. 24, 1989. CB
Virgie [pseudonym]. By Nanci Hollander. Chicago, Ill. 1965. Tape transcript in the possession of Todd Gitlin.
Ward, Hollye. By Chad Berry. Nashville, Tenn. Oct. 29, 1997. CB
Weatherford, John. By Chad Berry. South Bend, Ind. Dec. 19, 1989. CB
Whitten, Robert. By Chad Berry. Waynesboro, Tenn. May 17, 1985. CB
Williams, Ellie. By Chad Berry. Cypress Inn, Tenn. May 18, 1985. CB
Wilson, Joseph R. By Greer T. Warren. Anderson, Ind. Feb. 19, 1982; Mar. 19, 1982. IUOHRC
Wright, Howard and Bessie. By Chad Berry. Cypress Inn, Tenn. May 26, 1985. CB

Other Sources

Adamic, Louis. "The Hill-Billies Come to Detroit." *Nation* 140 (Feb. 13, 1935): 177–78.
Akers, Elmer. "Southern Whites in Detroit." Typescript. Ann Arbor, 1936. Available from University Microfilms International.
Alexander, John W. "Industrial Expansion in the United States, 1939–1947." *Economic Geography* 28 (Apr. 1952): 128–42.
Allen, Barbara. "Story in Oral History: Clues to Historical Consciousness." *Journal of American History* 79 (Sept. 1992): 606–11.
Anderson, Nels. *Men on the Move.* Chicago: University of Chicago Press, 1940.
"Appalachian Workers in Columbus Surveyed." *Columbus Business Forum* 3 (Mar. 1967): 37.
Arnow, Harriette. *The Dollmaker.* New York: Macmillan, 1954.
Asbel, Bernard L. "National Barn Dance." *Chicago* 1 (Oct. 1954): 20–25.
Averill, Patricia. "'Can the Circle Be Unbroken': A Study of the Modernization of Rural Born Southern Whites since World War I Using Country Music." Ph.D. diss., University of Pennsylvania, 1975.
Babcock, Glenn D. *History of United States Rubber Company: A Case Study in Corporation Management.* Bloomington: Indiana University Press, 1966.

Bailey, Rebecca J. "'I Never Thought of My Life as History': A Story of the Hillbilly Exodus and the Price of Assimilation." *Journal of Appalachian Studies* 3 (Fall 1997): 231–42.

Baker, Robert A. *The Southern Baptist Convention and Its People, 1607–1972.* Nashville, Tenn.: Broadman, 1974.

Banks, Alan, Dwight Billings, and Karen Tice. "Appalachian Studies, Resistance, and Postmodernism." In *Fighting Back in Appalachia: Traditions of Resistance and Change,* edited by Stephen L. Fisher, 283–301. Philadelphia: Temple University Press, 1993.

Beck, P. G., and M. C. Forster. *Six Rural Problem Areas: Relief-Resources-Rehabilitation.* Washington, D.C.: U.S. Department of Agriculture, 1935.

Berry, Chad. "The Great *White* Migration, Alcohol, and the Transplantation of Southern Protestant Churches." *Register of the Kentucky Historical Society* 94 (Summer 1996): 265–96.

Beynon, Erdmann Doane. "The Southern White Laborer Migrates to Michigan." *American Sociological Review* 3 (June 1938): 333–43.

Biggar, George C. "The Early Days of WLS and the National Barn Dance." *Old Time Music* 1 (Summer 1971): 11–13.

———. "The WLS National Barn Dance Story: The Early Years." *JEMF Quarterly* 7 (Autumn 1971): 105–12.

Biles, Roger. *The South and the New Deal.* Lexington: University Press of Kentucky, 1994.

Billings, Dwight B., and Kathleen M. Blee. "Agriculture and Poverty in the Kentucky Mountains: Beech Creek, 1850–1910." In *Appalachia in the Making: The Mountain South in the Nineteenth Century,* edited by Mary Beth Pudup, Dwight B. Billings, and Altina L. Waller, 233–69. Chapel Hill: University of North Carolina Press, 1995.

Bodnar, John. *The Transplanted: A History of Immigrants in Urban America.* Bloomington: Indiana University Press, 1985.

Borman, Kathryn M. *Urban Appalachian Children and Youth at Risk.* Cincinnati: University of Cincinnati, 1991.

Borman, Kathryn M., and Phillip J. Obermiller, eds. *From Mountain to Metropolis: Appalachian Migrants in American Cities.* Westport, Conn.: Bergin and Garvey, 1994.

Borman, Kathryn M., and Delores Stegelin. "Social Change and Urban Appalachian School Children: Youth at Risk." In *From Mountain to Metropolis: Appalachian Migrants in American Cities,* edited by Kathryn M. Borman and Phillip J. Obermiller, 167–80. Westport, Conn.: Bergin and Garvey, 1994.

Breckinridge, Mary. "The Corn-Bread Line." *Survey* 19 (Aug. 15, 1930): 423–24.

Brinkley, Alan. *Voices of Protest: Huey Long, Father Coughlin, and the Great Depression.* New York: Knopf, 1982.

Brown, James S. "The Family behind the Migrant." In *Appalachia in the Sixties: Decade of Reawakening,* edited by David S. Walls and John B. Stephenson, 153–57. Lexington: University Press of Kentucky, 1972.

———. "The Social Organization of an Isolated Kentucky Mountain Neighborhood." Ph.D. diss., Harvard University, 1950.

Bruno, Hal. "Chicago's Hillbilly Ghetto." *Reporter* 30 (June 4, 1964): 28–30.

Cabestro, Peggy, and Ann Hill. *Appalachian Culture: A Guide for Students and Teachers.* Columbus, Ohio: [Columbus Public Schools], 1976.

Caldwell, Morris G. "The Adjustment of Mountain Families in an Urban Environment." *Social Forces* 16 (Mar. 1938): 389–95.

Campbell, Brewster, and James Pooler. "Hallelujah in Boom Town." *Collier's* 113 (Apr. 1, 1944): 18–19, 52–53.

Carney, George O. "Spatial Diffusion of the All-Country Music Radio Stations in the United States, 1971–74." *JEMF Quarterly* 13 (Summer 1977): 58–66.

Carson, Clayborne. *In Struggle: SNCC and the Black Awakening of the 1960s.* Cambridge, Mass.: Harvard University Press, 1981.

Cash, Wilbur J. *The Mind of the South.* New York: Knopf, 1941.

Caudill, Harry M. *Night Comes to the Cumberlands: A Biography of a Depressed Area.* Boston: Little, Brown, 1962.

Chicago Fact Book Consortium. *Local Community Fact Book: Chicago Metropolitan Area, Based on the 1970 and 1980 Censuses.* Chicago: Chicago Review, 1984.

Cincinnati Enquirer Staff. *The Urban Appalachians.* Cincinnati: Cincinnati Enquirer, 1981.

Clarkson, Atelia, and W. Lynwood Montell. "Letters to a Bluegrass DJ: Social Documents of Southern White Migrants in Southeastern Michigan, 1964–1974." *Southern Folklore Quarterly* 39 (Sept. 1975): 219–32.

Clive, Alan. *State of War: Michigan in World War II.* Ann Arbor: University of Michigan Press, 1979.

Cobb, James C. "From Rocky Top to Detroit City: Country Music and the Economic Transformation of the South." In *You Wrote My Life: Lyrical Themes in Country Music,* edited by Melton A. McLaurin and Richard A. Peterson, 63–79. Philadelphia: Gordon and Breach, 1993.

Coles, Robert. *Migrants, Sharecroppers, and Mountaineers.* Boston: Little, Brown, 1971.

———. *The South Goes North.* Boston: Little, Brown, 1971.

Collins, Henry Hill. *America's Own Refugees: Our 4,000,000 Homeless Migrants.* Princeton, N.J.: Princeton University Press, 1941.

Council of the Southern Mountains. *Are You Thinking of Moving to the City?* Berea, Ky.: Council of the Southern Mountains, 1965.

———. *Report on a Meeting Held in Connection with the Opening of the Chicago Office of the Council of the Southern Mountains.* [Chicago: Council of the Southern Mountains], 1963.

Crissman, James K. "An Analysis of the Family Structure and Family Values of Central Appalachian Migrants in Akron, Ohio." Ph.D. diss., University of Akron, 1980.

Crouse, Joan M. *The Homeless Transient in the Great Depression: New York State, 1929–1941.* Albany: State University of New York Press, 1986.

Crowe, Martin J. "The Occupational Adaptation of a Selected Group of Eastern Kentuckians in Southern Ohio." Ph.D. diss., University of Kentucky, 1964.

Cunningham, Earl Harold. "Religious Concerns of Southern Appalachian Migrants in a North Central City." Ph.D. diss., Boston University, 1962.

Daniel, Pete. *Breaking the Land: The Transformation of Cotton, Tobacco, and Rice Cultures since 1880.* Urbana: University of Illinois Press, 1985.

———. *Standing at the Crossroads: Southern Life since 1900.* New York: Hill and Wang, 1986.

Daniel, Wayne W. "The National Barn Dance on Network Radio: The 1930s." *Journal of Country Music* 9, no. 3 (1983): 47–62.

Deaton, Brady J. "The Private Costs and Returns of Migration from Eastern Kentucky to Cincinnati, Ohio." Ph.D. diss., University of Wisconsin, 1972.

Denby, Charles. *Indignant Heart: Testimony of a Black American Worker.* London: Pluto, 1979.

"Depression Migrants and the State." *Harvard Law Review* 53 (Apr. 1940): 1031–42.

Drake, Chad. "The Recession Is Far from Over in the Southern Mountains." *Mountain Life and Work* 34, no. 4 (1958): 36–37.

Dunaway, Wilma A. *The First American Frontier: Transition to Capitalism in Southern Appalachia, 1700–1860.* Chapel Hill: University of North Carolina Press, 1996.

———. "Speculators and Settler Capitalists: Unthinking the Mythology about Appalachian Landholding, 1790–1860." In *Appalachia in the Making: The Mountain South in the Nineteenth Century,* edited by Mary Beth Pudup, Dwight B. Billings, and Altina L. Waller, 50–75. Chapel Hill: University of North Carolina Press, 1995.

Dunn, Durwood. *Cades Cove: The Life and Death of a Southern Appalachian Community.* Knoxville: University of Tennessee Press, 1988.

Elfers, Robert A., Mae H. Ashworth, and Bette V. Reed. *Impact: The Exploration of an Idea.* New York: Friendship, 1960.

Eller, Ronald D. *Miners, Millhands, and Mountaineers: Industrialization of the Appalachian South, 1880–1930.* Knoxville: University of Tennessee Press, 1982.

Faue, Elizabeth. *Community of Suffering and Struggle: Women, Men, and the Labor Movement in Minneapolis, 1915–1945.* Chapel Hill: University of North Carolina Press, 1991.

Feather, Carl E. *Mountain People in a Flat Land: A Popular History of Appalachian Migration to Northeast Ohio, 1940–1965.* Athens: Ohio University Press, 1998.

Fisher, Stephen L. "Victim-Blaming in Appalachia: Cultural Theories and the Southern Mountaineer." In *Appalachia: Social Context Past and Present,* edited by Bruce Ergood and Bruce E. Kuhre, 185–94. Dubuque, Iowa: Kendall/Hunt, 1983.

———, ed. *Fighting Back in Appalachia: Traditions of Resistance and Change.* Philadelphia: Temple University Press, 1993.

"Flight from the City." *Nation* 137 (July 12, 1933): 32–33.
Fligstein, Neil. *Going North: Migration of Blacks and Whites from the South, 1900–1950.* New York: Academic, 1981.
Flynt, J. Wayne. *Dixie's Forgotten People: The South's Poor Whites.* Bloomington: Indiana University Press, 1979.
———. "Southern Baptists: Rural to Urban Transition." *Baptist History and Heritage* 16 (Jan. 1981): 24–34.
Ford, Thomas R. "Status, Residence, and Fundamentalist Religious Beliefs in the Southern Appalachians." *Social Forces* 39 (Oct. 1960): 247–61.
———, ed. *The Southern Appalachian Region: A Survey.* Lexington: University of Kentucky Press, 1962.
Fowler, Gary L., and Christopher S. Davies. "The Urban Settlement Patterns of Disadvantaged Migrants." *Journal of Geography* 71 (May 1972): 275–84.
Franklin, Jimmie Lewis. *Born Sober: Prohibition in Oklahoma, 1907–1959.* Norman: University of Oklahoma Press, 1971.
Friedlander, Peter. *The Emergence of a UAW Local, 1936–1939: A Study in Class and Culture.* Pittsburgh: University of Pittsburgh Press, 1975.
Galloway, Lowell, Charles McBride, and Richard Vedder. "The Mobility of Appalachian Americans." *Review of Regional Studies* 2 (Fall 1971): 53–64.
Galpin, C. J., and T. B. Manny. *Interstate Migrations among the Native White Population as Indicated by Differences between State of Birth and State of Residence.* Washington, D.C.: U.S. Department of Agriculture, 1934.
Gibbons, Charles E. "The Onion Workers." *American Child* 1 (Feb. 1920): 413–15.
Giffin, Roscoe. "Appalachian Newcomers to Cincinnati." In *The Southern Appalachian Region: A Survey,* edited by Thomas R. Ford, 79–84. Lexington: University of Kentucky Press, 1962.
Giffin, Roscoe, and Mayor's Friendly Relations Committee. *Report of a Workshop on the Southern Mountaineer in Cincinnati.* Cincinnati: Mayor's Friendly Relations Committee, 1954.
Gissen, Ira. "The Mountain Migrant: The Problem Centered Workshop at Berea." *Journal of Human Relations* 4 (Autumn 1961): 67–73.
Gitlin, Todd, and Nanci Hollander. *Uptown: Poor Whites in Chicago.* New York: Harper and Row, 1970.
Goodrich, Carter, Bushrod W. Allin, C. Warren Thornthwaite, Hermann K. Brunck, Frederick G. Tryon, Daniel B. Creamer, Rupert B. Vance, and Marion Hayes. *Migration and Economic Opportunity: The Report of the Study of Population Redistribution.* Philadelphia: University of Pennsylvania Press, 1936.
Gottlieb, Peter. *Making Their Own Way: Southern Blacks' Migration to Pittsburgh, 1916–1930.* Urbana: University of Illinois Press, 1987.
Green, Archie. "Hillbilly Music: Source and Symbol." *Journal of American Folklore* 78 (July–Sept. 1965): 204–28.
Gregory, James N. *American Exodus: The Dust Bowl Migration and Okie Culture in California.* New York: Oxford University Press, 1989.
———. "The Southern Diaspora and the Urban Dispossessed: Demonstrat-

ing the Census Public Use Microdata Samples." *Journal of American History* 82 (June 1995): 111–34.

Grossman, James R. *Land of Hope: Chicago, Black Southerners, and the Great Migration.* Chicago: University of Chicago Press, 1989.

Grundy, Pamela. "'We Always Tried to Be Good People': Respectability, Crazy Water Crystals, and Hillbilly Music on the Air, 1933–1935." *Journal of American History* 81 (Mar. 1995): 1591–1620.

Guy, Roger. "The Chicago Southern Center: Appalachian Culture and Unity in Uptown, 1963–1971." Paper presented at Twenty-first Appalachian Studies Conference, Boone, N.C., Mar. 20, 1998.

———. "Diversity to Unity: Uptown's Southern Migrants, 1950–1970." Ph.D. diss., University of Wisconsin–Milwaukee, 1996.

Halbrooks, G. Thomas. "Growing Pains: The Impact of Expansion on Southern Baptists since 1942." *Baptist History and Heritage* 17 (July 1982): 44–54.

Hall, Jacquelyn Dowd, James Leloudis, Robert Korstad, Mary Murphy, Lu Ann Jones, and Christopher B. Daly. *Like a Family: The Making of a Southern Cotton Mill World.* Chapel Hill: University of North Carolina Press, 1987.

Hankins, Barry Gene. "Saving America: Fundamentalism and Politics in the Life of J. Frank Norris." Ph.D. diss., Kansas State University, 1990.

Hanrahan, Charles E. "Public Budget Effects of Eastern Kentucky Migration to Cincinnati, Ohio." Ph.D. diss., University of Kentucky, 1973.

Harriette Simpson Arnow, 1908–1986. Directed by Herb E. Smith. Appalshop Film and Video, 1987.

Harwood, Edwin S. "Work and Community among Urban Newcomers: A Study of the Social and Economic Adaptation of Southern Migrants to Chicago." Ph.D. diss., University of Chicago, 1966.

Hawkins, Helen S. *A New Deal for the Newcomer: The Federal Transient Service.* New York: Garland, 1991.

Hawley, Amos H. *The Population of Michigan, 1840 to 1960: An Analysis of Growth, Distribution, and Composition.* Ann Arbor: University of Michigan Press, 1949.

Henderson, George. "Poor Urban Whites: A Neglected Urban Problem." *Journal of Secondary Education* 41 (Mar. 1966): 111–14.

Herman, Mildred M. "Uptowners Call Him 'Preacher.'" *Presbyterian Life,* Oct. 1, 1965, 11–14.

High Lonesome: The Story of Bluegrass Music. Directed by Rachel Liebling. Shanachie Entertainment, Newton, N.J., 1994.

Hill, Edwin G. *In the Shadow of the Mountain: The Spirit of the CCC.* Pullman: Washington State University Press, 1990.

Hilliard, Raymond M., and Deton J. Brooks Jr. *A Study of Families from the Southern Appalachian Region Receiving Public Assistance.* Chicago: Cook County Department of Public Aid, 1960.

History of Michiana Association. Poplar Bluff, Mo.: General Baptist Association, n.d.

Hofstra, Warren R., and Robert D. Mitchell. "Town and Country in Backcountry Virginia: Winchester and the Shenandoah Valley, 1730–1800." *Journal of Southern History* 59 (Nov. 1993): 619–46.

Hopkins, Harry L. *Spending to Save: The Complete Story of Relief.* New York: Norton, 1936.

Horstman, Dorothy. *Sing Your Hear Out, Country Boy.* New York: Dutton, 1975.

Hsiung, David C. *Two Worlds in the Tennessee Mountains: Exploring the Origins of Appalachian Stereotypes.* Lexington: University Press of Kentucky, 1997.

Hundley, John R. "The Mountain Man in Northern Industry." *Mountain Life and Work* 31 (Spring 1955): 34–38.

Hutchens, Raymond Paul. "Kentuckians in Hamilton: A Study of Southborn Migrants in an Industrial City." M.A. thesis, Miami University, 1942.

Inscoe, John C. *Mountain Masters, Slavery, and the Sectional Crisis in Western North Carolina.* Knoxville: University of Tennessee Press, 1989.

Johnson, Leland, and Daniel Schaffer. *Oak Ridge National Laboratory: The First Fifty Years.* Knoxville: University of Tennessee Press, 1994.

Jones, Carmel L. "Migration, Religion, and Occupational Mobility of Southern Appalachians in Muncie, Indiana." Ph.D. diss., Ball State University, 1978.

Jones, Jacqueline. *The Dispossessed: America's Underclasses from the Civil War to the Present.* New York: Basic Books, 1992.

Kaufman, H. F. *Religious Organization in Kentucky.* Kentucky Agricultural Experiment Station, Bulletin 524. Lexington: Kentucky Agricultural Experiment Station, 1948.

Keith, Jeanette. *Country People in the New South: Tennessee's Upper Cumberland.* Chapel Hill: University of North Carolina Press, 1995.

Kentuckians of Michigan, Inc. *Annual Picnic, '74.* Detroit: Kentuckians of Michigan, 1974.

Killian, Lewis M. "Southern White Laborers in Chicago's West Side." Ph.D. diss., University of Chicago, 1949.

———. *White Southerners.* New York: Random House, 1970.

Kimbrough, David L. *Taking Up Serpents: Snake Handlers of Eastern Kentucky.* Chapel Hill: University of North Carolina Press, 1995.

Kirby, Jack Temple. *Rural Worlds Lost: The American South, 1920–1960.* Baton Rouge: Louisiana State University Press, 1987.

Kukin, Dorothy, and Michael Byrne. *Appalachians in Cleveland.* Cleveland: Institute of Urban Studies, Cleveland State University, 1973.

"Labor Conditions in the Onion Fields of Ohio." *Monthly Labor Review* 40 (Feb. 1935): 324–35.

Lake View Newcomer Committee. *Summary of Visits to Southern White Families.* Chicago: Lake View Newcomer Committee, 1961.

Landy, Marc. "Country Music: The Melody of Dislocation." *New South* 26 (Winter 1971): 67–69.

Lee, Alfred McClung, and Norman D. Humphrey. *Race Riot (Detroit, 1943).* New York: Dryden, 1943.

Lemann, Nicholas. *The Promised Land: The Great Black Migration and How It Changed America.* New York: Knopf, 1991.

Leybourne, Grace G. "Urban Adjustments of Migrants from the Southern Appalachian Plateaus." *Social Forces* 16 (Dec. 1937): 238–46.

Lively, C. E., and Conrad Taeuber. *Rural Migration in the United States.* Washington, D.C.: Government Printing Office, 1939.

Livingston, William Richard. "Southern Baptists in Michigan: A Study of Transcultural Expansion and Displacement." Ph.D. diss., Wayne State University, 1992.

Long Journey Home. Directed by Elizabeth Barrett. Appalshop Film and Video, 1987.

Lynd, Robert S., and Helen Merrell Lynd. *Middletown: A Study of Modern American Culture.* New York: Harcourt, Brace, 1929.

Malone, Bill C. *Country Music, U.S.A.* Austin: University of Texas Press, 1985.

———. "Writing the History of Southern Music: A Review Essay." *Mississippi Quarterly* 45 (Fall 1992): 385–404.

Maloney, Michael E. "The Prospects for Urban Appalachians." In *The Invisible Minority: Urban Appalachians,* edited by William W. Philliber and Clyde B. McCoy, 163–73. Lexington: University Press of Kentucky, 1981.

Marks, Carole. *Farewell—We're Good and Gone: The Great Black Migration.* Bloomington: Indiana University Press, 1989.

Matthews, Ellen Nathalie. *Children in Fruit and Vegetable Canneries: A Survey in Seven States.* Washington, D.C.: Government Printing Office, 1930.

Matusow, Allen J. *The Unraveling of America: A History of Liberalism in the 1960s.* New York: Harper and Row, 1984.

Maxwell, James A. "Down from the Hills and into the Slums." *Reporter* 15 (Dec. 13, 1956): 27–29.

Mayor's Friendly Relations Committee of Cincinnati. *When Cultures Meet: Mountain and Urban.* Cincinnati: Mayor's Friendly Relations Committee, 1962.

McBeth, Leon. "Expansion of the Southern Baptist Convention to 1951." *Baptist History and Heritage* 17 (July 1982): 32–43.

McCauley, Deborah Vansau. *Appalachian Mountain Religion: A History.* Urbana: University of Illinois Press, 1995.

McCoy, Clyde B., James S. Brown, and Virginia McCoy Watkins. "The Migration Stream System of Southwest Ohio and Its Relation to Southern Appalachian Migration." Urban Appalachian Council, Cincinnati, Ohio. Manuscript.

McCoy, Clyde, and Virginia Watkins. "Drug Use among Urban Ethnic Youth: Appalachian and Other Comparisons." *Youth and Society* 12 (Sept. 1980): 83–106.

McDonald, Michael J., and John Muldowny. *TVA and the Dispossessed: The Resettlement of Population in the Norris Dam Area.* Knoxville: University of Tennessee Press, 1982.

McDonald, Michael J., and William Bruce Wheeler. *Knoxville, Tennessee: Continuity and Change in an Appalachian City.* Knoxville: University of Tennessee Press, 1983.

McKinney, Gordon B. "Economy and Community in Western North Carolina, 1860–1865." In *Appalachia in the Making: The Mountain South in the Nineteenth Century,* edited by Mary Beth Pudup, Dwight B. Billings, and Altina L. Waller, 163–84. Chapel Hill: University of North Carolina Press, 1995.

McLaurin, Melton A., and Richard A. Peterson, eds. *You Wrote My Life: Lyrical Themes in Country Music.* Philadelphia: Gordon and Breach, 1993.

McWilliams, Carey. *Ill Fares the Land: Migrants and Migratory Labor in the United States.* Boston: Little, Brown, 1942.

Merten, Don Edward. "Up Here and Down Home: Appalachian Migrants in Northtown." Ph.D. diss., University of Chicago, 1974.

Miller, James. *"Democracy Is in the Streets": From Port Huron to the Siege of Chicago.* New York: Simon and Schuster, 1987.

Minehan, Thomas. *Boy and Girl Tramps of America.* New York: Farrar and Rinehart, 1934.

Montell, William Lynwood. *Killings: Folk Justice in the Upper South.* Lexington: University Press of Kentucky, 1986.

———. *Singing the Glory Down: Amateur Gospel Music in South Central Kentucky, 1900–1990.* Lexington: University Press of Kentucky, 1991.

Montgomery, Bill. "The Uptown Story." *Mountain Life and Work* 44 (Sept. 1968): 8–18.

Montgomery, David. *Workers' Control in America: Studies in the History of Work, Technology, and Labor Struggles.* New York: Cambridge University Press, 1979.

Murphy, T. E. "The Orphans of Willow Run." *Saturday Evening Post* 218 (Aug. 4, 1945): 20, 109–10.

Myadze, Theresa. "Rethinking Urban Appalachian Ethnicity." *Journal of Appalachian Studies* 3 (Fall 1997): 243–52.

Natchez Trace Parkway Survey. Washington, D.C.: Government Printing Office, 1941.

Nelson, Daniel. *American Rubberworkers and Organized Labor, 1900–1941.* Princeton, N.J.: Princeton University Press, 1988.

Nelson, Hart M., and H. P. Whitt. "Religion and the Migrant in the City: A Test of Hilt's Cultural Shock Thesis." *Social Forces* 50 (Mar. 1972): 379–84.

Nettles, Tom J. "Southern Baptists: Regional to National Transition." *Baptist History and Heritage* 16 (Jan. 1981): 13–23.

Neville, Gwen Kennedy. *Kinship and Pilgrimage: Rituals of Reunion in American Protestant Culture.* New York: Oxford University Press, 1987.

1980 Public Use Microdata Samples, Sample B: One percent.

1990 Public Use Microdata Samples, Sample B: One percent.

1970 Public Use Microdata Sample: Five Percent Sample.

1960 Integrated Public Use Microdata Sample: One Percent Sample.

Obermiller, Phillip J. "The Question of Appalachian Ethnicity." In *the Invisible Minority: Urban Appalachians,* edited by William W. Philliber and Clyde B. McCoy, 9–19. Lexington: University Press of Kentucky, 1981.

———, ed. *Down Home, Downtown: Urban Appalachians Today.* Dubuque, Iowa: Kendall/Hunt, 1996.

Obermiller, Phillip J., and William W. Philliber, eds. *Too Few Tomorrows: Urban Appalachians in the 1980s.* Boone, N.C.: Appalachian Consortium Press, 1987.

O'Harrow, Dennis. *Preliminary Survey of County Planning Problems in Johnson County, Indiana.* Indianapolis: Indiana State Planning Board, 1936.

"Okies of the '60s." *Time,* Apr. 20, 1962, 3.

Oyler, Merton. *Natural Increase and Migration of Kentucky Population, 1920 to 1935.* Kentucky Agricultural Experiment Station, Bulletin 395. Lexington: Kentucky Agricultural Experiment Station, 1939.

Palmer, Vivien M. *Social Backgrounds of Chicago's Local Communities.* Chicago: [University of Chicago], 1929.

Patterson, Timothy A. "Hillbilly Music among the Flatlanders: Early Midwestern Radio Barn Dance." *Journal of Country Music* 6 (Spring 1975): 12–18.

Petersen, Gene B., Laure M. Sharp, and Thomas F. Drury. *Southern Newcomers to Northern Cities: Work and Social Adjustment in Cleveland.* New York: Praeger, 1977.

Peterson, Richard A. "Class Unconsciousness in Country Music." In *You Wrote My Life: Lyrical Themes in Country Music,* edited by Melton A. McLaurin and Richard A. Peterson, 35–62. Philadelphia: Gordon and Breach, 1993.

Philliber, William W. *Appalachian Migrants in Urban America: Cultural Conflict or Ethnic Group Formation?* New York: Praeger, 1981.

———. "Wife's Absence from the Labor Force and Low Income among Appalachian Migrants." *Rural Sociology* 47 (Winter 1982): 705–10.

Philliber, William W., and Clyde B. McCoy, eds. *The Invisible Minority: Urban Appalachians.* Lexington: University Press of Kentucky, 1981.

Photiadis, John D. *Social and Sociopsychological Characteristics of West Virginians in Their Own State and in Cleveland, Ohio.* Morgantown: West Virginia University, 1975.

Pickard, Jerome Percival. *Population and Net Migration Trends in the Appalachian Region.* Appalachian Regional Commission Current Statistical Report Number 1. Washington, D.C.: Appalachian Regional Commission, 1971.

———. *Population Change in the Appalachian Region.* Appalachian Regional Commission Current Statistical Report Number 3. Washington, D.C.: Appalachian Regional Commission, 1971.

Pierson, George W. "The M-Factor in American History." *American Quarterly* 14 (Summer 1962): 275–89.

Pudup, Mary Beth. "Town and Country in the Transformation of Appalachian Kentucky." In *Appalachia in the Making: The Mountain South in the Nine-*

teenth Century, edited by Mary Beth Pudup, Dwight B. Billings, and Altina L. Waller, 270–96. Chapel Hill: University of North Carolina Press, 1995.

Pudup, Mary Beth, Dwight B. Billings, and Altina L. Waller, eds. *Appalachia in the Making: The Mountain South in the Nineteenth Century.* Chapel Hill: University of North Carolina Press, 1995.

Quinn, M.—L. "Industry and Environment in the Appalachian Copper Basin, 1890–1930." *Technology and Culture* 34, no. 3 (1993): 575–612.

Rasmussen, Barbara. *Absentee Landowning and Exploitation in West Virginia, 1760–1920.* Lexington: University Press of Kentucky, 1994.

Reed, John Shelton. *The Enduring South: Subcultural Persistence in Mass Society.* Chapel Hill: University of North Carolina Press, 1972.

———. *Southern Folk, Plain and Fancy: Native White Social Types.* Athens: University of Georgia Press, 1986.

Rose, Gregory S. "Hoosier Origins: The Nativity of Indiana's United States–Born Population in 1850." *Indiana Magazine of History* 81 (Sept. 1984): 201–32.

Ross, Malcolm. *Machine Age in the Hills.* New York: Macmillan, 1933.

Salmond, John A. *The Civilian Conservation Corps, 1933–1942: A New Deal Case Study.* Durham, N.C.: Duke University Press, 1967.

Salstrom, Paul. *Appalachia's Path to Dependency: Rethinking a Region's Economic History, 1730–1940.* Lexington: University Press of Kentucky, 1994.

———. "Newer Appalachia as One of America's Last Frontiers." In *Appalachia in the Making: The Mountain South in the Nineteenth Century,* edited by Mary Beth Pudup, Dwight B. Billings, and Altina L. Waller, 76–102. Chapel Hill: University of North Carolina Press, 1995.

Sanderson, Ross W. "Gasoline Gypsies." *Survey* 53 (Dec. 1924): 265.

Schort, George V. *Preliminary Survey of County Planning Problems in Henry County, Indiana.* Indianapolis: Indiana State Planning Board, 1936.

Schwarzweller, Harry K. "Occupational Patterns of Appalachian Migrants." In *The Invisible Minority: Urban Appalachians,* edited by William W. Philliber and Clyde B. McCoy, 130–39. Lexington: University Press of Kentucky, 1981.

———. "Parental Family Ties and Social Integration of Rural to Urban Migrants." *Journal of Marriage and the Family* 26 (Nov. 1964): 410–16.

Schwarzweller, Harry K., James S. Brown, and J. J. Mangalam. *Mountain Families in Transition: A Case Study of Appalachian Migration.* University Park: Pennsylvania State University Press, 1971.

Schweiker, William F. "Some Facts and a Theory of Migration." In *Research Series 8* (Morgantown: Appalachian Center, West Virginia University), 1968.

Shackelford, Laurel, and Bill Weinberg, eds. *Our Appalachia: An Oral History.* New York: Hill and Wang, 1977.

Shifflett, Crandall A. *Coal Towns: Life, Work, and Culture in Company Towns of Southern Appalachia, 1880–1960.* Knoxville: University of Tennessee Press, 1991.

Stekert, Ellen J. "Focus for Conflict: Southern Mountain Medical Beliefs in Detroit." In *The Urban Experience and Folk Tradition,* edited by Américo Paredes and Ellen J. Stekert, 95–127. Austin: University of Texas Press, 1971.

Still, James. *River of Earth.* Lexington: University of Kentucky Press, 1942.

———. *The Wolfpen Poems.* Berea, Ky.: Berea College Press, 1986.

Stone, W. Clement. *The Success System That Never Fails.* Englewood Cliffs, N.J.: Prentice-Hall, 1962.

Taylor, Paul S., and Edward J. Rowell. "Refugee Labor Migration to California, 1937." *Monthly Labor Review* 47 (July 1938): 240–50.

Teaford, Jon C. *Cities of the Heartland: The Rise and Fall of the Industrial Midwest.* Bloomington: Indiana University Press, 1993.

Tennessee Valley Authority. *The Tennessee Valley Region: Three Decades of Population Change and Current Economic Status.* Knoxville: Tennessee Valley Authority, 1971.

Thompson, John Leslie. "Industrialization in the Miami Valley: A Case Study of Interregional Labor Migration." Ph.D. diss., University of Wisconsin, 1955.

Tichi, Cecelia. *High Lonesome: The American Culture of Country Music.* Chapel Hill: University of North Carolina Press, 1994.

Tolles, N. A. "Survey of Labor Migration between States." *Monthly Labor Review* 45 (July 1937): 3–16.

Tribe, Ivan M. "Cultural Preservation among Appalachian Migrants: Three Musical Case Studies." *Journal of Appalachian Studies* 3 (Fall 1997): 263–70.

———. "The Hillbilly versus the City: Urban Images in Country Music." *JEMF Quarterly* 10 (Summer 1974): 41–51.

Trotter, Joe William, Jr., ed. *The Great Migration in Historical Perspective: New Dimensions in Race, Class, and Gender.* Bloomington: Indiana University Press, 1991.

Tucker, Bruce. "Toward a New Ethnicity: Urban Appalachian Ethnic Consciousness in Cincinnati, 1950–87." In *Ethnic Diversity and Civic Identity: Patterns of Conflict and Cohesion since 1820,* edited by Henry D. Shapiro and Jonathan D. Sarna, 225–47. Urbana: University of Illinois Press, 1992.

Uhlenberg, Peter. "Noneconomic Determinants of Nonmigration: Sociological Considerations for Migration Theory." *Rural Sociology* 38 (Fall 1973): 296–311.

"Uptown Chicago Gains Community Clinic." *Mountain Life and Work* 54 (Dec. 1978): 34–36.

"Urban Migrants." Special issue of *Peoples' Appalachia* 2 (July 1972).

U.S. Bureau of the Census. "Estimates of the Population of States and Selected Outlying Areas of the United States, July 1, 1957 and 1956." In *Current Population Reports: Population Estimates.* Series P-25, No. 186. Washington, D.C.: Government Printing Office, Oct. 27, 1958.

———. *Fifteenth Census of the United States: 1930,* vol. 2, *Population.* Washington, D.C.: Government Printing Office, 1933.

———. *Fifteenth Census of the United States: 1930,* vol. 3, *Reports by States.* Washington, D.C.: Government Printing Office, 1932.

———. *Historical Statistics of the United States: Colonial Times to 1957.* Washington, D.C.: Government Printing Office, 1961.

———. *Historical Statistics of the United States, Colonial Times to 1957: Continuation to 1962 and Revisions.* Washington, D.C.: Government Printing Office, 1965.

———. *Statistical Abstract of the United States, 1931.* Washington, D.C.: Government Printing Office, 1931.

———. *U.S. Census of Population: 1950,* vol. 4, *Special Reports.* Part 4, Chap. A, State of Birth. Washington, D.C.: Government Printing Office, 1953.

———. *U.S. Census of Population: 1960, Subject Reports, Mobility for State Economic Areas.* Final Report PC(2)-2B. Washington, D.C.: Government Printing Office, 1963.

U.S. Congress. House. Select Committee Investigating National Defense Migration. *National Defense Migration: Hearings.* 77th Cong., 1st sess., 1941. Vols. 11–34.

———. Select Committee to Investigate the Interstate Migration of Destitute Citizens. *Interstate Migration: Hearings.* 76th Cong., 3d sess., 1940. Vols. 1–10.

———. Select Committee to Investigate the Interstate Migration of Destitute Citizens. *Interstate Migration Report.* Washington, D.C.: Government Printing Office, 1941.

U.S. Congress, Senate. Special Committee Investigating the National Defense Program. *Investigation of the National Defense Program.* 77th Cong., 1st sess.–80th Cong., 1st sess., 1941–48. Vols. 1–43.

U.S. Department of Agriculture. *Economic and Social Problems and Conditions of the Southern Appalachians.* Misc. pub. 205, Washington, D.C.: U.S. Department of Agriculture, 1935.

Vargas, Zaragosa. *Proletarians of the North: A History of Mexican Industrial Workers in Detroit and the Midwest, 1917–1933.* Berkeley: University of California Press, 1993.

Votaw, Albert N. "The Hillbillies Invade Chicago." *Harper's* 216 (Feb. 1958): 64–67.

Waller, Altina L. *Feud: Hatfields, McCoys, and Social Change in Appalachia, 1860–1900.* Chapel Hill: University of North Carolina Press, 1988.

Walls, David S., and John B. Stephenson, eds. *Appalachia in the Sixties: Decade of Reawakening.* Lexington: University Press of Kentucky, 1972.

Watkins, T. H. *The Great Depression: America in the 1930s.* Boston: Little, Brown, 1993.

Webb, John N. *The Transient Unemployed: A Description and Analysis of the Transient Relief Population.* Washington, D.C.: Works Progress Administration, 1935.

Webb, John N., and Malcolm Brown. *Migrant Families.* Washington, D.C.: Government Printing Office, 1938.

Webb, John N., and Albert Westefeld. "Industrial Aspects of Labor Mobility." *Monthly Labor Review* 48 (Apr. 1939): 796.

———. "Labor Mobility and Relief." *Monthly Labor Review* 48 (Jan. 1939): 16–24.

Webb, John N., M. Starr Northrop, Malcolm J. Brown, and Katherine Gordon. *A Survey of the Transient and Homeless Population in Twelve Cities: September 1935 and September 1936.* Washington, D.C.: Works Progress Administration, 1937.

Weiland, Steven, Thomas E. Wagner, and Phillip J. Obermiller, eds. *Perspectives on Urban Appalachians.* Cincinnati: Ohio Urban Appalachian Awareness Project, 1978.

Weisiger, Marsha L. *Land of Plenty: Oklahomans in the Cotton Fields of Arizona, 1933–1942.* Norman: University of Oklahoma Press, 1995.

Westefeld, Albert. *Michigan Migrants.* Washington, D.C.: Works Progress Administration, 1939.

Whisnant, David E. *All That Is Native and Fine: The Politics of Culture in an American Region.* Chapel Hill: University of North Carolina Press, 1983.

———. *Modernizing the Mountaineer: People, Power, and Planning in Appalachia.* Knoxville: University of Tennessee Press, 1994.

Wilgus, D. K. *Anglo-American Folksong Scholarship since 1898.* New Brunswick, N.J.: Rutgers University Press, 1959.

———. "Country-Western Music and the Urban Hillbilly." *Journal of American Folklore* 83 (Apr.–June 1970): 157–79.

Williams, Faith, Hazel K. Stiebeling, Idelia G. Swisher, and Gertrude Schmidt Weiss. *Family Living in Knott County, Kentucky.* Washington, D.C.: U.S. Department of Agriculture, 1937.

Williams, John R. "Appalachian Migrants in Cincinnati, Ohio: The Role of Folklore in the Reinforcement of Ethnic Identity." Ph.D. diss., Indiana University, 1985.

Wolfe, Margaret Ripley. "Appalachians in Muncie: A Case Study of an American Exodus." *Locus* 4 (Spring 1992): 169–89.

Woodward, Harry H., Jr. *The Southern White Migrant in Lake View.* Chicago: Lake View Citizens Council, 1962.

Woofter, T. J., Jr. "Rural Relief and the Back-to-the-Farm Movement." *Social Forces* 14 (Mar. 1936): 382–85.

Worley, William D. "Social Characteristics and Participation Patterns of Rural Migrants in an Industrial Community." M.A. thesis, Miami University, 1961.

Wright, Gavin. *Old South, New South: Revolutions in the Southern Economy since the Civil War.* New York: Basic Books, 1986.

Wyatt-Brown, Bertram. *Southern Honor: Ethics and Behavior in the Old South.* New York: Oxford University Press, 1982.

Zill, Barbara. "John Morris Talks about Old Homestead Records." *Pickin'* 3 (Nov. 1976): 22–24.

Zorn, Eric. "A Homestead for Unsung Talent." *Bluegrass Unlimited* 14 (Dec. 1979): 24–26.

Index

CHAD BERRY, the grandson of migrants from Tennessee, grew up in northern Indiana. He has a B.A. in American studies from the University of Notre Dame, an M.A. in folk studies from Western Kentucky University, and a Ph.D. in history from Indiana University. A member of Phi Beta Kappa, he is an assistant professor of history at Maryville College in east Tennessee.

Typeset in 9.5/12.5 Trump Mediaeval
Composed by Jim Proefrock
at the University of Illinois Press

University of Illinois Press
1325 South Oak Street
Champaign, IL 61820-6903
www.press.uillinois.edu